TRAINING OF
THE AMERICAN ACTOR

TRAINING OF THE AMERICAN ACTOR

Edited by Arthur Bartow

THEATRE COMMUNICATIONS GROUP
NEW YORK
2006

This publication is made possible in part with public funds from the New York State Council on the Arts, a State Agency.

TCG books are exclusively distributed to the book trade by Consortium Book Sales and Distribution, 1045 Westgate Drive, St. Paul, MN 55114.

LIBRARY OF CONGRESS CATALOGING-IN-PUBLICATION DATA

Training of the American actor /
edited by Arthur Bartow.— 1st ed.
p. cm.
Includes bibliographical references.
ISBN-13: 978-1-55936-268-9
ISBN-10: 1-55936-268-5
1. Method (Acting) I. Bartow, Arthur.
PN2062.T73 2006
792.02'8—dc22
2006007809

Art and cover design by John H Howard
Text design and composition by Lisa Govan

First Edition, September 2006

To the friends and colleagues who agreed to contribute these chapters about their lifework on the faith that they would be published, in gratitude for their profound dedication to passing on these techniques to future generations of actors:

Robert Bella
Per Brahe
Fritz Ertl
Victoria Hart
Tom Oppenheim
Mary Overlie
Carol Rosenfeld
Louis Scheeder
Anna Strasberg
Stephen Wangh

To TCG and Terry Nemeth for publishing these ideas.

To the person who encourages me, Judith.

The actor's technique is that personal
and very private means by which
you get the best out of yourself.

—HUME CRONYN

There is a logical succession to the formulas,
to methods of thought and expression.
Thus, art takes the same strides as humanity.

—EMILE ZOLA

CONTENTS

CONTENTS

PREFACE

The multitude of acting techniques taught in America can be bewildering to the beginning student and, certainly, to the parents of the beginner. Part of my role as artistic director of the drama department at New York University's Tisch School of the Arts is to articulate the differences among the various acting processes offered within its large program. The department has twelve studios, and each is devoted to a specific way of training—individual processes that have been developed through years of experimentation by acknowledged masters. Some fall into the category of traditional (i.e., Stanislavsky-based) training, and others were created in reaction to traditional ways of working. These techniques, with the possible exception of Viewpoints training, were originally appropriated from European sources and subjected to a process of Americanization. Singly and together these techniques have become the ways American actors are universally trained.

I once had breakfast with the father of an incoming student, who leaned across the table confidentially and asked which studio trained the actors who got the jobs. Perhaps he thought there was a secret handshake or some magic words that would guarantee success. I could only comfort him by pointing out that students who have trained at any of the studios have become working actors. The alchemy to training, if there is any, is matching the students to the method of training that is closest to their own belief systems, so they can progress with as little resistance as possible to the challenges of preparing themselves to act.

Although it is critically important, technique itself is not acting. Technique provides the framework within which actors can organize and exercise their talent, keeping it available and confident. The actor's technique provides a musculature similar to that developed through the dancer's barre work or the pianist's and singer's practice of scales. The key word is *command*. Actors with a superficial knowledge of technique will not be able to plumb the depths of their work. It takes time to master technique, and Americans tend to learn only as much information as is necessary to assist in the task at hand. To have a command of two or more techniques is useful, even obligatory, if an actor is to be versatile. At some point youth, passion, talent and experience can fail an actor, and without a reliable technique, there will be nothing else to rely on for support. Investing in technique is investing for a lifetime. Technique makes it possible for Barbara Cook to continue singing youthfully into her late seventies, and it enabled Uta Hagen to captivate audiences as she acted into her eighties.

Given the perceived mystery of how the various techniques actually function to develop the actor, it seems useful to have a single volume that describes them side by side, distinguishing one system from another, discussing how they overlap and relating how each theory originated. I've asked ten teachers with consummate knowledge of these techniques to describe them as they are currently taught. All have direct links to the founders of these methods, and some, like Mary Overlie, who created the Six Viewpoints, are themselves the founding creators. Inevitably, these methods of working have evolved over time to fit the needs of a changing society. But, as described and analyzed in this book, these methods are as close to the founders' intentions as you are likely to find.

August 2006
New York City

ACKNOWLEDGMENTS

The authors are grateful to the following for their assistance, insightful feedback and support:

Ellen Adler, the Stella Adler Studio of Acting, Ida Bagus Alit, Ida Bagus Anom, Diana Ascher, the Atlantic Theater Company and the Atlantic Acting School, Carole Axel, Judith Bartow, the Herbert Berghof Studio, Lendley C. Black, Lee Breuer, William Carden, the students of the Classical Studio, William Esper, the Experimental Theatre Wing, Maggie Flannigan, Michael Grenham, Joseph Hart, Megan Hart, Rebecca Hart, David Jaffe, Kevin Kuhlke, Paul Langland, William H. Macy, David Mamet, Michael Massee, Mary McCann, Edith Meeks, Aole T. Miller, Michael Miller, New York University, Jeff Padgliano, Neil Pepe, Darci Picoult, Rosemary Quinn, Ryan Tresser . . .

. . . and especially to TCG editors Mollie Wilson, Kathy Sova and Cassandra Johnson.

INTRODUCTION

The actor's art cannot be taught. He must be born with
ability; but the technique, through which his talent can
find expression—that can and must be taught.

—RICHARD BOLESLAVSKY

ACTING IN AMERICA

No historical evidence exists to pinpoint when the first professional
actors appeared in America. We know there were amateur the-
atricals as early as 1598 in the territories that were to become
America, and records exist of a strolling player arriving from England in 1703. A theater, probably the first, was built in Williamsburg,
Virginia, in 1716. It housed a resident company of actors headed by
Charles and Mary Stagg, about whom little is known. Walter Murray
and Thomas Kean headed a company of comedians that performed
in Philadelphia in 1749, in New York in 1750, and in Williamsburg
in 1751. They continued performing for twenty years without distinction. For the most part, early settlers were too preoccupied with
their practical needs for shelter, food, worship and safety to make
culture a major concern. What cultural references they knew had
been brought with them from their mother countries. Colonized
America had not yet developed its own social history.

The first professional company of *comedians* to arrive in the
colonies was led by Lewis Hallam (1714–1756), the brother of
British theatrical manager William Hallam (1712–1758). William
Hallam's theatrical enterprise had run into bankruptcy in London,

but the generosity of his creditors allowed him to retain his costumes, properties and moveable scenery. Looking for new ways to revive his fortunes, he struck on sending a repertory of twenty-four plays and farces to the uncivilized colonial Americans. Lewis led a group of ten actors from London to America in 1752, but William remained in London and never saw his colonial American company perform. The company's strategy was to land in Royalist Williamsburg, which they considered more congenial to theater than Puritan New England. They performed in Williamsburg for eleven months, establishing a solid reputation, and by 1753, the company was given permission to perform in the northern colonies. They proceeded to build the first American theater in New York City. Rumblings from religious leaders suggesting that the troupe was in league with the devil limited their audiences and made it obligatory for them to spend much of their time touring to other cities. It was a politically arduous task to overcome the religious objections of the local fathers and gain permission to perform in the few cities large enough to provide sufficient patrons.

Theater, with its royal, seventeenth-century hierarchical organization, had a difficult time taking root in a country that was actively throwing off any suggestion of aristocracy. Even more threatening was the notion of outside groups siphoning off money that local leaders considered essential to keep in the community. Cities were small and the populations not so prosperous, so it was necessary for touring companies to rotate their repertoires from night to night in order to maximize income. This pattern of traveling companies, rather than resident companies, prevailed until the colonial war for independence, when it became hazardous for actors to be identified as British. During the war, Hallam's company kept a low profile by temporarily residing in the West Indies.

During the period between the Revolution and the Civil War, the United States expanded its boundaries while its population doubled every ten years. Major cities established resident theaters, and when certain actors gained in popularity over others, the star system developed. These entrepreneurial stars could divide their time among several companies, creating financial success for all. Although the number of actors increased, training remained informal, a combination of practical experience onstage and mentoring by older, established company actors.

After the Civil War, America's second industrial revolution vastly transformed the way the country functioned. The assembly line, with workers endlessly repeating a single task, introduced cost-efficiency to manufacturing. Such notions of efficiency also affected the theater: stars began to limit their repertories while moving from city to city with their own groups of featured players, engaging local actors (ringers) to fill small roles. But the disastrous economic depression of the 1870s eliminated most local companies, so the traveling star and his retinue were required to be self-sufficient. As a result, companies began presenting single plays that moved from theater to theater, with the star becoming a specialist in a single role. With cities in the expanded country now easily reachable by rail, a star could perform the same role for years. One such actor was James O'Neill (1849–1920), the father of playwright Eugene O'Neill (1888–1953), who became rich repeating the role of Edmund Dantes in *The Count of Monte Cristo* for over thirty years.

By the 1880s, New York City was becoming America's primary theater center. It was the country's chief commercial city and the entry point for immigrants, who brought with them a rich cultural history that often included a love of theater and live entertainment. There was a boom in the construction of playhouses, including such technical innovations as electric lighting and movable stages that accommodated the use of newly introduced three-dimensional scenery. Broadway productions were replicated and sent on road tours by rail. Sometimes multiple touring companies were created for popular plays. The sets were ponderous to move and costly to produce, so shows needed longer runs in order to recoup their investment. In these companies, actors were instructed to replicate the mannerisms and stage business of the original stars in order to provide an authentic New York experience for theater patrons across the country.

THE FIRST DIRECTORS, THEN THE FIRST ACTING SCHOOL

After 2,000 years of theater built around the playwright and the actor/manager, a new figure, the producer-director, arose. It was the responsibility of the producer-director to unify and integrate all production details. By the end of the nineteenth century, the director, or regisseur, had become the dominant force in the theater. The star actor continued to be important, but for the most part, actors became only one element of the production. Augustin Daly (1838–1899) was America's first regisseur, with David Belasco (1853–1931) and Steele MacKaye (born James Morrison MacKaye, 1842–1894) following his example.

Steele MacKaye was a director, playwright, actor, theater manager, inventor and visionary who wanted American theater to become an important art form. An erratic genius, he began by studying art and was influenced by the French Barbizon school, which emphasized naturalistic painting. As an actor, he was the first American to play Hamlet on the London stage, in 1873. He penned thirty plays, nineteen of which were produced in New York. Several of the plays were durable enough to continue being performed into the twentieth century. He was one of the most important innovators of playhouse design, with over one hundred inventions to his name, including folding theater seats, overhead lighting, fireproof scenery and the first double stage elevator, created for rapid scene changes. His emergence as one of America's first professional directors coincided with theater becoming big business in New York.

MacKaye wanted to establish a consistent acting company with the ability to perform exciting work, such as he had seen in the court theater established by director Duke George II of Saxe-Meiningen (1826–1914). Duke George's company was also a source of inspiration for André Antoine (1858–1943), who founded Théâtre-Libre in Paris in 1887, and Konstantin Sergeyevich Stanislavsky (1863–1938), who cofounded the Moscow Art Theatre with Vladimir Ivanovich Nemirovich-Danchenko (1859–1943) in 1898. MacKaye was searching for ways to emulate the new European sense of theatrical realism. But to create a company of actors, he needed a process for obtaining uniform results, a way of creating a common artistic language. In 1884, MacKaye established the first school for American actor training, the Lyceum Theatre School.

The Lyceum Theatre School for Acting was modeled after the Paris Conservatoire and centered on the techniques of François Delsarte (1811–1871), with whom MacKaye had studied in Paris. Delsarte was a French teacher of dramatic and musical expression who promoted naturalistic acting by devising and charting a complex vocabulary of face and body positions that communicate theatrical meaning. MacKaye added his own ideas of gymnastics to Delsarte's training vocabulary. (The system was a forerunner of modern kinesics, which designates various aspects of body motions and gestures as communicative behavior.) Delsarte was evidently searching for an external pathway to access the actor's inner life. His search presaged the psychodynamic theories of Sigmund Freud (1856–1939), which influenced Stanislavsky's subsequent experiments to find ways for the conscious to draw upon the emotional repository of the subconscious. Unfortunately, from what we know of its results, the Delsarte training did nothing to connect American actors to techniques more truthful than those in vogue since the days of actor Edwin Forrest (1806–1872). Forrest's acting was described by a contemporary critic as "the muscular school; the brawny art; the biceps aesthetics; the tragic calves; the bovine drama; rant, roar, and rigmarole."[1] Forrest's stage image embodied the emerging American character; his bravura style of acting was more about scoring points than bringing truth to the stage. Forrest was best known for playing rebels—two of his most popular roles were the gladiator Spartacus and the Native American Metamora, a role he played for forty years. This is not to say that more subtle acting didn't exist in America—the restrained acting of Edwin Booth (1833–1893), a generation after Forrest, was highly admired, but his genius was not easily emulated.

Although the Lyceum School failed to establish a lasting legacy of physical acting, it played a significant role in the beginnings of actor training, as it transitioned later into the American Academy of Dramatic Arts. The AADA replaced the Delsarte curriculum with a theoretical system similar to that developed by Stanislavsky. That school exists today, predominantly teaching the Meisner technique.

Acting departments were slowly introduced into university systems, beginning with the University of Michigan in 1906. Playwriting as a scholarly discipline had established itself two years earlier, notably with the course given by George Pierce Baker (1866–1935) at Radcliffe in 1904, which in 1905 moved to Harvard and drew students who would become America's first group of distinguished playwrights. While Baker's Harvard course was instrumental in developing first-class writers, there is no evidence that the establishment of the early university schools for the study of theater had any influence whatsoever on the acting profession. They were conduits for introducing foreign plays and new theatrical ideas on a community level, but it was not until conservatory-style preparation was introduced into universities in the 1960s that such programs became major training grounds for professional actors.

In Europe, the search for a new art of the stage led to experiments in naturalistic realism beginning around 1887. Almost immediately, this sparked a counterrevolution in nonrealistic theater, represented variously by productions created in 1890 by the French symbolist poet Paul Fort (1872–1960), in 1896 by the surrealist writer Alfred Jarry (1873–1907), and through the design theories of Swiss-born Adolphe Appia (1862–1928) and Englishman Edward Gordon

Craig (1872–1966). America followed slowly, with some admirable experiments in expressionism in the 1920s by playwrights Eugene O'Neill and Elmer Rice (1892–1967). But American public taste could never quite adjust to nonrealism. Even in stylized dramas, American audiences prefer to be tethered to acting behavior they perceive as real. For Americans, perceived reality equals truthfulness. That perception of realism has changed through the decades: in the nineteenth century, the most popular form of realism was melodrama, a style that we would consider hammy and insincere. Initially, America's embrace of realism came not through acting style but through surprisingly realistic stage effects. Producer David Belasco gained a reputation for highly detailed settings, sometimes created by transporting actual interiors from their sites to the stage, and amazed audiences with motorized special effects like realistic rain storms, water flowing from stage faucets and bacon sizzling on the stove. However, the plays remained third-rate romantic melodramas without subtle acting, except for the occasional star with a genius for moving audiences.

Americans were exposed to examples of splendid, disciplined ensemble acting during a visit from Dublin's Abbey Players in November of 1911, followed closely by the famous German director Max Reinhardt (1873–1943), whose company performed the expressionistic play *Sumurun* in January 1912. Then, in 1923, the Moscow Art Theatre—the acting ensemble whose theories, in practice, would become the basis for all American acting—arrived to galvanize the New York theater community.

STANISLAVSKY AND THE FOUNDATION OF AMERICAN ACTOR TRAINING

By 1923, Konstantin Stanislavsky, cofounder and director of the Moscow Art Theatre, had synthesized the early phase of his theories about acting, based on his own considerable acting experience and his observations of the results of the great actors of his time. This labor of creating a repeatable technique consumed his attention for the balance of his life. In total, Stanislavsky devoted some forty years to his study of the actor's way of working. As he reduced his ever-evolving theory to a system, the Art Theatre became his living laboratory of trial and error.

By 1906, at age forty-three, Stanislavsky had gathered a great deal of experience about the craft of acting, and he intuitively knew that there was more to acting than the artificial patterns into which the actor could easily fall. During his early years in the theater, Stanislavsky had haphazardly collected ideas on the art of acting that lacked coherence and were, therefore, useless for application in training his company. He began to research the laws that governed acting in order to create a useful system. He studied the work of the Italians Tommaso Salvini (1829–1915) and Eleonora Duse (1858–1924), held to be the greatest realistic actors of their time. He wanted to analyze and catalogue the elements of their genius.

It was the age of the modern scientific method and the early beginnings of psychology. Stanislavsky believed that feeling and truth were strategic to opening the door of creative intuition. He also believed that the pathway to the command of truthful performing lay through the subconscious. The subconscious automatically harmonizes the thousands of moment-to-moment decisions and actions of everyday life. But in the imaginary world of the stage, the subconscious knows it is not encountering reality, and therefore cannot perform its customary function. Onstage the subconscious loses its ability to serve as an automatic pilot. Stanislavsky wished to find a pathway from the conscious to the subconscious and back, to reinstate an imaginary belief that would summon lifelike behavior. His was the first effort to develop a psycho-technical system for training the actor. This approach was in sync with his times and, as we shall see, all art parallels and progresses at the same rate as the society around it. Art does not improve from one period to the next; it simply changes according to the belief needs of the times.

The Moscow Art Theatre actors were serving up realism at a time when some American playwrights were departing from it. O'Neill and Rice were experimenting with expressionism and symbolism, but the popular staples in American playhouses continued to be romantic melodramas, poetic dramas, comedies, and an ever-diminishing number of Shakespearean productions. Stanislavsky's actors impressed New York with their depth and technical perfection, their innovative ensemble work and their versatility in playing character and age. The Moscow actors appeared able to play any role, even those for which they were perhaps too old, as they transformed from character to character each night in rotating repertory. The Moscow Art Theatre planted the seed of desire for deeper American acting and set the stage for experiments that would eventually define the American acting style.

Richard Boleslavsky (1889–1937), a former member of the Moscow Art Theatre who was exiled as a result of the Russian Revolution, had made his way to New York in the early 1920s and was present to welcome his old friends when they arrived in 1923. During the run of their performances (which were spoken in Russian), Boleslavsky delivered some English-language lectures translating Stanislavsky's methods. Interest in these lectures generated the financial backing that enabled Boleslavsky to found the American Laboratory Theatre for actors and directors. He prevailed upon Moscow Art Theatre actress Maria Ouspenskaya (1876–1949) to teach in the Lab. When the Moscow Art Theatre returned to Russia in 1924, Ouspenskaya resigned in order to remain with the school and teach Stanislavsky's system, which included psychological investment and ensemble playing. Among the Lab's early students were Lee Strasberg (born Israel Strassberg, 1901–1982) and Stella Adler (1901–1992), both of whom became key figures in the development of American acting.

Lee Strasberg remained in the Lab classes only long enough to absorb Stanislavsky's basic principles as laid out by Ouspenskaya. Boleslavsky himself had stated that Americans must find an American way of using these techniques, and Strasberg took that to heart, preferring to experiment on his own. This was consistent with his lifelong pattern of learning—he had dropped out of school early and educated himself through the passionate pursuit of reading.

While acting in some of the sketches in the Theatre Guild's 1925 production of Rodgers and Hart's *Garrick Gaieties*, Strasberg became friends with Harold Clurman (1901–1980), who was stage-managing. In spite of their differences in temperament, the two were drawn together for a period of five years, engaging in passionate conversations about creating an important new theater that would embed genuine meaning for American audiences. They wanted a company of actors capable of ensemble work, such as they had observed during the Moscow Art Theatre visit, not a group of commercially trained actors without a common technique. Ultimately, Clurman became the evangelistic theorist for the founding of the Group Theatre, and Strasberg became the man with ideas for turning these theories into unified practice.

In 1931, Lee Strasberg was working for the Theatre Guild along with Harold Clurman and Cheryl Crawford (1902–1986). The Guild was the Broadway producing organization that operated in the manner of a noncommercial art theater. Of all Broadway theater producing institutions, it was the most dynamic and risk-taking. Even so, Strasberg, Clurman and Crawford felt that the Guild was too commercial, that it offered no real opportunity for them to grow as working actors and that it was time for a true ensemble of actors to emerge, one that would present plays that conveyed the life of their times. Strasberg had been experimenting as a director and teacher, expanding on what he had learned at the American Lab. Together, the three formed the Group Theatre (with a band of twenty-eight actors, most of whom would become legends in the history of American acting) and began a turbulent nine-year odyssey that to this date identifies them as America's greatest acting ensemble. Lee Strasberg acted as the Group's director. In his book *The Fervent Years*, Harold Clurman described the Group's work under Strasberg's guidance as "never stagy. Its roots are clearly in the intimate experience of a complex psychology, an acute awareness of human contradiction and suffering, a distinguished though perhaps a too specialized sensibility."[2]

The Theatre Guild generously helped the fledgling Group by giving it the rights to Paul Green's play *The House of Connelly* and $2,500 toward production, and then presenting the production under its auspices as a nonsubscription offering.[3] This first Group Theatre production was exultantly launched and enthusiastically received. Strasberg unified the company by exercising his beliefs in actor training. As Clurman recalled, "Strasberg was a fanatic on the subject of true emotion. Everything was secondary to it. He sought it with the patience of an inquisitor, he was outraged by trick substitutes . . . Here was something new to most of the actors, something basic, something almost holy. It was revelation in the theater; and Strasberg was its prophet."[4]

Group actor Bobby Lewis organized a Group Theatre school, with the intention of training the next generation of Group actors and making money for the company. It lasted only one year because of the company's extensive touring schedule, but it inspired the creation of other schools, and Bobby Lewis would eventually become a major director and teacher and the cofounder of the Actors Studio.

Looking back on their efforts, today's actors can only draw admiration and inspiration from the nine-year struggle of the Group Theatre (which lasted from 1931–1940). It developed some of America's greatest actors and produced a number of landmark productions, notably those of playwright Clifford Odets, who began as an actor in the company. The work of the company also formed a crucible to test what would become the major branches of American acting techniques. The Group realized its ideal of reconnecting the theater of ideas to the American society, but it was not able to sustain that success by Broadway's standards—the company's actors were admired, but Broadway is about making money. The Group could survive only as long as it could satisfy this insatiable need, and few of the plays it produced by other playwrights had the success rate enjoyed by Odets.

Although the Group's financial woes were the major reason for its ultimate demise, it was also rocked with personality clashes and internal controversy over its processes. After a few years, some company members felt that they were stagnating. Even though they were considered some of the best actors in America, they knew that they had to continue experimenting and growing. Company actress Stella Adler, daughter of the preeminent Yiddish actor Jacob P. Adler (1855–1926), led a contingent that was uncomfortable with Strasberg's ironhanded control over the company's acting method. In 1934, she worked with Stanislavsky in Paris for a few weeks and returned to the company to announce that Strasberg's use of the Stanislavsky system, with his emphasis on emotion as the guiding force for actors, had been incorrect. Stanislavsky was now working on the actor's use of his imagination to create the play's action. She lectured the company about the revelations she had experienced in Paris. This was the first challenge to Strasberg's hold on Stanislavsky-based training. Adler's classes on Stanislavsky's latest work led to the eventual establishment of her own conservatory in 1949. Another acclaimed Group Theatre actor, Sanford Meisner (1905–1997), began his own teaching experiments in 1935 based on what he had learned from Strasberg and Adler as well as his experiences as an actor in the company.

The acting techniques that arose in America as the twentieth century progressed were designed either to emphasize certain aspects of Stanislavsky's work or to react against it. Together, Strasberg, Adler and Meisner came to represent the troika of Stanislavsky-based approaches to American acting—each focused on a different facet of his forty-year process. Simplistically, the work of these three can be described as dominated respectively by emotion, imagination and spontaneity. Each teacher would have passionate adherents. Each would produce successful actors.

Despite widespread admiration for the Group Theatre actors, their process for acting did not filter into mainstream American culture until the confluence of events following World War II.

In the first chapter, Louis Scheeder takes up the story of how American acting suddenly became internationally prominent post–World War II. He sets the scene for this cultural phenomenon in his analysis of Lee Strasberg as the right man in the right place at the right time.

But first, a chronological context for the acting techniques in this book . . .

THE TRAINERS AND THE TRAINING

It takes twenty years to become an actor.

—SANFORD MEISNER

Actor training in America has transitioned from on-the-job apprenticeships, when techniques were handed down within a theatrical company from one generation of actors to the next; to being taught by master teachers running their own professional studios; to largely being the responsibility of universities, as is currently the case. In this latest shift from professional studios to the academy, it must be admitted that some of the ferocity of teaching has been lost. The previous system of apprentice-style teaching by older actors, who had been raised in a "get it right or get out" way of life, has given way to the academy's more nurturing sense of responsibility toward the emotional health of younger, less mature students.

Why are so many young people interested in studying acting today? NYU's drama program alone receives nearly 3,000 applications annually. This desire to perform cannot be based solely on insubstantial dreams of stardom and the American preoccupation with the foibles of tabloid personalities. It is explained best by Vicki Hart's summation within her chapter on Meisner training: "Our feelings signify what the world means to us . . . Students must learn what these feelings are, how to gain access to them and what to do with them. During this process they must be dedicated to finding their own truth." Living in a society that demands conformity, where emotions and opinions are withheld to avoid public scrutiny and criticism, what better way to practice being human than in imaginary circumstances where young people are permitted, even required, to experience the full range of themselves in the service of speaking truthfully?

Beginning in the 1950s and burgeoning during the 1960s, professional not-for-profit theaters proliferated across the nation. The creation of these theaters coincided with shrinking Broadway activity, and Broadway producers blamed not-for-profit theaters for their diminishing commercial revenues. But it was the escalating costs of production, lack of opportunity for new playwrights and actors, and paucity of good theater on Broadway that fueled the regional theater movement. These new theaters expected to maintain resident companies and needed trained actors capable of playing a broad range of styles. No longer would it be sufficient for an actor to be proficient in a narrow range of personality roles and styles, as rewarded in films and television and by Broadway producers. Schools that already had established academic acting departments revised them in favor of developing new curricula that would meet the needs of company actors. These actors were expected to be proficient in performing the classics and contemporary plays in realistic and nonrealistic styles, demands that triggered the establishment of conservatory-style programs at universities.

The chapters in this book represent ten frequently studied approaches to actor training. Most of these approaches, or variations on them, are widely taught throughout the United States. The chapters roughly follow the chronological order in which the approaches came to full prominence. Each, to some extent, borrows or reacts to what has come before. All these approaches, in one way or another, sprang from Stanislavsky's investigation of the actor's process, surely the most complete exploration ever undertaken. Some of these techniques focus on a specific portion of his system, some were developed in opposition to his methods, but all use Stanislavsky's vocabulary as a foundation from which to work. There are other theories of acting not covered here with which the well-educated actor will be familiar; for example, the writings of Antonin Artaud (1896–1948), the biomechanics of Vsevolod Emilievich Meyerhold (1874–1940) and the philosophy and exercises of Bertolt Brecht (1898–1956). Frequently, these can be part of the American actor's study, but they seldom serve as the primary focus in his development.

Successful acting must reflect a society's current beliefs. The men and women who developed each new technique were convinced that previous methods were not equal to the full challenges of their time and place, and the techniques in this book have been adapted to current needs in order to continue to be successful methods for training actors. The actor's journey is an individual one, and the actor seeks a form, or a variety of forms, of training that will assist in unlocking his own creative gifts of expression.

Many of these techniques include exercises designed to access the inner life of the actor. But in order to effectively evoke the inner life, it is vital that actors spend an equal amount of time developing the vehicle for this expression, the physical skills of a flexible and evenly produced voice, a supple and strong body, musical rhythm and controlled, relaxed movement. Equally important is an inquiring mind for history, politics, psychology and culture. It is easy to see why most teachers refer to the acting profession as a lifetime of learning.

Among the techniques described in these chapters there are conflicting ideas about what kind of training will make an actor, as well as much that overlaps or is complementary. But the goal in all cases is to develop an actor with range, power and depth. If every human organism reacted in the same way to the same information, we would need only one technique, we would all be the same, and the world would be a boring place.

So we begin this investigation of technique with the training espoused by Lee Strasberg. Significantly, he was the first and, therefore, perhaps the most important person to develop and popularize an American acting method. Like Stanislavsky, Strasberg's investigation took place through decades of thought and experimentation. However, it was not until the 1950s that his ideas caught fire in American culture. His work finally corresponded to his time.

LEE STRASBERG'S METHOD FROM ANNA STRASBERG

> In acting everything is done unconsciously as a process of memory.
>
> —LEE STRASBERG

Although he had seen and appreciated the ensemble work of Stanislavsky's Moscow Art Theatre, it was through classes at the American Theatre Lab, led by Richard Boleslavsky and Maria Ouspenskaya, that Lee Strasberg was introduced to the techniques employed by the Russian master. Boleslavsky had been an actor in the Moscow Art Theatre's company from 1906 to 1919, the period in which Stanislavsky had begun his investigations. Boleslavsky had graduated from acting to directing in the MAT Studio. He introduced Stanislavsky's principles to Americans and, later, he successfully directed on Broadway and in the film industry.

Boleslavsky published a small book in 1933 that described six lessons for the actor—concentration, memory of emotion, dramatic action, characterization, observation, and rhythm. At the American Theatre Lab, Lee Strasberg found these lessons to be a revelation, but he left the Lab as soon as he had absorbed their significance. He felt that he could better apply these principles to American realism through his own experimentation than through classes with the Russian Boleslavsky. The American Theatre Lab classes, particularly in concentration and affective memory, formed the foundation for Strasberg's lifelong work. He called this his *method* and, at some point, Strasberg's work became known as the Method, a term implying that Strasberg's technique and Stanislavsky's work were synonymous.

By all reports, Strasberg had a contradictory personality, combining a brute force of will with an almost unapproachable intellectualism. A teacher who could unlock the doors to real emotion, he himself did not voice his own feelings easily. He had an enduring effect on the acting of the Group Theatre, but personality clashes with Clurman and Crawford led to Strasberg's resignation in 1937.

Without the artistic protection and home base of the Group, Strasberg was thrown back into the vicissitudes of working in commercial theater and film. His work in New York and Hollywood over the next ten years was without distinction, and he might have been relegated to a significant but minor position in theatrical history had events not combined to place him at the center of post–World War II theater training. Against his better judgment, but out of need, director Elia Kazan (1909–2003), the former Group Theatre actor who had become America's preeminent stage director and who was now in the process of becoming one of Hollywood's best film directors, asked his old nemesis/mentor, Strasberg, to direct the acting and directing program at the Actors Studio. Kazan, with Bobby Lewis and Cheryl Crawford, had founded the Studio as a place where commercial actors could learn a unified way of acting for the stage and films. After initially declining the invitation, Strasberg finally agreed. Within three years, Kazan acknowledged that Strasberg *was* the Actors Studio.

Throughout his lifetime, Strasberg, like Stanislavsky, was a lightning rod attracting those who devotedly emulated his work, and driving those who rejected it to create their own oppositional acting techniques. Either way, it can be said that Strasberg fathered American acting.

Anna (Mizrahi) Strasberg, Lee's former student, second wife and widow, and now the artistic director of the Lee Strasberg Theatre Institute in New York and Los Angeles, describes Strasberg's technique as it is being taught today at the Institute, carefully respectful to every detail of his legacy. Because he taught for such a long period of time, and his principles were so popular and successful at a time when acting and playwriting were ascendant in the culture, Strasberg's techniques are the most quoted, admired, reviled, beloved, hated and written-about of the American acting techniques.

STELLA ADLER TECHNIQUE FROM TOM OPPENHEIM

> Jacob Adler said that unless you give the audience something that makes them bigger—better—do not act.
>
> —STELLA ADLER

Stella Adler was born into theater royalty. Her father, Jacob Adler, the preeminent actor of the Yiddish-American theater, was born in Russia and immigrated to America in 1887. He founded the Independent Yiddish Art Company. His Shylock in *The Merchant of Venice* was so impressive that it played on Broadway in 1903 and 1905, with Adler performing in Yiddish while his fellow actors performed in English. When he died, 150,000 people gathered at his funeral procession to pay their respects. Stella Adler's mother, Sara, was a leading actress in her own right, and her brother Luther, sister Julia and niece Pearl were highly admired actors. Her cousin Francine Larrimore (1898–1975) was a Broadway star, with a long career performing such roles as Roxie Hart in *Chicago* (1926), Kitty Brown in *Let Us Be Gay* (1929) and Abby Fane in *Brief Moment* (1931). Sara and Jacob had five children and two stepchildren. All in all, there were sixteen Adler actors working simultaneously. It was said that no curtain went up in New York without an Adler on the stage. Every member of the family, it seems, possessed the acting gene. They did not have to train for the theater; they simply walked onto the stage. Today the Adler gene is lodged in Stella's grandson, Tom Oppenheim, the artistic director of the Stella Adler Studio of Acting in New York. (Oppenheim's father, David, is the highly admired clarinetist who performed under Leonard Bernstein and was an influential dean of the Tisch School of the Arts at NYU.)

Stella Adler joined the Group Theatre in 1931 and worked under Lee Strasberg's direction in Paul Green's *The House of Connelly*, Maxwell Anderson's *Night over Taos* and John Howard Lawson's *Success Story* and *Gentlewoman*. When she joined the company, she was already a professional actress. She was tempestuous by nature, so perhaps it was not surprising that she conflicted with Strasberg and was a ringleader among the actors who revolted against his iron determination that emotion was predominant in all acting. Her sense of revolt crystallized when she journeyed to Paris and told Stanislavsky, "I enjoyed acting and the theater until you came along, and now I hate it." Stanislavsky listened to her reading of a scene from *Gentlewoman*, and asked about her training. When she described Strasberg's approach, he responded that her training was correct, but by this time he had moved his own study of acting to the actions, or "beats," that served the truth of the playwright's central action of the play, which he called the "super-objective." He now believed that emotion could arise naturally if the actor was true to his character's through-line in the play. Adler returned from Paris and triumphantly questioned Strasberg's approach to training. Strasberg defended his work, saying that action was meaningless without emotion. It was the beginning of the end of Strasberg's absolute control over the company, and the beginning of a second branch of Stanislavsky-based training in America.

We have learned that the theater and its acting styles change as society changes, and certain acting styles are more suitable in one time period than another. It may be that an emphasis on action rather than emotion would have been better suited to the theater during the social upheavals of the 1930s. However, it is a fact that under Strasberg the Group actors gained the reputation of being the finest acting ensemble in America. And it is also a sad fact that the Group Theatre was never financially successful. Strasberg's vision of actor training did not catch hold and become a phenomenon until the 1950s. Timing is everything.

Stella Adler opened her training institute in 1949. Her method is rooted in script analysis and exercises for the imagination. It is reputed that the day Lee Strasberg died in 1982, Adler asked her students to rise, saying, "A man of the theater has died . . . and it will take the theater one hundred years to get over him."

SANFORD MEISNER TECHNIQUE FROM VICTORIA HART

The foundation of acting is the reality of doing.

—SANFORD MEISNER

Sanford Meisner was the third member of the Group Theatre to develop his own training method based on Stanislavsky. (A fourth member, Bobby Lewis, was a successful director and teacher, but did not leave behind a theory and curriculum that could be replicated.)

Meisner always cited Strasberg as his mentor, but he developed a method for training actors to access their emotions that did not rely on sense memory. Instead, he utilized exercises to force the actor into spontaneous reaction. Although it appears to be utterly simple, the most difficult task for an actor in the theater is to listen. Meisner is the only technician to place a major emphasis on exercises designed to allow for a true, unpremeditated response by the actor through listening and responding. In order to accomplish this, Meisner places the actor's focus on his acting partner. His famous repetition exercise basically wears down the actor's defenses until he responds truthfully.

> The smallest social unit is not the single person but two
> people. In life too we develop one another.
>
> —J. WILLETT

Being just as human as the next person, an actor, with or without experience, has natural defenses that get in the way of honest, seemingly unplanned line readings and emotional reactions. In other words, how do you train an actor who knows the script, who knows the story, who knows his objective, to live in the moment? This is particularly true when the task at hand, the play, provides technically difficult physical and emotional challenges. Meisner believed that he had found the way.

BEYOND MICHAEL CHEKHOV TECHNIQUE:
CONTINUING THE EXPLORATION THROUGH THE MASK
FROM PER BRAHE

> For artists with mature imaginations, images are living
> beings, as real to their minds' eyes as things around us
> are visible to our physical eyes.
>
> —MICHAEL CHEKHOV

Michael Chekhov (born Mikhail Alexandrovich Chekhov, 1891–1955) made innovative contributions to acting technique based on his experience as one of the twentieth century's great character actors, and Stanislavsky's most brilliant student. His explorations led him to look at acting as "spiritual logic." Thus, Chekhov developed exercises and theories with a greater emphatic metaphysical approach than those of the other techniques. Actors with an accessible inner life will immediately respond to the terminology Chekhov used to stimulate the actor's psyche. Chekhov's images communicate directly to the actor's artistic inner life without first needing to be cerebrally translated.

Accepted into the Moscow Art Theatre when he was twenty-one, Chekhov worked under Yevgeny Bagrationovich Vakhtangov (1883–1922) in MAT's experimental First Studio. He professed complete confidence in the Stanislavsky system, yet he and Stanislavsky fought over Chekhov's methods during rehearsals. But Stanislavsky could not deny the extraordinary results of Chekhov's interpretations in performance. Chekhov believed that imagination was more important than Stanislavsky's ideas on the use of affective memory. Rather than using personal experiences as artistic stimuli, he urged actors to build character through fictional imaginings. Perhaps it was the influence of Chekhov that moved Stanislavsky away from affective memory and toward experiments with the imagination. When Stella Adler met with Stanislavsky in Paris in the 1930s, she was told that, if she ever came across Michael Chekhov, she should take the opportunity to work with him.

To his reliance on imagination, Chekhov added a belief in anthroposophy. The Austrian Rudolf Steiner (1861–1925) founded the anthroposophy movement, which, according to the *Encyclopaedia Britannica*, taught that "man once participated more fully in spiritual processes of the world through a dreamlike consciousness but had since become restricted by his attachment to material things. The renewed perception of spiritual things required training the human consciousness to rise above attention to matter. The ability to achieve this goal by an exercise of the intellect was believed theoretically innate in everyone."[5] This belief was translated into a movement technique Steiner called eurythmy, largely adopted by expressionists who sought to show characters as symbols rather than people. As a result of this combination of beliefs, Chekhov's characterizations were considered by Stanislavsky to be overly physical, employing techniques of grotesque comedy. Charles Baudelaire (1821–1867) wrote of the laughter this type of comedy engenders: "The grotesque is a creation mixed with a certain imitative faculty of elements found in nature. The laughter caused by the grotesque has about it something profound and primitive."

Whatever the means Chekhov used to discover and refine his techniques, it is the clarity of his imagistic language to actors that sets him apart from other acting theorists. His found words and images are immediately perceived and inculcated by actors through a gut reaction rather than through a cerebral understanding.

While teaching in Russia, the Danish teacher Per Brahe was introduced to Chekhov technique and saw that the spiritual elements of Chekhov's experiments perfectly complemented his work with the mask, which, in turn, was inspired by Balinese dance. Brahe has linked these three theatrical disciplines into one performance theory.

UTA HAGEN TECHNIQUE FROM CAROL ROSENFELD

> Talent alone is not enough. Character and ethics, a point of view about the world in which you live and an education, can and must be acquired and developed.
>
> —UTA HAGEN

Carol Rosenfeld discusses the exercises that Uta Hagen (1919–2004) created for her highly influential classes at the Herbert Berghof (HB) studio, and Rosenfeld's experience teaching them there under Hagen's tutelage. The reader will recognize many of the terms applied in these exercises as originating from Stanislavsky, also in familiar usage in other techniques. There is no focus on the direct development of emotion that one finds in Strasberg or Meisner technique—Hagen's methods eschew sentimentality in acting and focus clearly on the development of imagination and spontaneity (similar to Meisner's goals). She places great emphasis on the use of realistic props and furniture to create a base of environmental reality for the student.

Uta Hagen's performance work and teaching personified her pursuit of truthful acting. Acting into her eighties, Hagen displayed a vitality and freshness onstage that was the envy of younger actors. Hagen's acting output was not abundant—she devoted herself primarily to teaching—but the major roles that she essayed were legendary. Anyone who saw her characterization of Martha in Edward Albee's play *Who's Afraid of Virginia Woolf?* (1962) will never forget it. I recall watching the show from the back row of the highest balcony in the Billy Rose Theatre. Her performance reached up to me with complete clarity and power. Some weeks later, I had the opportunity to attend a gypsy run-through of the play while Hagen and her costar Arthur Hill were preparing replacement actors in the secondary roles of Nick and Honey for the London production. This time I sat in the third row of the orchestra section. Hagen's performance was the same twenty feet from the stage as it had been at the back of the highest section of the theater. Seen from near the stage, Hill's performance seemed larger-than-life, as he was projecting to the back of the house. Hagen was not projecting. She was not *acting*. I realized that Hagen was simply filling the entire theater with her presence.

Hagen credited Harold Clurman, from the Group Theatre, for rekindling her dedication to a "true life in the theater" when he directed her in *The Whole World Over* in 1947—yet another example of the spirit of dedication and craft from that premier band of American actors being passed to the next generation.

PHYSICAL ACTING AFTER JERZY GROTOWSKI
FROM STEPHEN WANGH

The body does not have memory, it is memory.

—JERZY GROTOWSKI

Jerzy Grotowski (1933–1999) received a conventional Stanislavsky-based training in his native Poland. After graduating from the theater school in Kraków, he received a scholarship to study directing at the Lunacharsky State Institute of Theatre Arts (GITIS) in Moscow. There he encountered the theories of Vsevolod Meyerhold, which had been developed both in sympathy with and contradiction to the work of his mentor and colleague, Stanislavsky. Meyerhold had experimented with a physical approach to theater that he called "biomechanics." Grotowski also became familiar with Vakhtangov's synthesis, an aggressive means of expression, and the oriental theater techniques employed in the Peking Opera, Indian Kathakali and Japanese Noh theater.

Grotowski discovered the teachings of Delsarte, whose physical techniques had formed the basis for the first acting school in America. While the translation of Delsarte's work to America from France had done nothing to help American actors develop a modern approach to truthful behavior, Grotowski was able to connect these physical actions to a deeper understanding of the human organism. Grotowski's work reflected a combination of intellectualism, extreme physical control, social passion and mysticism.

In 1959, Grotowski began his experiments on a new aesthetic for the theater in Opole, Poland, when the local authorities gave him the Theatre of Thirteen Rows. The Opole People's Council granted a meager subsidy and permitted the establishment of the only professional experimental theater in Poland. Even with the subsidy, the theater was so poor that its actors almost starved. "Poor Theater" was at first a necessity that later became a favored style of work. Grotowski was committed to the idea of ensemble and turning the craft of acting into an art. His actor training required great effort to develop accomplished physical dexterity and powerful vocal abilities. Grotowski explored the actor's entire organism in order to tell the story. Performances in Communist Poland were censored, while rehearsals were not. So Grotowski's laboratory experiments, where he explored his interest in ritual and the actor's physiology, became more interesting to him than performing. Performances were primarily a way to explore the actor-audience relationship. Late in Grotowski's life, the laboratory experiments became the whole of his work.

In 1967, Stephen Wangh studied with Jerzy Grotowski for four weeks at NYU. Grotowski was just becoming internationally known, and these were the first classes he had taught in America. Wangh readily admits that he teaches "after" Grotowski. Since Grotowski emphasized experimentation and was constantly changing, growing, it would be impossible for anyone to say that they taught Grotowski's method. Apparently, he never intended to create a system to be meticulously followed, and even if he had, such rigorous physical and emotional work would require a degree of commitment daunting to anyone but the most dedicated actors. But Grotowski's exercises and theories have inspired followers who agreed with him that precision and discipline are the keys to great acting.

THE SIX VIEWPOINTS FROM MARY OVERLIE

The most important feature of the new viewpoint on dynamics, popularly known as chaos theory . . . is the development of a whole series of novel techniques for extracting useful information from apparently random behavior.

—*ENCYCLOPAEDIA BRITANNICA*

Mary Overlie, the creator of Viewpoints theory, is similar to Stanislavsky and Strasberg with respect to her long quest to define artistic deconstruction[6] and put it to practical application. She explored her theories initially through her dance company, and then by teaching them to a generation of acting and directing students. Just as Stanislavsky observed the great realistic actors of his time and catalogued techniques to replicate their processes, Overlie has observed the work of extraordinary abstract artists to inform her process.

Taking what she observed of the elements of classical and modern theatrical forms as they applied to acting, she separated these hierarchical elements into six materials and arranged them side by side, horizontally, giving them equal importance. These *deconstructed* materials could then be reconstituted in any combination or order of hierarchy, or be applied singly. When practicing this, the actor discovers new information that might not be so easily encountered through traditional methods of working. This postmodern deconstruction process is highly democratic, with each material possessing potential equality. Perhaps this stress on the democracy of the elements of artistry makes Viewpoints the first truly indigenous American innovation in actor training and performing. Lee Strasberg had attempted to Americanize Stanislavsky's Russian-based system of creating realistic acting. Here, Overlie has sublimated the theatrical hierarchy of realistic acting to the needs of its individual components. While the avant-garde was rooted in France before being transplanted to America, Overlie's method of investigation is not inherited from another country, but it does rely upon the definitions of traditional Western form. Actors who have already studied conventional actor training are quickly able to grasp the idea of deconstruction because they recognize the six theatrical materials of Viewpoints that Overlie identifies as integral, hierarchical components of classic and modern theater:

- Space (ability to perceive physical relationships)
- Story (ability to perceive and collect information over a period of time and make conclusions)
- Emotion (ability to perceive states of feeling and to be put into states of feeling)
- Shape (ability to respond to form)
- Time (ability to perceive duration and systems designed to regulate duration)
- Movement (ability to identify kinetic states through memory).

Foremost among those embracing Viewpoints is renowned teacher and director Anne Bogart, who was introduced to this theory and practice while teaching with Overlie. Bogart has since developed a company around her own, expanded version of Viewpoints vocabulary, combining it with the physical work of Tadashi Suzuki, a prominent figure in contemporary Japanese theater. His techniques, developed to anchor Japanese actors to a new Asian tradition of theater, have been utilized in America largely as exercises to focus concentration and strengthen the actor.

As a training tool, Viewpoints is especially valuable for actors who are struggling with self-imposed blocks, blocks that stand in way of their own confidence and ability to reach a deeper concentration in their work. Because the technique is not judgmental and requires an intense concentration on discovery and internal observation that is not focused primarily on the self, the young actor slips into a better way of *being* onstage.

Overlie's richly dense description of Viewpoints is also a clearly articulated description of postmodern deconstruction in practice.

PRACTICAL AESTHETICS FROM ROBERT BELLA

> All that is under your control is your intention.
>
> —DAVID MAMET

The roots of Practical Aesthetics lie in elements of Meisner technique. Just as Viewpoints training defines a way of taking apart theatrical hierarchy so it can be examined for new information, Practical Aesthetics tends to delimit traditional training, paring away emotional and character work to create a systematic shorthand for the actor.

In 1983, playwright David Mamet delivered a series of lectures in the drama department at NYU's Tisch School of the Arts. These talks described his theories about acting. Excited by what they heard, a group of students approached Mamet to ask that he take them under his wing for training and to create a theater company. Under the tutelage of Mamet and actor William H. Macy, the students began summer retreats in Vermont over the next two years. By the summer of 1984, the actors felt sufficiently prepared to write *A Practical Handbook for the Actor* under Mamet's watchful eye. This bible of Mamet's beliefs outlined the principles of Practical Aesthetics, as it came to be known. Subsequently, the Atlantic Theater Company was formed and took up residence at Lincoln Center Theater, where Mamet's old friend and director from Chicago days, Gregory Mosher, was the artistic director. The company was successfully launched when they produced Howard Korder's play *Boy's Life*. Today, the Atlantic Theater Company owns its own theater performance space on West 20th Street, and a school where it conducts a three-year curriculum for NYU based around Practical Aesthetics.

Practical Aesthetics may be the first theory created by a playwright to be translated into a curriculum for training actors. Brecht theorized and left a list of exercises, but these were not formalized into a curriculum. Mamet is first and foremost a playwright, just as Stanislavsky was first and foremost an actor. Mamet, being one of the major American playwrights straddling the twentieth and twenty-first centuries, has dictated a way of working for actors that fits the needs of the writer.

Mamet briefly studied with Sanford Meisner, evidently a difficult experience for both of them. One might imagine that Meisner's comment, "An ounce of behavior is worth a pound of words," would not sit well with a playwright. Mamet discontinued taking Meisner's classes after the first year, which stresses spontaneity of the actor playing self, and before the second-year training, which introduces character development, and came away with a disdain for techniques that employ direction by indirection to put the actor in contact with his emotions. He adopted Meisner's credo that acting is about what characters do, not what they feel. Feelings do not tell the playwright's story. He believes that there is a direct way in which to teach craft that anyone can learn. While talent is probably necessary to get commitment from an actor, to Mamet, lack of it is not necessarily an impediment to learning the craft. Anyone can make a shoe. Some make a more beautiful shoe than others, but anyone who applies himself can make a shoe.

Frequently, the characters in Mamet's plays are emotionally stunted or unable to express their feelings. They represent contemporary society in its most repressed condition, largely able to express only anger. In this same context, Mamet has nothing against actors who are in touch with their feelings; he simply feels that it is a waste of time for them to try to make a connection with something that can be as fickle as genuine, repeatable emotion. He has written caustically about techniques that, at their center, train to reach the emotions and place an emphasis on the primacy of the actor. Undoubtedly, as a playwright, he has encountered actors who are searching for the subtext in his plays at the expense of its action. As might be expected, he believes that the only salvation for an actor is study of the text.

One technique Mamet lifted from Meisner was the repetition exercise. Mamet could see its value in training spontaneity and, in a sense, eliciting a genuine emotional reaction from the actor. He also agreed with Meisner's belief that "to act is to do." So it is action, the action gleaned from deciphering the script, that is at the heart of Practical Aesthetics.

Mamet also believes that it is wasteful for actors to spend time on character work. "It is impossible for you to become the character you are playing. In the theater, character is an illusion created by the words and given circumstances supplied by the playwright and the physical actions of the actor."[7] Mamet relieves the actor of the burden of becoming someone else. Like Viewpoints, Practical Aesthetics is democratic; it's American. You are what you say. (Politicians discovered this long ago.) Ironically, Mamet's view of the actor *being* the character is similar to Strasberg's expectation that the actor must bring himself into the role, although Mamet's view does not include the need for internal work such as Strasberg's exercises in affective emotional memory. The reader will also note some crossover of beliefs between Mamet's philosophy and Louis Scheeder's Neo-Classical emphasis on Thought in Action.

Practical Aesthetics is a young technique that continues to be tested and refined through the practices of the Atlantic Theater Company. It is quintessentially American. It is fast, no-nonsense and easily accessible, and requires only hard work to master. As the reader will see, Practical Aesthetics is practical in every way.

INTERDISCIPLINARY TRAINING FROM FRITZ ERTL

[The Group Theatre] demanded a basic understanding of a complex artistic principle; that all people connected with this theater, the actor, designer, playwright, director, etc., had of necessity to arrive at a single point of view which the theme of the play also expressed.

—STELLA ADLER

Fritz Ertl's chapter on interdisciplinary training might very well describe a way of teaching that brings actor training full circle, since the idea of the inclusive actor who knows every facet of theatrical production takes us back to the days when Steele MacKaye did it all, not as an actor specialist, but as a theater worker.

Ertl makes the case that in order for actors to fully understand their function in the creation of theater, they should study other disciplines—in this case, directing. He describes his role in the interdisciplinary training provided by the Playwrights Horizons Theater School's curriculum, which is part of the drama department at NYU's Tisch School of the Arts. Ertl's training recognizes that, in a sense, the very best actors direct themselves. They are partners with the director and playwright in creating stage space and finding a dramatic way of framing the play. It seems that what goes around comes around. Ertl makes the case for the versatile actor who uses all of himself in multiple capacities—acting, writing, directing, designing, dramaturgy, etc. This trains the actor to revert to an earlier period, before the mass production of theater, when he was at the center, leading and managing the company. Perhaps this is the future—to return to the past, as theater periodically does to cleanse and revitalize itself through a contemporary sensibility.

NEO-CLASSICAL TRAINING FROM LOUIS SCHEEDER

Training, if it is to advance, should ideally function as a laboratory in which hypotheses are posited, tested, refined, and retested.

—LOUIS SCHEEDER

Louis Scheeder's chapter concludes the book, using contemporary rationales for performing classical texts. Although he confines himself to applying this work to Shakespearean text, his implication is that this approach is viable for any text work, be it classical, contemporary or nonsensical.

Many schools profess to provide classical training. But what does that really mean, since these schools certainly are not limiting their students exclusively to work on plays with elevated language? In most cases, classical training refers to a course of study that gives equal weight to rigorous voice and text work, stage combat, singing, relaxation and isolation of physical movement, dance, and some form of traditional (Stanislavsky-based) acting technique, scene work and performance. It is the integration of these enlivened facets of the actor's self that results in a whole larger than the sum of its parts.

Scheeder defines his approach to acting technique as Thought in Action—text as subtext, character and action all rolled into one. He does not seek to layer text onto an acting technique or vice versa, but rather states that the proper use of text *is* the technique.

Louis Scheeder has developed and tested his theories as director of the Classical Studio, an advanced training program of the NYU drama department.

Arthur Bartow
August 2006
New York City

ENDNOTES/SOURCES

Epigraphs:

(Page xv) Quoted by Edith J. R. Isaacs in her introduction to *Acting: The First Six Lessons* by Richard Boleslavsky, New York: Theatre Arts Books, 1933.

(Page xxv) Quoted by Sydney Pollock in his introduction to *Sanford Meisner on Acting* by Sanford Meisner and Dennis Longwell, New York: Vintage, 1987, p. xv.

(Page xxvii) Hull, S. Loraine, *Strasberg's Method as Taught by Lorrie Hull*, Woodbridge, CT: Ox Bow, 1985, p. 19.

(Page xxix) Adler, Stella, *Stella Adler on Ibsen, Strindberg, and Chekhov*, Barry Paris, ed., New York: Knopf, 1999; Vintage, 2000, p. 3.

(Page xxx) Meisner, Sanford, and Dennis Longwell, *Sanford Meisner on Acting*, p. 16.

(Page xxxi) Willet, J., *Brecht on Theatre*, London: Methuen, 1964, p. 197.

(Page xxxi) Chekhov, Michael, *On the Technique of Acting*, Mel Gordon, ed., New York: HarperCollins, 1991, p. 4.

(Page xxxiii) Hagen, Uta, with Haskel Frankel, *Respect for Acting*, New York: Wiley, 1973, p. 13.

(Page xxxiv) Wolford, Lisa, "Grotowski's Vision of the Actor," *Twentieth Century Actor Training*, Alison Hodge, ed., London: Routledge, 2000, p. 203.

(Page xxxv) *Encyclopaedia Britannica*, "17th and 18th Century Mathematics" (article 1, article 2), analysis, ordinary differential equations, dynamical system theory and chaos, Ultimate Reference Suite CD-ROM, 2003.

(Page xxxvii) Mamet, David, Introduction to *A Practical Handbook to the Actor* by Melissa Bruder et al., New York: Vintage, 1986, p. xi.

(Page xxxix) Adler, Stella, *Stella Adler on Ibsen, Stridberg, and Chekhov*.

(Page xl) Scheeder, Louis, "Neo-Classical Training" (essay included in this book).

1. Curtis, George William, "The Editor's Easy Chair," *Harper's Magazine*, vol. 28, December 1863, pp. 132–33.

2. Clurman, Harold, *The Fervent Years: The Group Theatre & the '30s*, New York: Knopf, 1945; Da Capo Press, 1983, p. 61.

3. Ibid., p. 55.

4. Ibid., p. 44–45.

5. "Steiner, Rudolf," *Encyclopaedia Britannica Online*, 2006.

6. Deconstructionist theory began as a literary method of inquiry in post–World War II France, fathered by philosopher Jacques Derrida. It became popular in the United States in the 1970s and was applied by avant-garde artists, either consciously or unconsciously, to their work. Jonathan Kandell's obituary of Derrida (*New York Times*, vol. CLIV, no. 52, Oct. 10, 2004, p. 1) reported that deconstruction "asserted that all writing was full of confusion and contradiction" due to an author's inability to "overcome the inherent contradictions of language itself." This theory was used to explore the fundamental inconsistencies of Western culture.

7. Mamet, David, Introduction to *A Practical Handbook to the Actor* by Melissa Bruder et al., p. 74.

RECOMMENDED READING LIST

Bentley, Eric, *The Theory of the Modern Stage*, New York: Applause, 1997.
Bentley shepherds fifteen essays about ten modern theater makers with historical overviews. David Magarshack's essay on Stanislavsky, pp. 219–274, provides a definitive description of the great theorist's early work, surpassing in clarity Stanislavsky's own writings.

Boleslavsky, Richard, *Acting: The First Six Lessons*, New York: Theatre Arts Books, 1933.
In this slim volume, Boleslavsky reviews the lessons he taught in America's first exposure to Stanislavsky's methods.

Hewitt, Barnard, *Theatre U.S.A., 1665 to 1957*, New York: McGraw-Hill, 1959.
Hewitt has compiled an authoritative and complete history of American theater by combining comprehensive narrative with historical reviews.

Hodge, Alison, ed., *Twentieth Century Actor Training*, New York: Routledge, 2000.
Alison Hodge has assembled excellent essays that tell the story of actor training from an international perspective. There are descriptions of some American methods, but most of the theories described in this book have been more influential in Europe than in the United States.

Rimer, J. Thomas, trans., *The Way of Acting: The Theatre Writings of Tadashi Suzuki*, New York: Theatre Communications Group, 1986.
Tadashi Suzuki has received international attention for his work, which is intended to serve the goals of the entire spectrum of Japanese theater. Many American actors have participated in extended workshops at Suzuki's spiritual home for his company in the small village of Toga. Some American training programs have adopted his techniques, principally for their benefits in concentration and strengthening the lower body.

Smith, Wendy, *Real Life Drama: The Group Theatre and America, 1931–1940*, New York: Knopf, 1990; Grove/Atlantic, 1992.
This is a tremendously well-told saga of the Group Theatre and the artists who participated in its nine-year life.

TRAINING OF
THE AMERICAN ACTOR

STRASBERG'S METHOD AND THE ASCENDANCY OF AMERICAN ACTING

Louis Scheeder

Against the background of the Cold War and the depredations of the McCarthy era, Lee Strasberg transformed Russian theatrical practice into a symbol of American freedom and nationalism and elevated American acting into an international art form. Strasberg developed the Method in two stages: first as a founder and director of the Group Theatre, and later as the artistic director of the Actors Studio. In the 1930s, Strasberg worked to create emotional life; in the 1950s he sought to release and theatricalize that emotional life. Strasberg believed that the training of internal skills was "the fundamental work of the actor."[1]

When Strasberg, Harold Clurman and Cheryl Crawford founded the Group Theatre, the ideals of Stanislavsky were paramount. However, the trio was not only idealistic, they were also self-proclaimed revolutionaries in the field of acting.[2] Strasberg had studied "other revolutions, political and artistic" and consciously created "an artistic revolution" with the Group.[3] Strasberg later characterized the Group years as "a period of utilizing previous discoveries in the process of actual professional production" during which he concerned himself with "practical application rather than theory."[4]

Strasberg directed the majority of the Group's productions in its early years and assiduously applied Stanislavsky's previous discoveries—i.e., affective memory–based techniques—to the Group's productions. Opposition to Strasberg's commitment to emotion surfaced when, in 1934, Stella Adler traveled to Paris and met with Stanislavsky. While the director assured her that what she had learned about his system was essentially correct, he also emphasized what he considered to be the "crux of the whole system," which was the concept of the "through-line action and task": rather than a pure emphasis on emotion, he advocated that the actor concentrate on a through-line of actions, which he defined as the psychological intent of the character articulated in verbal form. [5] He had come to believe that the actor should work on individual moments of action so that the character might attain the stated objective of a given scene. Adler returned to New York determined to apply these new concepts to the Group Theatre's work, and eventually, in March 1937, Strasberg resigned from the Group because of the factionalism and feuds that arose from his commitment to affective memory.[6] He continued to direct on Broadway, with limited success, before venturing to Hollywood, where he prepared actors for screen tests. Strasberg achieved excellent results: more than ninety-five percent of those tested were given contracts. However, under the direction of others, the majority of Strasberg's charges failed to sustain their early promise, which testified to the effectiveness of his ministrations.[7] After World War II, Strasberg returned to New York, resumed his directing career, taught acting and coached actors, though without any institutional affiliation.

In the fall of 1947, Group founder Cheryl Crawford, along with Group veterans Elia Kazan and Robert Lewis, founded the Actors Studio. The three Broadway professionals wanted a pool of trained actors from which they could draw for their commercial ventures. They divided the Studio into two classes: Kazan worked with the younger students and Lewis with the more experienced professionals. Kazan focused on exercises, including work with animal imagery and improvisations, and stressed the importance of actions and specific acting intentions that called for the actor to seek a defined goal or objective for each scene. Lewis inspired and challenged the more established actors by having them work on roles in which they would not normally be cast. Kazan found that Lewis stressed the "bolder, imaginative side of acting, rather than emphasizing the interior emotional event."[8] While there was a general agreement that they were teaching in the tradition of Stanislavsky and of the Group, teachers and students referred to the "Lewis method" and the "Kazan method."[9] Lewis, however, resigned from the Studio after the first year as a result of a personal conflict with Kazan. Subsequently, Kazan and Crawford sought someone whom they could "give the Studio to," as he was increasingly busy directing films and she was an active producer. [10]

Earlier, Kazan had insisted that the one person they had to keep away from the Studio was Strasberg.[11] Robert Lewis recalled: "Kazan opposed Strasberg right from the beginning. When they had to bring in a teacher they tried Meisner, (Josh) Logan—anybody but Strasberg."[12] Cheryl Crawford, who had been Strasberg's biggest supporter in the Group days, was the chief lobbyist for his association with the Actors Studio.[13] When Kazan finally approached Strasberg, he had to pressure him into getting involved; he recalled that Strasberg "hesitated, he backed off, he qualified, he did everything in the world to try and get out of it. I just persisted."[14] Kazan and Strasberg engaged in a courtship that was at once delicate and challenging: while Kazan had come to doubt his own abilities as a teacher, Strasberg was critical of Kazan's emphasis on and attention to "actions." By September of 1948, Kazan had enticed Strasberg to participate as one of several teachers. By the following year, Strasberg was listed as a member of the "new guiding directorate" of the Studio, and he received the first of what would prove to be intermittent payments for his teaching.[15] According to Kazan, the failure of Strasberg's January 1951 production of Ibsen's *Peer Gynt* (starring John Garfield) was the final blow that drove Strasberg from the commercial theater to a permanent position with the Studio.[16] By the fall of that year, he was the sole acting teacher and had assumed the title of artistic director.

While the Studio was the performative offspring of the Group, striking differences between the two organizations soon emerged. While the Group had set up an alternate model to the organization and ethos of Broadway, its direct assault had failed to change the system. However, Strasberg embarked on a second and far more effective revolution as he and his actors proceeded to reconstitute American acting. They set out to "infiltrate and transform from within the entire commercial system."[17] While Stella Adler, Robert Lewis, Sanford Meisner and other Group veterans battled over who was the true heir to the Stanislavsky tradition, Strasberg broke with Stanislavsky and created a style of acting that was reflective of the concerns and anxieties that coursed through postwar America. Adler brought back from Paris a call for action and intention that suited the Group and the country in the 1930s, but by the 1950s, society was ready for Strasberg and his fascination with affective or emotional memory. His Method was predominant in a period when America turned away from social concerns and immersed itself in "private life and personal preoccupations."[18] For the postwar era, Strasberg was "the right man in the right place at the right time."[19]

Senator Daniel Patrick Moynihan has declared that secrecy during this period of American life "took on the overtones of ritual." It became a "performance intended to demonstrate who was in and who was out."[20] Strasberg's full-time commitment to the Studio transpired against this background of secrecy, as well as the fear engendered by the blacklist, the secret and unacknowledged practice of actively denying employment to individuals on the basis of their prior, legal political beliefs and sympathies. Once the prison terms of the original "Hollywood Ten" had been upheld by the federal courts, a second and more virulent round of Congressional hearings began inquiring into supposed Communist influence in the film industry. Former Group members John Garfield, J. Edward Bromberg and Morris Carnovsky refused to cooperate and were blacklisted by the film, radio and television industries. Other Group alumni, like Clifford Odets and Studio president Elia Kazan, participated in the ritual performance of publicly "naming names"—identifying colleagues who previously had been members of the Communist party, a political affiliation that was not illegal at the time.

While there remains a widely held opinion that the theater had virtually no blacklist, this did not mean that professional anti-Communists did not seek to instigate one, nor did it mean that the atmosphere for serious plays was not altered. While Broadway may have seemed immune to the worst depredations of the era, it was nonetheless seriously infected by the plague as it unconsciously proceeded to modify its behavior. Writers and directors perceived a difference in the type of play that was produced. Looking back at the blacklist era after four decades, Arthur Miller saw that "the cultural effects are all over the place. They're obvious in the theater, for example. For the longest time until even now, the idea of a theater which is engaged with the society gradually withered away until theater became just mere entertainment and lost its audience, by and large."[21] In a 1956 colloquy at New Dramatists, Arthur Miller had discussed the "social pressures of today." He declared that Americans no longer "believe in the validity of the individual will," but instead defined the "good citizen" as one "who adjusts himself to what we call reality, who gets along." Miller sensed that most people "express a helplessness about life because of the fact that they can't seem to find any leverage on it from which to exercise their will."[22] Harold Clurman found that the "political constriction" that began in 1947 and "reached a sort of climax" in 1953 made "almost everybody disinclined to commit themselves to any opinion that suggested anything specific beyond 'loyalty.'" For Clurman, what began as a "political terror inducing a political hush, gradually deteriorated to a cessation of all serious discussion of any kind whatsoever and, to a large extent, even of thinking."[23] He confessed, "What happened to most of us was that we came to desire nothing more than to be inconspicuous citizens, with no other thought than 'to get on,' no other ideal than celebrity or success."[24]

Against this background of secrecy, investigations, and conformity, the Actors Studio became a player's place, a place apart: studio members were "often warned not to include the fact of their memberships in their bios in theater programs." The influential publication *Red Channels* highlighted the Studio membership of any member it smeared or blacklisted.[25] In the privacy of the Studio, "Strasberg effectively guided his students away from discussion about the relation between the actor and the audience and the possible politics of actors' theatrical choices."[26] Strasberg "was a big adviser on what to do. His position was that artists have no place in politics, and if you get caught you get out."[27]

As the process, rather than the product, became the grail in that politically sensitive time, Strasberg turned the Actors Studio into a realm of pure research. He developed the cultural equivalent of Los Alamos, a secret site dedicated to nurturing explosiveness. The closed-door policy of the Studio "generated intrigue and helped make those teachings *top secret*" (emphasis in original).[28] Strasberg's Method, what has been termed a "top secret invention," implied that a chosen few could discover the mysteries of creativity and performance.[29] During the worst ravages of the McCarthy era, the Studio developed into an intense and contained institution, a secret society, akin to the CIA and the secret societies of the Ivy League that supplied that agency with its personnel.

Strasberg utilized secrecy to foster an "abstract, scarcely defined, notion of nationalism in acting" that served the needs of the Cold War. While other Group alumni pledged their adherence to Stanislavsky, Strasberg built "systematically on the dogma of inherent American superiority" to the Russian director.[30] Under Strasberg's guidance, Method acting became "a marker of cultural value to shore up the identity and purpose of the national culture" during the Cold War.[31] Strasberg took Stanislavsky's theories, which some had earlier considered "an excrescence on the American theater,"[32] and transformed them into "a sign of patriotism rather than communism."[33] The new style of acting proceeded to elevate the values of individualism over collectivity and to exalt the personal over the political.

Strasberg's reconstruction of Russian practices corresponds to the other great appropriation of the period. Serge Guilbaut has controversially argued that during and after the Second World War, New York "stole" modern art from the French and made itself into the capital of the art world.[34] Strasberg likewise engineered a complicated maneuver whereby he posited that New York, if not the Studio itself, was the center of the postwar theatrical landscape. In doing so, he elevated American acting from the ranks of entertainment and made it an art.

Strasberg's invention of the Method created a new standard of emotional honesty for English-language acting. He completed his maneuvers by casting our closest allies, the British, in the role of the cultural enemy by dismissing their acting as effete, poised, formal and overly articulate, and glorifying American acting as spontaneous, intense and emotionally rich. As the Truman Doctrine proclaimed American dominance over former European spheres of influence, the Method overshadowed European styles of performance.

While the impact of the Method proved to be international in scope, the revolution was internal and domestic, as Strasberg dodged all taint of internationalism and Communism with his proclamations that his work and that of the Studio were wholly American. He displayed a belief in American exceptionality when he told Britain's *Plays and Players*, "We at the Studio are proud and flattered to see that our work has aroused such interest throughout the world. But the work we do there and the methods we use cannot be exported."[35]

The Method actor became a symbol of freedom and independence by creating from the self, from the interior. The new actor abandoned portrayals based on historical models or traditional characterizations and disdained techniques that might be tainted by European models or theatrical tradition. The secret to creating the new type of characterization lay in the uniqueness of the American individual— within the Method universe, the actor is not playing a character; rather, the actor "is *playing himself*" (emphasis in original).[36] The job of the Method actor was to "find new qualities of his own individuality, which will in turn apply to the character he is portraying."[37]

Whereas the Group Theatre had reveled in language, the Actors Studio found words to be suspect. Characters in plays from the 1930s believed in language; they knew that words allowed ideas to be communicated and were the very essence of protest. The Method "took a position at least implicitly suspicious of language as a tool of reason and articulation."[38] Strasberg empowered his actors to elevate their emotional responses to a level of primacy over the text of a play. His distrust of language may also have been an unconscious tactic by which he demonstrated his "Americanness" and differentiated himself from Russian cultural mores.

The Method allowed, not for collective, but for individual cultural protest, which was carried out not with text or with dialogue but with behavior as gesture. Movement became the Method actor's form of "writing with erasure." Whereas the Group had wielded language, the Method flaunted behavior as actors adhered to "the Method motto," the practice of "acting between the lines."[39] All the mannerisms of the method actor—the twitches, grunts, mumbles and shrugs—freed the actor but also undermined, erased and destabilized the text. The Method actor, no longer an interpreter, rose in stature to become a coauthor of the theatrical event.

With the actor elevated to the status of cocreator, it was perhaps inevitable that commentators began to employ religious metaphor in writing about the Actors Studio. In *Theatre Arts* magazine, Maurice Zolotow described the "often painful and terrifying rites" that took place at the Studio, which was "a temple, a church, a shrine" at which actors dedicated themselves "as sacrificial lambs in a dramatic experiment. The acting studio was no longer a place of craftsmanship, but was a site of 'inspiration.'"[40]

The Method had proved successful in bringing the independent, individualized emotional response of actors to a variety of roles. However, the technique had its greatest success in film and other genres of popular entertainment, such as television and popular song, in which the performances that enchanted and impressed critics and audiences were neurotic and intense. The destruction of illusion and revelation of truth proved problematic, since what was believable and truthful in the classroom was often not nearly theatrical enough for the stage. Harold Clurman grew concerned about the inadequacies of postwar American acting and lamented the passing of actors with "grandeur and sweep," who had been replaced by "limited, almost uniform" actors who produced only "a new kind of pathetic naturalism." Clurman deplored the emphasis on the psychological and mourned "an insufficient regard to the external—visual, musical, graphic, formal aspects."[41]

The studied antitheatrical naturalism of Strasberg's innovative work spawned a counterrevolution against the Method. The controversy over a *means* of aesthetic creation spilled over into two public forums. First, Harvard University invited Michael Redgrave to give the 1956 Theodore Spencer Memorial Lectures; second, in the spring of the following year, Robert Lewis gave a series of eight lectures, entitled "Method—Or Madness?" at Broadway's Playhouse Theatre. Lewis was forced to resort to an application form for potential attendees; "some five thousand" people applied to hear the director's thoughts about the new acting technique.[42] Demand was such that both lecture series were published in book form in 1958.[43]

Redgrave branded Strasberg as a "deviationist" from the original (or Stanislavsky-based) Method.[44] He acknowledged the standards set by the Group Theatre and paid obeisance to the work of luminaries such as Brando, Julie Harris and Eli Wallach, as well as Harold Clurman and Kazan. Just three years earlier, Redgrave had stated that some of Stanislavsky's "best ideas" survived "in the work of Elia Kazan and his Actors' [*sic*] Studio."[45] However, by 1956 Redgrave had appeared on Broadway with members of the Studio. He claimed that Strasberg's conviction that "the actor's work on himself was paramount" was "paralyzing and destructive" and "a damn nuisance in the theater."[46] Redgrave called for a concern with form and content, the exterior aspects to art, rather than the emotive presence of the performer. However, when he admitted that style "has become a dirty word," it was almost as if he was aware that he was engaged in a cultural Dunkirk—a real need to beat a strategic retreat from foreign shores.[47]

In the lectures, Lewis set out to "lift the veil of what some people feel is secrecy" surrounding the Method.[48] He called for a return to the principles of Stanislavsky that held sway in the Group Theatre after Strasberg's departure. He alluded to a "High-Priest attitude of some of the 'propagators of the faith.'" He waved copies of Stanislavsky's *An Actor Prepares* and *Building a Character* and informed his audience that "they only have to read the two volumes; everything is in there."[49] He invoked Redgrave's early encomiums as proof that the Method in its pure form could appeal to all actors, and could be used for classical theatrical endeavors, not just naturalistic family dramas.[50] Lewis might well have been the first person to address publicly the problems caused by the lag between the two major Stanislavsky books and the resulting overemphasis on emotion. However, Lewis was fighting a battle from a previous war. Acting theorist Duane Krause has reported that Lewis, like Stella Adler, believed that Strasberg was "mistaken" and that the Actors Studio "reempowered him" to "make the same mistakes over again."[51] Strasberg's adversaries did not realize that the Method had found its moment in the private fears and anxieties of the postwar era, which were notably different in scope and intent than the economic and political concerns of the Depression.

While the claimants of the Stanislavsky legacy regarded him as an apostate, Strasberg never claimed to be a strict devotee of the Russian director. Strasberg avowed that the Group had "emphasized elements that [Stanislavsky] had not emphasized and disregarded elements which he might have considered of greater importance." Further, Strasberg was "critical of the way in which Stanislavsky used his own work in some of his productions," and characterized the methods of both the Group and the Actors Studio as an "adaptation of the Stanislavsky System."[52]

Strasberg continued to adapt and refine Stanislavsky's practices at the Actors Studio. After rereading Stanislavsky's dictum about the necessity of the actors being private in public, Strasberg created the private moment exercise, which became one of his most effective and controversial conceptions. Its development in 1956 and 1957 tacitly acknowledged Clurman's lament about the absence of theatricality from the naturalism that Strasberg's emotional work fostered. Strasberg viewed the exercise as a corrective for actors who were inhibited by the presence of an audience. By enacting a moment of true privacy in front of people, Strasberg hoped to get them to confront the issue and conquer it. Strasberg desired "to strengthen the actor's expressiveness" by having the actor "go beyond his everyday, casual behavior" that limited his work onstage.[53]

Strasberg realized that "we do private things when we are alone, and we know they are really private when we cannot continue them if somebody comes into the room." Thus, in the private moment, the actor is asked to do something "that they do in life, but which even in life is so private that, although they do it and it is real, when anyone comes in, they have to stop doing it."[54] The exercise compelled the actor to achieve a greater degree of concentration, which then allowed for a heightened emotional state and increased theatricality. Consequently, actors sang, danced and even performed rituals of private grooming. The exercise was clearly not for everyone; Strasberg noted, "For certain people I have found it highly useful . . . for others the private moment has no value."[55] Nonetheless, Strasberg found that many actors expressed themselves with "startling abandon."[56]

Since privacy is central, the exercise most often takes place in a room, as opposed to a public, outdoor space. The actor is requested to create the sensory surrounding of his or her space. To that end, actors are encouraged to bring in household objects to create the environment. The exercise might have been called the secret moment because it is based not necessarily on privacy, but on secrecy, on the idea that anything one does in the exercise would have to stop in the presence of an observer. Strasberg was no longer retreating into the private; he was pushing the boundaries of methodology in taking the private public.[57]

Strasberg's new exercise was vilified from many quarters as word of it spread through the theatrical community. The exercise quickly became a symbol of all that was wrong with the Method, and was called "a sinister indulgence in sexual and scatological display" by its detractors.[58] Stanislavsky acolyte Sonia Moore charged that Strasberg had transformed the Russian master's "public solitude" into a "sinister private moment." She attacked the exercise as a "distortion, offensive to the name of Stanislavsky, and also to human privacy."[59] In untrained hands, the exercise became a voyeuristic enterprise, a peep show for the classroom audience. One anonymous Studio member observed: "This kind of thing in different forms is done all over town. A large percentage of them turn out to be bedroom scenes."[60] As mores changed with the advent of the sixties, many actors did take the concept further than originally intended. The presence of nudity and changing standards in the public performance of sexuality in the sixties and seventies demanded that professionals be able to work on aspects of sexuality not hitherto called for on the stage or screen. However, Strasberg developed the private moment well before the sexual revolution as an exercise for mature, professional actors working in a shielded environment, not as a tool for training novices.

Strasberg was denigrated during this period as a "poor man's psychiatrist." While he would often discuss psychological problems with members or students out of personal concern, Strasberg more often urged, though he did not insist, that they seek professional care.[61] Many did; others did not, mainly because of a fear of losing their creativity as a result of analysis. In 1957, an article in *The Saturday Evening Post* revealed the extent to which Studio members relied upon analysis: Strasberg stated, "to the extent that being psychoanalyzed helps an actor know more aspects of himself, it helps him to be a better actor."[62] Geraldine Page had worked with her psychoanalyst to develop the role of Alma in Tennessee Williams's *Summer and Smoke,* and Anne Bancroft also testified to the benefits of psychoanalysis in her work.[63] Strasberg's and the Studio's approach to acting centered on the personal and private psychology of the individual—the emotions, memories, fears, doubts and dreams—and, inevitably, certain members and students veered into narcissism and psychological dependency.

Strasberg, unfortunately, committed little to paper.[64] On his return from Russia in 1934, he brandished his distrust of language when he composed an appreciation of Meyerhold for *New Theatre* in which he lauded the Russian experimentalist for bringing out the "sharpness of the Molière grotesque" so that audiences "might listen without getting bored by the long monologues and altogether foreign dialogue."[65] His 1947 introduction to *Acting: A Handbook of the Stanislavsky Method* hailed Stanislavsky for representing "a sharp break with traditional teaching" and for inspiring works which "are never copies or imitations of one another."[66]

Strasberg has been dismissed as being a "talker" rather than a writer, a label that disparages not only Strasberg but also the entire oral tradition of the teaching of acting. However, there may be a kernel of truth within that caustic comment. For, if we are to understand Strasberg, we should perhaps think of him as a performer rather than a writer. His chief legacy seems to be the series of audiotapes transcribed by Robert Hethmon in the mid-1950s.[67] In addition to his celluloid appearances in *The Godfather: Part II* and other films, he left other performances behind: the Lee Strasberg Theatre Institute possesses a trove of videotapes from classes held there in the 1970s. However, these have yet to be cataloged or disseminated—they are, for now, secret.

ENDNOTES/SOURCES

1. Strasberg, Lee, *A Dream of Passion*, New York: Plume, 1987, p. 116.
2. Vineberg, Steve, *Method Actors: Three Generations of an American Acting Style*, New York: Schirmer Books, 1991, p. 51.
3. Kazan, Elia, *Elia Kazan: A Life*, New York: Anchor Books, 1989, pp. 61–62.
4. Strasberg, pp. 92–93.
5. Garfield, David, New York: Macmillan, 1980, p. 35.
6. Hirsch, Foster, "Standing Up for Strasberg," *American Theatre*, March 2001, p. 55.
7. Adams, Cindy Heller, *Lee Strasberg: The Imperfect Genius of the Actors Studio*, Garden City, NY: Doubleday, 1980, p. 189.
8. Kazan, p. 302.
9. Garfield, pp. 56–58.
10. Kazan, p. 302.
11. Rogoff, Gordon, "Lee Strasberg: Burning Ice," *Tulane Drama Review*, Winter 1964, p. 136.
12. Gray, Paul, "Stanislavsky and America: A Critical Chronology," *Tulane Drama Review*, Winter 1964, p. 43.
13. Smith, Wendy, *Real Life Drama: The Group Theatre and America, 1931–1940*, New York: Knopf, 1990, p. 418.
14. Ciment, Michel, *Kazan on Kazan*, New York: Viking, 1974, p. 37.
15. Garfield, pp. 80–82.
16. Kazan, pp. 302–303.
17. Carnicke, Sharon M., *Stanislavski in Focus*, Amsterdam, the Netherlands: Harwood Academic Publishers, 1998, p.48.
18. Smith, p. 182.
19. Ibid., p. 418.
20. Moynihan, Daniel Patrick, *Secrecy*, New Haven and London: Yale University Press, 1998, p. 18.
21. Fariello, Griffin, *Red Scare: Memories of the American Inquisition*, New York: W. W. Norton, 1995, p. 345.
22. *Broadway's Fabulous Fifties: How the Playmakers Made It Happen*, New Dramatists Alumni Publications Committee, ed., Portsmouth, NH: Heinemann, 2002, p. 66.
23. Clurman, Harold, *The Fervent Years: The Group Theatre & the '30s*, New York: Knopf, 1945; Da Capo Press, 1983, p. 285.
24. Ibid., p. 285.
25. Garfield, p. 88.
26. McConachie, Bruce, "Method Acting and the Cold War," *Theatre Survey*, May 2000, p. 57.
27. Navasky, Victor, *Naming Names*, New York: Viking, 1980, p. 219.
28. Baron, Cynthia, "The Method Moment: Situating the Rise of Method Acting in the 1950s," *Popular Culture Review*, August 1998, p. 100.

29. Ibid., p. 89.

30. Rogoff, p. 137.

31. Conroy, Marianne, "Acting Out: Method Acting, the National Culture, and the Middlebrow Disposition in Cold War America," *Criticism*, Spring 1993, p. 250.

32. Clurman, p. 279.

33. Baron, p. 90.

34. Guilbaut, Serge, *How New York Stole the Idea of Modern Art: Abstract Expressionism, Freedom, and the Cold War*, Chicago and London: University of Chicago Press, 1983.

35. "Actors Studio is *Not* a School," *Plays and Players*, February 1957, p. 9.

36. Easty, Edward Dwight, *On Method Acting*, New York: Ballantine Books, 1981, p. 45.

37. Ibid., p. 18.

38. Braudy, Leo, "'No Body's Perfect': Method Acting and '50s Culture," *Michigan Quarterly Review*, Winter 1966, p. 198.

39. Ibid., p. 198.

40. Zolotow, Maurice, "A Study of the Actors Studio," *Theatre Arts*, August 1956, p. 91.

41. Clurman, Harold, "Actors in Style—and Style in Actors," *New York Times Sunday Magazine*, December 7, 1952, pp. 34, 38.

42. Lewis, Robert, *Method—or Madness?*, New York: Samuel French, Inc., 1958, p. 6.

43. The theatrical climate was decidedly different in November and December of 1990, when Robert Lewis reprised and expanded upon his famous lectures on successive Sunday evenings. "Method—or Madness? II" was presented in the tiny Van Dam Playhouse in SoHo. Approximately 60 people, a number enlisted as invited guests of the sponsor, were in attendance.

44. Redgrave, Michael, *Mask or Face: Reflections in an Actor's Mirror*, New York: Theatre Arts Books, 1958, p. 62.

45. Redgrave, Michael, *The Actor's Ways and Means*, London: Nick Hern Books, 1995, p. 32.

46. Redgrave, *Mask or Face*, p. 29.

47. Ibid., p. 63.

48. Lewis, p. 7.

49. Ibid., p. 7.

50. Ibid., p. 4.

51. Krause, Duane, "An Epic System," *Acting (Re)Considered: Theories and Practices*, Phillip B. Zarilli, ed., London: Routledge, 1995, p. 268.

52. Garfield, pp. 168–169.

53. Strasberg, p. 143.

54. Hethmon, Robert, ed., *Strasberg at the Actors Studio*, New York: Viking, 1965; Theatre Communications Group, 1991, p. 118.

55. Ibid., p. 115.

56. Ibid., p. 116.

57. The "private moment" exercise paved the way for much of the performance art that would surface in the late 1970s and early 1980s. In many instances, the process became the performance. Richard Schechner has noted this performative genealogy in a 1981 essay. He wrote that "performers were encouraged to show the audience their private selves as well as their assumed characters. Exercise after exercise took Stanislavsky's and Strasberg's idea of "public solitude" further. And these exercises were not designed finally to help an actor portray a role or build a character. The very process of preparation and rehearsal was made public." (Schechner, Richard, "The Decline and Fall of the [American] Avant-Garde," Part Two, *Performing Arts Journal* 15, 1981, vol. V, no. 3, p. 11)

58. Garfield, p. 172.

59. Moore, Sonia, *Training an Actor: The Stanislavsky System in Class*, New York: Viking, 1968, p. 40–41.

60. Gray, Paul, "Stanislavski and America," *Tulane Drama Review*, Winter 1964, p. 49.

61. This signaled another break with the political past. The Communist Party had a long-standing rule against psychoanalysis. The Party claimed that the process was used to justify inequality by attributing systemic failures to personal flaws. The Party also feared that its status as a secret organization would be compromised, since the analysand was encouraged to reveal everything to the analyst. (Navasky, p. 131) In Russia itself, psychoanalysis was prohibited as "contrary to state political ideology." (Fermi, Laura, *Illustrious Immigration: The Intellectual Migration from Europe 1930–1941*, Chicago and London: University of Chicago Press, 1968, p. 146)

62. Zolotow, Maurice, "The Stars Rise Here," *The Saturday Evening Post*, May 18, 1957, p. 86.

63. Gray, p. 47.

64. The privileging of and dependence on publication is clearly demonstrated in Joseph R. Roach's book *The Player's Passion*. In this study of the "science of acting," as the subtitle calls it, Roach does not differentiate Strasberg from other twentieth-century American figures; rather, he groups him (along with Harold Clurman and Stella Adler) as an adherent of Richard Boleslavsky's "scientific psychology." (Roach, Joseph R., *The Player's Passion: Studies in the Science of Acting*, Cranbury, NJ: Associated University Presses, 1985, pp. 215–216)

65. Strasberg, Lee, "The Magic of Meyerhold," *New Theatre*, September 1934, p. 15.

66. Strasberg, Lee, Introduction to *Acting: A Handbook of the Stanislavsky Method*, Toby Cole, ed., New York: Lear, 1947.

67. Detractors have argued that the introduction of the tape recorder at Studio sessions starting in 1956 encouraged Strasberg's notorious volubility as he began to speak for posterity. (Garfield, p. 145)

LEE STRASBERG TECHNIQUE

Anna Strasberg

I don't teach you to act; I teach you to live.

—LEE STRASBERG

There is a passage in a book by Max Reinhardt, the great early twentieth-century director and acting teacher, which resonated with Lee: "Before you enchant an audience, you must enchant yourself."

Lee was one of those rare human beings who studied everything and loved to teach. He had to learn something new every day. His approach to life was one of curiosity. No knowledge was wasted. He immersed himself in books and studied the great masters of the theater—Stanislavsky, Vakhtangov, Meyerhold, Reinhardt and all forms of theater throughout history—before they became required reading for actors and directors. He read the masterpieces of world literature and the works of great philosophers and scientists. Lee had a thorough knowledge of all the arts.

One of his most inspired moments occurred when he saw Eleonora Duse in *Ghosts* and *The Lady from the Sea*. He walked out of the theater astounded at what he had experienced. "Why is she a great actress? She is not particularly glamorous and she doesn't speak English, yet when she is onstage I understand all of her pain. I understood the play and I cannot get her out of my head." If Duse was going to lean against a tree, she studied it and became one with the tree. I think that is where Lee's ideas about the method came from.

Lee taught actors, not to act, but to *live*, expressing their truths; and then, as an actor, to live the character truthfully. If you see a list of any of the exercises Lee developed, it is obvious how necessary they are to living. Lee never asked actors to be abstract in any of the exercises. He said, "You must not give abstract answers to acting problems. You have to take a specific problem and address it. Acting is not a theory. A theory is something that hasn't been proven. The record shows this has been proven. This work is an aesthetic. And with each person it varies." He taught you to make personal connections to create your reality, your experience, your sense of truth. People must know and understand the exercises before they reject them.

Lee's technique does not teach people anything they do not already know. The reality is that we live in a society that reinforces the negative. As a child, you naturally explore with your senses, but if you try to touch a glass and are told, "No, no, no! Don't touch!" you stop exploring with the sense of touch. Society begins to retrain your senses. One day, a well-known and successful actress who was studying with Lee was crying after she had done a scene in class. Lee asked, "What am I doing to you? All I'm doing is introducing you to yourself." He was teaching her to reconnect with her sensory life. The Method teaches actors to re-create—not to copy, not to make believe, but to connect with what you know and use it as a character. Simple things create simple realities. In its basic form, the Method teaches actors to use their five senses. They start with themselves, the individual, being absolutely unique and original.

The first exercises we teach, and the most important exercises being taught in this method, are *relaxation* and *concentration*, and you can take them to the bank. You cannot be anything great without the art of concentrating and relaxing.

RELAXATION

Lee said, "The process of relaxation deals with habits that interfere with and confine expression. We must encourage you to find new ways of expression that are held back by habits." No other approach to the actor's problems deals with the role of habits and expression, except in a purely external and mechanical way. The basic habitual behavior of a human being leads to the habitual behavior of the actor. The sense of yourself is an important force in making you do what you do and behave as you behave. Most people have little sense of themselves and have great difficulty seeing themselves.

You must go further than your habits permit. Habits get in the way of impulses. In training, we start with the mental tension in the brow and relax that, and then move to the eyes, which are the hardest-working parts. You relax them, and then you relax the muscles in the mouth. We've been taught not to express things, not to say the truth. We say to a child, "Go kiss Aunt Martha." "I don't want to kiss Aunt Martha." "Kiss Aunt Martha!" And the poor kid kisses Aunt Martha, and everything around the mouth is tense, and he begins to protect himself. That's the first of the antic dispositions we put on.

This relaxation is not the Buddhist relaxation. It isn't removing oneself, because that's a solution for stress. We're not working with stress. Stress and tension are two different things. We teach actors to relax the face, the neck, and then the back, because the back carries all those muscles that connect to the lungs. They're like bellows, the lungs—if they don't get the air, the lungs can't support the sound. We teach the students to know where they carry their tension. Some carry it in their eyes. For many people, the body area from the neck to the thighs does not exist, because we are taught to be ashamed. Do you ever see people try to kiss by leaning forward, not touching below the neck? The only time this doesn't hold true is when they are dancing. Then they go wild and release all the tension in the back, hips and legs. This is the kind of relaxation we try to help actors achieve.

CONCENTRATION

Lee loved sports. He would say, "Look at that batter. Watch him as he comes to the plate. He's concentrated. He doesn't hold the bat so tight that he's frozen." I remember an interview with a baseball player who said, "I don't fool around when I come to the stadium. I come to do the things I do, so I have to concentrate." Before a performance, all of your impulses are running wild with no place to go, so they need to be released and focused. The concentration exercises focus on objects, on place, and on the sense of touch. You concentrate on an object you know very well, examining the weight of it, how it feels warm on your fingers, the look of it, what you see. You pay attention to things that you know so well that you don't have to think about them—the smell, the taste. That's concentration on simple realities.

Lee always said, "I don't teach you to act. I teach you to live out on the stage or in front of the camera the life of that character posited by the playwright." It's the truthfulness of that living process that needs the concentration. You need to pay attention to the details. It's like playing the piano. First you learn the notes, then the fingering, and then you work on developing the flexibility of the fingers and the technique. How good you become depends on the attention you pay to learning the notes, listening and being totally there. Acting is not really different from any of the other arts. A lot of young actors study for six months or a year and say, "I've got the secret; I can cry!" And that's all they can do. They learn one aspect of acting, and they fall in love with that. It's the ones who stay on course who emerge as actors.

We don't do any of the emotional work in the first year—we just go back to rediscover and reconnect with the senses. It's a combination of the technical and the inner life. Today, we don't know how to walk—we are the blue jeans generation. We walk and do everything as if we were wearing blue jeans and thick rubber boots. You might think that piercing the nose and the eyebrow and wearing skimpy little outfits indicate that students are free. Big mistake. They are doing it because they are so closed-off, yet they feel the need to belong. The people who are going to be actors, who are going to be artistic, break away from that need to be part of a group.

AFFECTIVE MEMORY

When Stanislavsky said that "emotional memory" didn't work, Lee said, "He's right. But why doesn't it work?" Stanislavsky discovered that an actor has to feel the genuine emotion; in other words, the actor has to be human. To awaken the actor's imagination depends on the ability to stimulate the emotional memory. Stanislavsky wondered whether there was a way actors could control that memory and feed the creative mood or spirit. Could the actor deliberately recall emotions and bring them alive at will? Stanislavsky said emotions cannot be directly turned on or stimulated, but can only be reached indirectly through sense memory.

Lee explored these questions with his students and discovered that emotional memory is the key to unlocking the secret of creativity. When anybody creates, he is unconsciously using memories of senses and emotions. All people have emotional memories, but not everyone can re-create them. The emotional memory exercise provides a technique for doing so. The emotional memory is used for intense emotional experiences onstage, and Lee always felt that teachers of his technique should be careful that individuals are ready to be subjected to these emotionally powerful exercises. "It is best that you do the exercises for the first time with a teacher who is there to relieve your fears or worries that you might not be in control," he said. "There is no danger in anything done with will and awareness."

Sense memory becomes a crucial part of creating a usable emotional memory in the actor's work. Lee would ask actors, "Describe where you are, what you see, hear, touch, taste, smell, experience kinetically, through the five senses. You are there in your mind's eye. Relive sensations. What is the shape, size, form, texture, length, thickness, color of the object? Do you see light in the room? There are different degrees of light. Do you see a reflection? Is it hot or cold? What sensations do you feel in your body, and where? Is there a smell in the room? Where do you smell it—in your nose, throat or mouth? Ask, what's under your feet? Say, 'I'm hearing, I'm touching.' That's when it starts to work. Control it. Define it clearly. Force your attention into detail. Make everything precise and definite." The actors would try to tell Lee their story, because that's what actors do. He didn't want to know the story or event. He wanted to know the things around that event.

These exercises are not meant to be a performance. They are homework for the actor. They are there to help the actor when he or she is having trouble. The actor shouldn't use all of the exercises at once; use one element and apply that one element to help evoke whatever connection you need.

THE PROGRESSION OF THE WORK

This method works in three parts. The first part is getting to trust the sensory work. Then the actors try sensory work in a monologue. We don't care that the monologue is a shambles, because the students are not really ready to bring the senses and the text together. Sometimes they make it work, and sometimes they fake it. But they begin to know that there is something more than just the surface and coloring to the words. The playwright was paramount to Lee: "The play's the thing." None of that is apparent in the early training, because none of it has to do with text. The beginning part of the work is really getting back to trusting yourself, your instincts and your realities, and getting to trust the exercises.

The second part of the method is taking the sensory work and affective memories and putting them into scene work, to test whether they stand up under the pressure of a scene. The second year is hard for the students because they have to put the things they've learned in the first year into the text. It's difficult to concentrate on what they learned in their first year while they're saying the lines, and sometimes the concentration stops because they tense up. You have to do the work and then leave yourself alone to see where it will take you. You can't manipulate it. You can't say, "Oh, that song makes me cry, so therefore I'll think of that song every time I . . ." whatever. The whole point is you leave yourself alone. You start the exercise. If there's a song attached, you do the song; if there's a smell, you do that. We teach you to use the five senses. Not every sense is equally strong with each person—some people have no sense of smell, but they have a keen sense of hearing or taste. Some people can't do the sense of touch because they've been slapped so much on the hands that they can't create that. It doesn't matter, because we can retrain the senses.

Actors sometimes think they must have an exercise for every if, and, or but. Lee said, "Actors! They take medicine when they don't need it." After scene night, the students say, "This didn't work, and that didn't work." That is because they worked on too many things. Lee used to say, "You must start with one thing, one truth. Trust it. Don't manipulate it. Let it carry you. You can only prepare for the first moment. You can't prepare for the whole scene." The Method was meant to be consciously invoked only if you're in trouble during a performance. That's the technique—only if you need it. Young actors prepare for the whole scene. They say, "Wait until my big blowup, and people will see what I can really do." But the people who do the homework get it, and if they don't do the homework, they can't wing it. Because when they wing it, they have to make constant adjustments. The adjustments always have to be in the here and now, the living-out process. It's a process of work, a technique that you can use for anything—sports, architecture, art, anything.

Once in a class, someone tried to use many different techniques—an inner monologue, a song, a private moment, a scene—just to show that she could do them. Lee took his watch off and showed it to the class. "You see this watch? Very expensive . . . it has diamonds in it." And he passed the watch around to the class, asking, "Do you see any diamonds?" And the class said, "No, Lee, no diamonds." He said, "But there are diamonds in there. It does tell time accurately. The diamonds are there to help make the movement accurate." He was trying to tell them that you don't have to show everything. It has to come out in the character, in the work. *Seamless* is a word he used a lot, comparing acting to music. When a great musician, like Isaac Stern, moves from one note to another it's all one, it's seamless. That's what we try to achieve with acting.

Not all of the exercises work for everybody. For instance, if a person could naturally express a full range of emotions, Lee did not have them do the emotional exercises. If a student's mind moved so fast that it skipped over things, he would have them focus on the concentration exercises. He said, "You have to do one thing fully before you do the next thing." That is a very hard lesson to learn, and a lot of the actors say, "Oh, that's boring." But once you connect, it becomes kinetic. It's really very liberating. When you bite into something you ate in childhood, you're not biting into that food; you're biting into your childhood. So it's important to reawaken useful senses. Music is valuable. That's what Lee used when he acted in *The Godfather: Part II*—a piece of music in his head, and a very difficult mathematical problem. An NYU student came to class and sang a Sunday-school song, and it opened up a whole world for her. These things are valid. You can't use all of them, and you don't need to. You build a repertory of things that you can use, that are truly meaningful and truthful to you.

The third part is the character work. This is the homework. Great actors do their homework. They find the walk, they practice the way the character holds his hands, during the journey of discovery that they take before the performance. The whole satisfaction is being one with the character, not having to work at it. The audience must not catch you working. You have to be that character, and convince the audience. It's the revelatory moments in those simple gestures and that simple reality that get the audience believing along with you. All great art is revelatory. It isn't putting on the antic disposition. That's another form of acting. Actors get away with it, but the audience doesn't feel for you. They come out and say, "Boy, that is an actor. He really acted."

There is the story in Henry Fielding's *Tom Jones* of a farmer being taken to see Garrick playing Hamlet. The people taking him to the performance want to know if an ordinary person who doesn't regularly go to the theater would recognize great acting. At the end of the play they ask the farmer who he thought was the great actor on the stage. He answers, "The king, without doubt." One of his hosts replies, "Indeed . . . you are not of the same opinion with the town;

for they are all agreed, that Hamlet is acted by the best player who ever was on the stage." To this, the farmer responds, "He the best player! . . . I know you are only joking with me; but, indeed, madam, though I was never at a play in London, yet I have seen acting before in the country; and the king for my money; he speaks all his words distinctly, half as loud again as the other. —Anybody may see he is an actor."

THE PRIVATE MOMENT EXERCISE

The private moment exercise is really concentration. An example of a private moment is a scene in Clifford Odets's *The Country Girl*: the wife is beleaguered; the husband is drinking again, and he's in a play; they're going to lose the income; the director is being tough on her and she has a kind of need for him. She has no friends, and she's in this room alone. The radio is playing music and she begins to dance, and all of her feelings are in this dance. The director walks in, and she stops, chagrined. That's a private moment. Another classic example of this is the balcony scene from *Romeo and Juliet*, when Juliet thinks she is alone and muses on her love for Romeo. Once a person told Lee that she never sang in public because she hit the wrong notes. Lee's reply was, "If you hear yourself hitting the wrong notes, then you can hear yourself hitting the right notes."

In Europe they have centuries of tradition—the English theater, the German theater, the Italian commedia dell'arte—centuries of a tradition that evolved and grew. In America it really started when the Group Theatre broke with tradition in the 1930s, and it wasn't very popular. Lee was never popular in theater because he changed the face of that theater. He was aware that he was changing the perception of acting. Once Harold Clurman said to Lee, "I heard you said nice things about me in an interview. But we fight all the time." Lee said, "Of course we fight, but we fight for ideas." The fighting among members of the Group was always about ideas. The roots among those people went so deep, and they were so intertwined, that you could not pull them apart. Each believed in his mission, his ideal. They laid the foundation for a new American theater. Lee's life was with the Group Theatre. It was his real life.

For Lee Strasberg, always.

—A. S.

RECOMMENDED READING LIST

Chekhov, Michael, *To the Actor: On the Technique of Acting*, New York: Routledge, 2002.
Originally published in 1953, this book is particularly interesting for Chekhov's use of the psychological gesture.

Hethmon, Robert H., ed., *Strasberg at the Actors Studio, Tape-Recorded Sessions*, New York: Theatre Communications Group, 1991.
Transcripts of sessions at the Actors Studio, with Lee Strasberg's direction elucidating major aspects of the actor's technique.

Keats, John, *Selected Letters of John Keats*, Grant F. Scott, ed., Cambridge, MA: Harvard University Press, revised edition, 2002.
Keats' letters contain many insights into art, truth, and the poetic process.

Murry, John Middleton, *Keats and Shakespeare, A Study of Keats' Poetic Life from 1816 to 1820*, London: Oxford University Press, 1925.
Chapter Three discusses Keats' aesthetics of "Sensations," which lead to "intuition" and "essential Beauty, which is essential Truth."

Proust, Marcel, *Swann's Way*, Mineola, NY: Dover Publications, 2002.
First published in 1913, the first volume of Proust's *In Search of Lost Time* includes a vivid description of affective memory and how it can be recalled (in the famous passage about dipping a madeleine into tea).

Sheehy, Helen, *Eleonora Duse: A Biography*, New York: Knopf, 2003.
Sheehy describes how the great actress applied techniques such as affective memory to her work.

Strasberg, Lee, *A Dream of Passion: The Development of the Method*, Evangeline Morphos, ed., New York: Plume, 1987.
Lee Strasberg's guide to creativity and the acting process.

_____, "Acting," *Encyclopaedia Britannica*.
A concise overview of major influences in the development of modern acting technique.

ISRAEL LEE STRASBERG, the youngest of four children, was born to Baruch Meier Strasberg and Chaia (Ida) Diner on November 17, 1901 in Budzanów, Poland, Austria-Hungary (now Budanov, Ukraine). The family immigrated to New York City, landing at Ellis Island in 1909.

In 1920, Strasberg was invited to join the Students of Art and Drama, an amateur group at the Chrystie Street Settlement House, where he investigated different directing styles. In 1923, he began training as an actor at the American Laboratory Theatre. A year later, Strasberg joined Philip Loeb's Theatre Guild and began his professional theatrical career as an assistant stage manager for *The Guardsman* at the Garrick Theatre, as well as making his professional acting debut as the First Soldier in *The Processional*, another Theatre Guild production at the Garrick.

Strasberg cofounded the Group Theatre in 1931 with Harold Clurman and Cheryl Crawford. For the Group, Strasberg directed *The House of Connelly* (1931), *Success Story* (1932) and Sidney Kingsley's *Men in White* (1933), which received the Pulitzer Prize. In 1936, Strasberg directed his last production for the Group, Paul Green's comedy *Johnny Johnson*, based on Brecht's *The Good Soldier Schweik*, with music by Kurt Weill, one of the first antiwar plays presented in America. In this year, he also became a United States citizen.

A daughter, Susan, was born to Strasberg and his wife, Paula (Miller), in 1938. A son, John, was born in 1941.

Strasberg resigned from the Group in 1937, and the Group disbanded in 1941. Strasberg directed sixteen plays between 1938 and 1951, and began working with actors in Hollywood in 1943.

Strasberg joined the Actors Studio in 1947 and within a year became its artistic director. By 1960, a directors unit had been established at the Studio to encourage exploration of form and style. In 1966, a West Coast branch of the Actors Studio was established in Los Angeles. In 1967, Strasberg married Anna Mizrahi, whom he had met at the Los Angeles Actors Studio. They had two children, Adam Lee (1969) and David Lee (1971).

Lee Strasberg came to be regarded as a spokesman for American theater. In 1957, he wrote the definition of "Acting" for the fourteenth edition of the *Encyclopaedia Britannica* (in use to this day), replacing Stanislavsky's text. He also wrote the introduction for the new edition of Diderot's *Paradox of Acting*. In 1963, Strasberg represented the American theater at the Stanislavsky Centennial celebration, held in Moscow.

The Lee Strasberg Theatre Institute was created in New York and Los Angeles in 1969. Strasberg also established the Young Actors Program for teenagers and nonactors.

Strasberg was nominated for an Academy Award for his film-acting debut, the role of Meyer Lansky in Francis Ford Coppola's *The Godfather: Part II* (1974). Subsequent film roles included parts in *The Cassandra Crossing* (1976), *And Justice for All* (1978) and *Boardwalk* and *Going in Style* (1979). In 1977, Hollywood's Walk of Fame dedicated a star to Lee Strasberg, located at 6757 Hollywood Boulevard.

Strasberg died in New York City on February 17, 1982. Later that year, he was inducted into the Theatre Hall of Fame, located in the George Gershwin Theatre.

ANNA STRASBERG cofounded the Lee Strasberg Theatre Institutes in New York and Los Angeles with her husband, Lee. As artistic director, she continues the vision and work of the legendary director, actor and master teacher. Mrs. Strasberg also founded and is the artistic director of the Lee Strasberg Creative Center, which provides a place for presenting new theater works by talented young actors, playwrights and directors.

In addition to teaching master classes at the Lee Strasberg Theatre Institutes, Mrs. Strasberg is an adjunct professor at Connecticut College. She has lectured at colleges and conducted acting seminars throughout the United States and the world, including Princeton University, Brown University and Trinity College in Dublin. She has produced and directed numerous award-winning plays at the Marilyn Monroe Theatre in Hollywood, as well as at other theaters in New York and Los Angeles.

STELLA ADLER TECHNIQUE

Tom Oppenheim

In your choice is your talent.

—STELLA ADLER

PART I: THE TRAINING

This simple, concise statement, "In your choice is your talent," which Stella Adler repeated over and over like a mantra as she taught, reflects the unique power, vision and spirit of her technique. For Stella Adler, an actor is first and foremost an ever-evolving human being, fiercely independent, informed and freethinking. The actor's primary obligation as a craftsperson and artist is to grow. Human growth and growth as an actor are synonymous. Although there are basic, practical aspects of the Stella Adler Technique—like understanding the given circumstances of a play, analyzing a text, or playing an action—human growth, mining the infinite depth of the imagination, and opening fully to the world and to life are woven into her Technique and are its principal aims.

"In your choice is your talent" is a reminder that actors must make choices, that those choices must be strong choices, and that the more self-realized the actor, the stronger, richer and fuller the choice. It was also a reminder that "in *your* choice is your talent," not in Stella Adler's choice or anyone else's.

For Stella Adler, three important sources of human growth and self-cultivation were the study of nature (including human nature), the study of art (including but by no means limited to theater art) and the study of history. In nature, Stella saw a great metaphor for the magnificence of life and also for the infinite depth of the actor's imagination. She advocated its study not biologically but poetically. A seminal exercise in her basic technique was to observe something from nature—a flower or leaf, for example—study it in its minute details and then describe it to the class so that they can see it. This is a way of using nature as text. Moreover, nature connects us to the eternal, to that which is greater than us. In Stella's words, "One must go to nature for images that live . . . Nature is large and timeless. Go to the things that are forever, like a stone or a flower. The stone was there before you were born. It is there for you to see now and it will be there after you die."[1]

This sense of going to nature applies also to human nature. "Actors are undercover agents," Stella said. "You must constantly spy on people, studying their character elements . . . Acting is hard because it requires not just the study of books, though that can be important too, but constant study of human behavior."[2]

"The currency of civilization is Art," said Stella. She saw the arts as a vitally important dialogue, a dialogue between people from diverse cultures and times, a dialogue that connects us to what is deepest in each other and ourselves, a dialogue that is ennobling. Stella would admonish her students, "You spend too much time in acting class. Go to a museum." Often, in the course of her teaching, she would read the letters of Vincent van Gogh, a poem, or a passage from a novel to illuminate a play or character. In order for actors to grow to their full stature as artists, they must grow through knowledge of painting, architecture, literature and music as well as theater.

For Stella, the study of history was also a form of self-expansion on a number of levels. It allows one to examine one's life within the greater canvas of human history and civilization. It helps one to understand similarities and differences in diverse historical periods and, therefore, how to be at home in any play, whether it is a period or contemporary piece. Finally, it allows one to see the particular and the universal in everyday life. She wrote:

We have accepted what's around us as just there. We accept it. We don't understand that what's around us has gone on for hundreds and hundreds of years, changing so slowly we don't see it happen. Therefore, we lose the sense of ourselves and where we come from. We lose the sense of the continuity of history—and the sense that history continues in everyday life. You are living or reliving history every moment of your life.

You see a man going out to buy a paper. How many years have men gone to buy the paper? . . . It's something that existed before you saw it. And it has a history. An awareness of history will help you stop taking life and its activities for granted . . .

You see a man holding hands with a girl. How long has that been going on? Adam and Eve. It is *not* ordinary. Though you may be tempted to think it's ordinary, it's up to the actor to see how it's different . . .

You must recognize the significance of living every moment . . . Recognize history. Recognize you're a continuation of history.[3]

This ability to see the particular everyday event, while simultaneously seeing its relationship to all of history and its universal implications, was important for Stella with respect to her understanding of the relationship between the actor and what the particular character he or she is playing represents.

None of these studies were to be pursued as academic disciplines for the sake of accumulating knowledge and information. Rather, they were ways of arousing the actor and helping the actor to grow as fully as possible. They were a way to help the actor become a worthy vessel for great dramatic literature and a life on the stage. Nature, art, all of history, the universe itself, are the actor's spiritual food and fodder for the actor's imagination.

"In your choice is your talent." The deeper the soul, the fuller the spirit, the richer, stronger and more complex an actor's choices tend to be. Stella taught that the path of the actor is demanding. It entails more than working on parts, more than auditioning, more even than working on stagecraft and technique. The path of the actor entails a life committed and forever recommitted to growth. The actor must choose over and over to replenish the source for his or her acting, to plunge into life, into the life of the imagination, passionately, over and over. "In your choice is your talent." The actor must choose to grow.

THE TECHNIQUE

There are three distinct branches of Stella's Technique: Foundation, Character and Script Interpretation. Before I describe them, let me say that these techniques are complex and take a long time to learn. My focus here is to outline them in the broadest possible terms in order to present their uniqueness and then to trace that uniqueness to Stella Adler's history.

Foundation

Stella Adler's Foundation work proceeds from her conviction that the primary source for one's acting is the imagination. The imagination contains everything from art, to ideas, to poetry, to the entire collective unconscious of all humanity, to one's personal past, to this present moment. Whatever you say, do, think or feel onstage must be filtered through the imagination. Whatever you see, real or imagined; whatever you hear, real or imagined; every prop, set piece or costume element must not be taken for granted or accepted by rote. It must be created or re-created through the imagination. For every present there is a past that must also be imaginatively created. Stella taught that the actor sees the world not through factual, literal eyes, but through the eyes of the imagination. The imagination warms the world, makes it matter—makes it, artistically speaking, real and useful.

The Stella Adler technique also embraces the point of view that acting is doing. It is an action-oriented technique. It proceeds from the conviction that truth is found in the given circumstances of the play.

Stella Adler devised many exercises to explore, expand and strengthen the imagination, to teach actions, to show how behavior is determined by one's circumstances—how what you do is determined by where you are. Often all three concepts are present in the same exercise. We have already touched on one of these—the flower exercise. In this one simple exercise, many fundamental, perhaps unique aspects of the technique are contained. The basic exercise is to observe a flower, studying it in minute detail, the way you will eventually study a script, totally owning it, knowing it better than you know yourself. Then you must learn to sequence the details so you can describe them clearly and logically. Then you stand or sit in front of the group and "give it away"—that is, describe the flower so vividly that the group can see it. This part of the exercise requires the important stage skills of making contact with another or others, having something inside in your mind's eye that you know so well you do not have to strain to see it, and then being able to reach your partner with the image. At a later stage of the flower exercise, you will substitute an image, thought, idea, action or need. This requires an open and responsive voice and an aligned and relaxed body. Also, you must have a strong point of view about the object described. This exercise also asks the actor to use only those words necessary to evoke the image. Thus the actor becomes aware of the power of words.

This in itself is unique to the Stella Adler Technique. It seems to me that in American actor training there is, at best, a kind of ambivalence toward words—an idea that words are the writer's business. The actor's work is elsewhere, underneath the words. Like other teachers, Stella also had this concern. She frequently warned, "The play has nothing to do with words. The play is about ideas." Nevertheless, Stella had great respect for words, for the emotional and intellectual potency and power of theatrical and poetic language. She insisted that her students become aware of their own use of language, and if they were limited by habitual speech patterns or a regionalism she would demand they "fix it." She wanted her students to develop an ear for and a love of language so that when they did the "work" to get underneath the words, their thoughts, feelings and impulses could fully inflect the playwright's language according to their own understanding of the character's needs.

This exercise runs throughout the basic Stella Adler Technique. Sometimes the objects are real. Sometimes they are made up. For example, there is a version of this exercise in which the student is asked to create an imaginary Fifth Avenue apartment. It must be created in minute detail. Each piece of furniture, each vase and ashtray must have a background. Where did it come from? How long has it been there? How did it get that chip or scratch? As in the flower exercise, the student must then "give it away." Therefore, you must see what is not there and describe it as though it were. The more specifically you have created it—that is, made *choices* about it—the clearer you can see it, the more confidence and comfort you have *on the stage*. You have more confidence on the stage because you are not on the stage but in a real place, a place you know because you created it. The last step is to live in the place. Stella would ask you to live in the place as a cat, because cats are uninhibited and instinctive in their movements. She would want you to use the place with feline fullness and dexterity. Thus she would introduce the concept of living truthfully in imaginary circumstances. The world you create, the background you endow objects with, now speaks to and through you. It tells you how to do what you do. The actor both creates the world and responds to it.

Another exercise in basic technique is to paraphrase an essay from Kahlil Gibran's *The Prophet*. Stella chose these essays because they were about large ideas, like friendship, sorrow and joy—ideas that uplift the spirit and engage the mind. Actors were asked to choose an essay, study it as carefully as they had the flower and then "give it away" in their own words. Stella would look for all the things demanded in the flower exercise—clarity of thought, economy of words, a relaxed body and opened voice—as well as a more personally engaged, non-pushed truth. For the first time, the actor is dealing with text, with ideas. It is therefore incumbent upon the actor not only to understand the author's words but also to have a strong relationship to or point of view about them, to make choices that center and animate. "In your choice is your talent."

An important idea running throughout these exercises is the clarification of the difference between what I find out there in the world and what I bring to it. For example, I find the flower in nature. It has specific details that provide its unique quality: its stem is so long, of a certain color and texture, the blossom is thus-and-such color, length and width. These are all facts. Then there is what I bring to the flower: I find it beautiful, exquisite and miraculous. It reminds me of this fabric, silk, for example; or of that time of day, dawn. There is the flower, and here I am. My job is to communicate my experience of that flower.

Stella believed that in understanding that the world is out there, objective, before you, and that your interior self is in here, with its memories, associations and musings, you become acutely aware of your imagination and of what you have to contribute. You also understand that you must go out to life, to embrace it, to experience it.

You will eventually substitute the text for the flower. The words are there on the page, black on white, objectively before you. They are the playwright's gift. You take them and create, interpret, make choices. "In your choice is your talent."

Character

The second branch of Stella Adler's technique, the Character class, is, within the context of American actor training, also unique. In my experience, American acting teachers and directors often seem skittish about Character work. Perhaps it is due to the medium of film and television. The fast pace at which they work in film causes producers, directors and casting agents to look not for an actor who can *play* the character, but for the character himself. Perhaps it is because of a national predilection for naturalism combined with a constricted sense of truth. Perhaps it is because the tendency in America to associate success with money causes actors to figure out their type and stick to it, and encourages casting agents play it safe and find someone who does not have to *act*. Whatever the reason, many a teacher and director repeat the same battle cry: "Just be yourself." Similarities between oneself and the character are focused on, while differences are diminished or disregarded.

Stella saw it otherwise. She had a passion for Character work combined with an expansive sense of self. For her, one's habitual daily self is a cleverly constructed character one plays. Underneath it exists an endless multiplicity of possible selves. She also had a great interest in otherness, other selves, other times, other cultures and socioeconomic classes. Like Goethe, Stella believed that nothing human was alien to her.

Paradoxically, Stella believed that the deeper you delve into Character, into other identities, the closer you get to yourself (or perhaps I should say *selves*). The more complete the mask, the more intimate the self-revelation. The actor is freed by the fiction to tell the truth. For Stella, the goal of Character work is not escape but self-fulfillment.

Her Character class offered a variety of approaches and exercises to help actors explore Character. Some of these exercises were outside-in approaches: they involved "shopping" in the world for images, examples of objects animate or inanimate that remind you of, or evoke for you, the character type. Once found, you were asked to physicalize the object and feel the inner resonance of its outer object, for example, taking on the physicality of a city bus to find one's way into the life of a bossy bullying type or the grandeur of a mountain to find one's way into regality.

Some of the exercises advocate inside-out paths to Character. For example, choosing a way of thinking, feeling or willing that seems appropriate for a given character and then exploring its anatomy. What, for instance, does timidity feel like, and what does it do? What are its inner movements and its relationship to the world? What do I know about timidity? When have I experienced it and why? And finally, how does this inform, for instance, the playing of a character like Laura in Tennessee Williams's *The Glass Menagerie*?

Another road into Character work is an exploration of what Stella referred to as the five major archetypes: the aristocracy, the military, the clergy, the middle class and the peasant class. Here she would use paintings, sculpture, architecture, period music, costume, and various forms of movement, including dance, military marches, walking, sitting, and standing in imaginary places and times. She would also employ dramatic texts to allow the actor to combine these explorations with theatrical language.

All of these techniques for Character work point to the exploration of otherness. They advocate that the contemporary American actor embrace self-transcendence and transformation as a necessary element in their development. However, underlying this conviction and sensibility is what might be described as a kind of Adlerian mysticism.

In Stella's words: "The actor has in him the collective consciousness. It's as if all knowledge and all wisdom are contained in his mind. Through his vast imagination he inherits the wisdom of his ancestors without having had the personal experience. The actor, throughout history, has always had a deep and cosmic understanding."[4]

And in her book *Acting with Adler*, Joanna Rotte quotes Stella: "You are everybody. In some area of your life you are a killer, a crook, a liar, and a whore. You are a genius, a god, and pure. You are everything. There goes a man who is going to be killed. There goes you. Somewhere, you are that man."[5]

It is noteworthy that although Stella Adler is best known for having created acting techniques for modern or Chekhovian realism—and rightly so—she nevertheless had a lifelong interest in and love for the avant-garde and heightened theater. This predilection is clearly manifest in her Character class, where she devised techniques for heightening Character. For example, Rotte wrote:

> Adler defined heightened character as the type externalized to its theatrical extreme. As in farce or melodrama, it is characterization so stylized on the outside that the inside can almost be forgotten. Drawn in broad strokes and vividly colored, heightened character requires a rather dualistic perspective. Things are pretty much black and white, not muted or subtle. Heightening takes what Adler called a slanted (biased) view, that results in the type's being theatricalized more than individualized.
>
> The technique for heightening a character is to see him through the eyes of his social opposite, or at least through the eyes of someone radically different. It may be to perceive the servant from the master's viewpoint, the capitalist from the socialist's, the Hollywood starlet from the Christian fundamentalist's, the doctor from the child's, the homosexual from the neo-Nazi's.[6]

Of course, to go along with these techniques for Character work, Stella insisted that characters must be multidimensional and grounded in oneself. They must be real human beings. But she does not shy away from painting characters in broad strokes. While she demands truth, she never shies away from size. While an actor thinking in terms of character types and heightening character might risk falling into stereotypes, this approach also promises an expanded sense of reality, of theatrical truth, of artistic possibility. This aspect of Stella's work has definite relevance not only for realistic and classical drama but also for the post-realistic drama of Beckett, Brecht, Shepard, etc.

Script Interpretation

The third aspect of Stella Adler's approach, Script Interpretation, grew out of her love for plays and playwrights—something she inherited from her father. This is not to suggest that other acting teachers cared less about plays than she, but none that I know of actually developed a technique for reading plays and analyzing them in quite the way Stella did.

Script Interpretation class directly applies the imagination-oriented Adler approach to specific plays and playwrights. She would take a playwright, enumerate issues, ideas and concerns common throughout his work and place them in their historical geographical and social context. Then she would zero in on one particular play, discussing its ideas, the impact it had on the theater and culture of its day, and its continued implications and meanings for our own times. Finally, she would work on one particular scene. She would go through it slowly and meticulously, supporting her reading with historical research and imaginative musing. Again, she worked not as a scholar, but as an actress, passionately endeavoring to create and discover the life underneath the text, carefully combing through the specific words the author has given to find the deeper voices within both the play and herself.

SUMMING UP

The three aspects of the Stella Adler Technique (Foundation, or basic technique, Character and Script Interpretation) are really a single approach—a challenging, demanding approach that requires that the actor's whole self be involved in the art of acting. It requires a profound willingness to change, to evolve, to grow. It requires the

conviction that human growth and growth as an actor are synonymous. It requires the courage to think for oneself and make choices.
"In your choice is your talent."

PART II: THE HISTORY OF TRADITION

> My first feeling of self, my first true consciousness, was
> not in a home, not in a room, but in a dressing room.
> A dressing room is not a room, it is something very dif-
> ferent. Costumes hang on the wall. There is a large mir-
> ror. On a table in the corner one sees wigs, hairpieces,
> mustaches. But most important is the dressing table with
> its colored sticks of theatrical makeup.
>
> Few people entered the dressing room. One almost
> did not dare to penetrate the loneliness there. The loneli-
> ness came from my father, putting on his makeup. There
> was a special quality in this choosing of his colors and
> placing them, like a painter, one next to the other, an
> almost religious sense of something being created.
>
> I watched this creation. I watched a man change
> into another man.
>
> —STELLA ADLER

In a special way, Stella Adler's ideas and her technique grew out of
her life in the theater. She was born in 1901 in New York City and
literally grew up in the Yiddish theater. More specifically, she grew up
in the theater of her father, the great Yiddish actor Jacob P. Adler. Her
mother, Sara Adler, was also a great actress, and Stella, like her brothers
and sisters, made her first stage performance at the age of four. They
played the great European repertory (Gogol, Ibsen, Gorky, Tolstoy).
They also acted in adaptations of Shakespeare—all this in Yiddish.

Furthermore, the atmosphere of the Adler home was totally
influenced by the theater and by acting, not only as a profession but as
a way of life, a means of communication as well as a sacred art form.
Stories were not merely told but acted out. Dinners were constantly
interrupted by family members standing up to show, as well as tell, a
joke, a description of the day's events, or a recollected piece of business from last night's performance. Home was itself an acting class.
Indeed, the atmosphere of the Adler household was entirely informed
by acting and by theater, but also, and above all, by laughter.

But perhaps the most indelible memories for Stella were of the serious side of the theater and of the ideas and ideals learned from her father. The theater that Jacob Adler created was a theater committed to great plays, to the highest theatrical and artistic standards, and to big ideas. Jacob Adler understood theater as a means to elevate and educate both himself and his people.

Born in the Russian city of Odessa in 1855, Jacob Adler was one of the most important figures of the Yiddish theater, which began in Romania in the 1870s and spread throughout Europe and finally to America.

The Yiddish theater grew out of a movement in Jewish history known as the Haskala (the awakening), a movement that corresponds to the revolutions of the eighteenth and nineteenth centuries as all of Europe climbed out from under the oppressive weight of monarchial governments and began to be democratic. For the Jews, the road to freedom involved education.

> Education was the battle cry of this Jewish revolution. If the world would not break the wall of the ghetto from the outside, the Jew must break it from the inside. Education—*secular* education—was the tool that would break the wall. Free, no longer isolated, the Jew would take his place in science, in art, in political action, in every great endeavor of the time.[7]

For Jacob Adler, this new freedom would eventually lead to a life in the theater. As a young man, he discovered the Russian theater. He also discovered the burgeoning expression of a uniquely Jewish theatrical voice in the so-called singers of Brod, beggars who would sing of ordinary Jewish life in the many taverns, wine cellars and street corners of Odessa. Jacob Adler fell in love with the theater and devoted his life to the development of the Yiddish theater. This lifelong devotion took him from Odessa through Europe to England, and finally to the Lower East Side of Manhattan.

The history of the Yiddish theater is complex and rich, and even the most general overview is beyond the scope of this history of the influences of Stella Adler. Suffice it to say that in its heyday it achieved a theatrical excellence to rival any such movement, from the Greeks to the Elizabethans. Its repertoire was broad and varied, encompassing styles from classical, to vaudeville, to realistic, to fantastical. It produced great actors and magnificent plays. It has made a significant impact on the theater of our time. As we shall see, members of the Group Theatre, including Lee Strasberg, Harold Clurman, Sanford Meisner and Robert Lewis, gained their first acquaintance with theater through the Yiddish theater.

As Jacob Adler's career advanced, his stature as an actor grew. Many critics, both Jews and Gentiles, considered him to be among the great actors of his time. Critic Henry Tyrell wrote of Adler's performance in Tolstoy's *Power of Darkness*: "If Adler could perform in English in a Broadway theater he would be idolized. Unfortunately, he is not sufficiently versed in the vernacular, yet, for that matter, neither are Bernhardt, Duse or Salvini, in whose class Adler belongs."[8]

Another measure of his stature and success as an actor was the fact that, late in his career, he was asked to play Shylock in Yiddish on Broadway, surrounded by an English-speaking cast. When he died on March 31, 1926, between 100,000–150,000 people lined the streets of the Lower East Side as his coffin passed.

Perhaps Jacob Adler's most important contribution to the Yiddish theater, beyond the greatness of his acting, was his impulse to elevate it through great plays. It is clear from his writing that this impulse can be traced back to his earliest days in the theater. In his memoir, he describes a talk he had with fellow actor Sonya Oberlander, the woman who was to become his first wife:

> She spoke to me of the Greeks, how they smeared their mouths with grape juice, rode about in wagons, played under the empty sky, and yet from this beginning made their great art. She spoke of Shakespeare's day. No scenery. Nothing but a shield with a word on it . . . She spoke of Molière's time, when actors traveled the countryside like vagabonds, and were reduced to stealing a chicken for their supper . . . And yet, the French theater rose to the heights on which it now stands. And today, Sonya said—when we have Hugo's *Hernani*, Gogol's *Revizor*, when we have a *Faust*, a *Wallenstein*, when France has given the world such immortals as Rachel and Bernhardt . . . when America has produced the genius of Booth, Italy the giant Salvini—what is the place of the theater today? Kings value it as their highest pleasure. Millionaires and aristocrats pay fortunes just to have a box at a play. Young intellectuals wait hours in the cold . . . just to drink in the art of some great actors . . . And

if from these lowly beginnings, these theaters rose to such loftiness and beauty, why cannot our Yiddish theater rise equally high?"[9]

Jacob Adler spent his life wrestling with that question. He spent his life endeavoring to dignify and educate his people by lifting the Yiddish theater from mere entertainment to a great art form. "In 1891," he wrote, "I formed a company of my own and took over the Union Theater on Broadway and Eighth Street . . . I opened the season with three [plays] from the standard European repertoire. It was time, I felt, that our theater touched on the deeper sides of life, time that plays of a more serious character found a place on our stage."[10]

In the same year, he met the playwright Jacob Gordin. Gordin wrote important plays such as *Siberia*, *The Yiddish King Lear* and *The Wild Man*. These were serious plays about ordinary Jewish life with realistic sets and recognizable characters. Adler produced these plays and acted in them, doing some of his greatest work. Adler and his company had to weather negative response and audience attrition, but he was resolved. "We opened [*Siberia*] on December 3, 1891," he wrote. "I knew from the first that a great step had been taken, a step from which there was no turning back."[11]

In 1892, despite continued audience attrition, a notice appeared in the Yiddish press: "The Union Theater, under the sole artistic direction of Jacob P. Adler, has been reorganized with the aim of driving from the Yiddish stage all that is crude, unclean, immoral, and with the purpose of lifting Yiddish theater to a higher level. The independent Yiddish Artists Company will present to the public only beautiful musical operas and dramas giving truthful and serious portrayals of life."[12]

Ultimately, the combination of Gordin and Adler won. The Yiddish theater was changed. It was for a time elevated to the heights of other great theatrical epochs. Jacob P. Adler's dream had become manifest. This was ten years prior to Stella Adler's birth.

The correlations between Stella Adler's theatrical predilections and those of her father are, I hope, clear. They both shared a passion for great dramatic literature. Clearly Stella's interest in character work came from her early exposure to her father's theater, where she witnessed the mystery of theatrical creation, "A man turning into another man." They both understood that great acting includes but transcends the truth of daily life. It includes the grandeur of the human spirit. The correlation between human growth and growth as an actor, and the idea of growing through great plays, is common to them both.

No wonder, also, that Harold Clurman's first memory of the theater was of his father taking him to see Jacob Adler in *Uriel Acosta*, and that ever since then he had, in his own words, "a passionate inclination toward the theater." In the Yiddish theater, Harold Clurman witnessed many of the virtues that years later he so passionately instilled in the Group Theatre.

Wendy Smith wrote in her book *Real Life Drama*, "The Yiddish theater enthralled [Clurman] with its productions of classical drama: Shakespeare, Tolstoy, Chekhov, and Gogol brought to life in performances of extraordinary realism by actors with an emotional fluency unknown to their English-language counterparts. Most of all, it was the intense relationship between and among actors and audience he adored, the sense of theater as a gathering place for the community."[13]

Stella Adler and Harold Clurman met in 1920. Their relationship was tumultuous and lifelong. They were colleagues, lovers, husband and wife, mortal enemies and the best of friends. They met at the American Laboratory Theatre, an actor training program created by two former members of the Moscow Art Theatre, Richard Boleslavsky and Maria Ouspenskaya.

By the time Harold met Stella, he had been friends with Lee Strasberg for some time. Their dream for what was to become the Group Theatre was well established. Both Clurman and Strasberg, as well as many other young actors, including Stella Adler, felt dissatisfied with the American theater of the twenties. However, it was Clurman's capacity to articulate that dissatisfaction and, by way of his ferocious, unrelenting idealism, to galvanize people, that gave birth to the Group, a theatrical movement that changed American theater and film forever.

Part of what made Harold's rhetoric so powerful was his capacity to see the shortcomings of the American theater in the context of America itself. Clurman understood that the materialism of the roaring twenties and the emphasis on individualism were artistically and spiritually hazardous for the country, and, by extension, for the theater. Theater had become a commodity, something to buy and sell and ultimately a mere form of entertainment; not what Harold thought it should be, a living expression of and connection to the needs and aspirations of the American people. Consequently, Clurman argued, the American people had become increasingly cut off from each other and from meaningful discourse and interaction.

Harold Clurman dreamed of a theater that would respond to this condition and, against all odds, mend it. He began weekly talks in which he described the kind of theater he felt the country needed: "A theater is created when people with common interests and tastes unite to devise ways and means whereby they may give their group feeling an adequate theatrical expression. They seek out people who, for all the superficial differences of their temperament, fundamentally share the same feeling. They seek them amongst directors, actors, playwrights, scene designers—confident all the time that the thing that binds them together must be a reflection of a sentiment that animates many people in the world about them."[14]

This philosophy led Clurman to insist that the Group would perform plays by American playwrights that dealt in a positive way with "the essential moral and social preoccupations of our time." The result was a theater that, like Jacob Adler's theater before it, spoke to, unified and elevated its public. Harold Clurman and the Group discovered that actors and audience must grow through great and relevant plays. The actor's work is animated by the material and its relevance to the audience.

For many of the new members of the Group, joining Harold's theater took real courage. They had to give up contracts and well-paying theater jobs in order to join a company with no capital and, at first, no play. Among these early members were Robert Lewis, Sanford Meisner, Ruth Nelson, Morris Carnovsky, Phoebe Brand, Clifford Odets, Franchot Tone, Luther Adler and, of course, Stella Adler. Later members included Elia Kazan, Lee J. Cobb and John Garfield, names that will live forever in the history of American theater.

Becoming a member of the Group may have been difficult for Stella Adler, since she was by nature not a *group* type. Though she started out in her father's theater, she was always fiercely independent, a leader, not a follower. By the time she met Harold Clurman, she was a seasoned actress in her mid-twenties and had been on the stage her whole life. She had already acted in great Yiddish Plays and translations of European classics. As a member of the Adler clan, she thought of herself as a member of theater royalty and not "one of the gang." There were many reasons why joining the Group was an unlikely road for Stella. But join she did. Harold Clurman's dream was irresistible. It resonated too strongly with the theater of her youth, the Yiddish theater of Jacob P. Adler. What Jacob Adler had done for his audience of immigrant Jews, Harold sought to do for the whole country. Stella recognized this. In her introduction to her father's memoir, she wrote: "Here in the Group I found what I had been searching for—a theater that had come together for something more meaningful than another Broadway hit. The plays of John Howard Lawson, the plays of Paul Green, the deeply moving plays of Clifford Odets, were chosen by the Group not because they would bring money into the box office, but because they had something to say about American life, something important that needed to be said.

"My years in the Group were difficult: a time of pain as well as a time of growth. There were deep divisions, fundamental differences. But when the Group broke up, when the actors dispersed, I felt I had lost my home."[15]

One of these "deep divisions" was between her and Lee Strasberg on their "fundamental difference" about acting. Strasberg had a lifelong fascination with emotional truth. The exercises he learned from Boleslavsky and Ouspenskaya emphasized affective memory, that is, recalling past events in as much sensorial detail as possible in order to resurrect the associated emotions. It became central to his way of working. Although this method of acting clearly had powerful results for many Group members, including Stella (some say her greatest work was done under Strasberg's direction), it nevertheless ran counter to her temperament and theatrical predilections.

Having worked for three years under Strasberg's guidance and direction, some of the other Group actors felt the same discomfort as Stella. While everyone recognized Strasberg's brilliance and uncompromising pursuit of truth, some began to feel limited by it. Perhaps because, for Strasberg, "truth" was always emotional truth, and emotional truth must be pursued head-on by way of affective memory; perhaps because they began to sense that creative potential could be mined from places other than one's personal past; perhaps because the internal nature of the work proved too painful for some—whatever the reason, they agreed that another way of working, a different approach, was needed.

In 1934, on a return trip from Russia, Stella and Harold stopped in Paris. There they met with the great Russian teacher, director, actor and father of modern actor training Konstantin Stanislavsky. This meeting would have huge consequences not only for Stella Adler, but also for the rest of the Group Theatre. Ultimately its impact would be felt far beyond that.

It is clear from the first words she spoke to Stanislavsky that Stella was in an artistic crisis at the time. "Mr. Stanislavsky," she said, "I enjoyed acting and the theater until you came along. And now I hate it." Thus began daily meetings between Stanislavsky and Stella, meetings that went on for five weeks. These meetings were in the nature of private classes or coaching sessions in which Stanislavsky tried to clarify for Stella how his system worked and certain changes it had undergone.

They spent their time working on a role Stella played in John Howard Lawson's *Gentlewoman*, a role in which Stella was ultimately dissatisfied with her performance. They carefully went over one scene from that play. It was then that Stella learned what would become some of the most important elements of her technique and her future work as both an actress and teacher. Most important, Stanislavsky taught her that she no longer had to attack emotion head-on through affective memory. He released her from the obligation to work on feeling in favor of choosing and playing actions and living imaginatively in the given circumstances of the play. She was encouraged to analyze the script, find the character's overall action, and then make choices about what actions might be played—that is to say, what the character must *do* to get what she wants, to achieve her objective. Truth was to be found not exclusively in one's personal past but through one's imagination and in the given circumstances of the play. Emotion would flow naturally out of the sequence of actions one chose to play in order to achieve one's objective. Emotion comes from doing.

It's important to note that, as Wendy Smith observed, "Willy Barton's notes from Adler's class reveal that the actress by no means rejected everything Strasberg had taught the Group. True emotion remained crucial; when listing the different areas of work on a part, she included the 'golden box' that contained the actor's personal source for the feelings needed in a scene. But she emphasized the conscious use of emotion, the interconnection between mind, will, and feeling: 'One cannot feel without the will and mind being concerned. They are the motor of our psychic life.'"[16]

In other words, Lee Strasberg's way of working, his insistence on real emotion and on using one's own life and personal past in pursuit of connecting fully to the material, was never completely denied. Rather it was reprioritized, perhaps de-emphasized. For Stella, mind and will came first and feelings followed. From the actor's point of view, what one wants, what one pursues and the thought process one utilizes to get it are primary. Furthermore, one's mind, ideas, what one stands for in the playwright's world must be fully understood. (For example, in Arthur Miller's *All My Sons*, if I'm playing Chris, what big idea do I stand for in the debate with my father? If he stands for the self-preservation and self-interest of big business, perhaps I stand for self-sacrifice and love of one's fellow man.)

Stella returned to America with a renewed sense of purpose. Acting had become fun again. Although she had taught classes prior to her trip to Paris and her work with Stanislavsky, I think it is fair to say that, upon her return, Stella Adler the teacher was born. She gave two talks to the Group about what she had learned in Paris. She explained what she understood to be a viable alternative way to work. The central message was action versus feeling—for Adler, the actor must first do, and feelings will follow; for Strasberg, the actor must first feel and doing will follow.

What liberated Stella liberated other Group members. A new way of working was introduced, an alternative not only for Group members but also for generations of actors to come. This indeed was an important moment in the history of theater and actor training in America and worldwide. If Lee Strasberg was the first American to interpret the Stanislavsky system and apply it to American actors in American plays, then Stella Adler was the first American to diversify methodology. Perhaps the measure of Stella's accomplishment as a teacher, beyond even the well-known actors she trained, is the fact that, in the Group years, among her most loyal and enthusiastic students were director Elia Kazan and teachers Robert Lewis and Sanford Meisner.

A biography on Stella Adler has yet to be written. When it is, it will certainly include Jacob Adler, Harold Clurman and Konstantin Stanislavsky as the three major influences on her life and work. Stella also credited her mother, the great Yiddish actress Sara Adler, for teaching her strength and fortitude both in life and on the stage and for what she described as a "kind of brave optimism." That same quality existed strongly in Harold Clurman and informed the work and never-say-die spirit of the Group Theatre, particularly through the plays of Clifford Odets. All this found expression in Stella's theatrical spirit and her technique. She was vehement about her students making "positive" choices. The voices of the past continue to speak from the Yiddish theater through the Group Theatre to this very day. They whisper to us of a theater of ideas, a theater that matters. They remind us of our own magnificence and provide a vision of fulfillment and the glory of the human spirit. Would that we could hear them still.

ENDNOTES/SOURCES

Epigraphs:
(Page 29) Adler, Stella, *The Technique of Acting*, New York: Bantam, 1988, p. 26.
(Page 38) Adler, Stella, Introduction to *Jacob Adler: A Life on the Stage—A Memoir* by Jacob Adler, New York: Knopf, 1999, p. xiii.

1. Adler, Stella, *The Art of Acting*, Howard Kissel, ed., New York: Applause, 2000, p. 48.
2. Ibid., p. 148.
3. Ibid., p. 43.
4. Adler, Stella, *The Technique of Acting*, p. 4.
5. Rotte, Joanna, *Acting with Adler*, New York: Limelight Editions, 2000, p. 134.
6. Ibid., p. 154.
7. Rosenfeld, Lulla, "A Yiddish Theater? How Did It Happen?" in *Jacob Adler: A Life on the Stage*, p. xxi.
8. Adler, Jacob, *Jacob Adler: A Life on the Stage*, p. 355.
9. Ibid., p. 100.
10. Ibid., p. 316.
11. Ibid., p. 321.
12. Rosenfeld, Lulla Adler, *The Yiddish Theatre and Jacob P. Adler*, New York: Shapolsky Publishers, 1988.
13. Smith, Wendy, *Real Life Drama: The Group Theatre and America, 1931–1940*, New York: Knopf, 1990; Grove/Atlantic, 1992, p. 184.
14. Ibid., p. 7.
15. Adler, Stella, Introduction to *Jacob Adler: A Life on the Stage*, p. xix.
16. Smith, p. 184.

RECOMMENDED READING LIST

Adler, Jacob, *Jacob Adler: A Life on the Stage—A Memoir*, Lulla Rosenfeld, trans., New York: Knopf, 1999; Applause, 2001.
This detailed history of Stella's father, the great Yiddish actor Jacob P. Adler, includes an introduction by Stella Adler and provides insight into the source of her epic vision.

Adler, Stella, *Stella Adler on Ibsen, Strindberg, and Chekhov*, Barry Paris, ed., New York: Knopf, 1999; Vintage, 2000.
This book is comprised of lectures Stella Adler gave on the three playwrights in her famous and unique Script Interpretation class.

_____, *The Technique of Acting*, New York: Bantam Books, 1990.

Clurman, Harold, *All People Are Famous (Instead of an autobiography)*, New York: Harcourt Brace Jovanovich, 1974.

_____, *The Fervent Years: The Group Theatre & the '30s*, New York: Knopf, 1945; Da Capo Press, 1983.
Clurman's impassioned opus describes the history of the Group Theatre and the many personalities and forces that made it work.

Kissel, Howard, ed., *Stella Adler: The Art of Acting*, New York: Applause, 2000.
This is a carefully crafted compilation of lectures, speeches and writings of Stella Adler giving the reader a clear view of her technique, ideas and approach to acting and to theater.

Rosenfeld, Lulla Adler, *The Yiddish Theatre and Jacob P. Adler*, New York: Shapolsky Publishers, 1988.
A great book for understanding Stella's legacy and the history that influenced her. With an introduction by Harold Clurman.

Rotte, Joanna, *Acting with Adler*, New York: Limelight Editions, 2000.
A lucid description of Stella's technique and philosophy, from a former student. With a foreword by Ellen Adler.

Smith, Wendy, *Real Life Drama: The Group Theatre and America, 1931–1940*, New York: Knopf, 1990; Grove/Atlantic, 1992.
An excellent, detailed account of the history of the Group Theatre.

STELLA ADLER was born in New York City on February 10, 1901, to Jacob P. and Sara Adler. She had many brothers and sisters: Charles, Jay, Julia, Luther, Florence and Frances; and a half-brother and half-sister (born from Jacob's first marriage): Abram and Celia. All would become actors.

Adler first appeared on stage in 1906 at the age of four in *Broken Hearts*, which was produced at her father's Yiddish theater. In 1907 she appeared as a young prince in Richard III and continued to appear in productions at her father's theater for the next ten years. Her career in the theater and in film and television continued throughout her life.

She was married to Horace Eleaschreff (with whom she had one daughter, Ellen, who is the mother of Tom Oppenheim), Harold Clurman and Mitchell Wilson.

She died on December 21, 1992, in Los Angeles.

On August 4, 2006, Stella Adler received a star on the Hollywood Walk of Fame.

Adler's extensive theater, film and television work include (in chronological order):

Actor

Naomi, *Elisha Ben Avia*, Pavillion Theatre, London, 1919; Apatura Clythia, *The World We Live In*, Jolson's 59th Street Theatre, New York, 1922; the Orpheum Vaudeville Circuit (national tour), 1923–24 (billed as Lola Adler); Baroness Crème de la Crème, *The Straw Hat*, American Laboratory Theatre Production, New York, 1926; Elly, *Big Lake*, American Laboratory Theatre Production, 1927; Beatrice, *Much Ado about Nothing*, American Laboratory Theatre Production, 1927; various roles in Yiddish theater, the Irving Place Theatre, New York, and on tour in Latin America and Western Europe, 1927–1930; various roles, *The God of Vengeance*, *The Lower Depths*, *Liliom*, *The Witch of Castile* and *Jew Suss*, the Yiddish Art Theatre, New York, 1930–31; Geraldine Connelly, *The House of Connelly*, Group Theatre Production, Martin Beck Theatre, Broadway, 1931; Dona Josepha, *Night Over Taos*, Group Theatre Production, 48th Street Theatre, New York, 1932; Sarah Glassman, *Success Story*, Group Theatre Production, Maxine Elliott's Theatre, Broadway, 1932; Myra Bonney, *Big Night*, Group Theatre Production, Maxine Elliott's Theatre, 1933; Hilda Cassidy, *Hilda Cassidy*, Martin Beck Theatre, 1933; Gwyn Ballantine, *Gentlewoman*, Group Theatre Production, Cort Theatre, New York, 1934; Adah Isaccs Menken, *Gold Eagle Guy*, Group Theatre Production, Morosco Theatre, Broadway, 1934; Bessie Berger, *Awake and Sing!*, Group Theatre Production, Belasco Theatre, Broadway, 1935; Clara, *Paradise Lost*, Group Theatre Production, Longacre Theatre, Broadway, 1935; Catherine Carnick, *Sons and Soldiers*, Morosco Theatre, 1943; Clothilde Hilyard, *Pretty Little Parlor*, National Theatre, Broadway, 1944; Zinida, *He Who Gets Slapped*, Theate Guild revival, Booth Theatre, Broadway, 1946; Madame Rosepettle, *Oh Dad, Poor Dad, Mama's Hung You in a Closet and I'm Feeling So Sad*, Piccadilly Theatre, London, 1961.

Director

Golden Boy (director of the L.A./London tours), 1938–39; *Manhattan Nocturne*, Forrest Theatre, Broadway, 1943; *Johnny Johnson*, Off-Broadway revival, 1945; *Polonaise*, Alvin Theatre/Adelphi Theatre, New York, 1945; *Sunday Breakfast*, Coronet Theatre, Broadway, 1952.

FILM

Actor

Linda Craven, *Love on Toast*, Paramount Pictures, 1937 (billed as Stella Ardler); Claire Porter, *Shadow of the Thin Man*, MGM, 1941; Mrs. Faludi, *My Girl Tisa*, United Artists, 1948; as herself, *American Masters*, "Harold Clurman: A Life of Theatre," 1988, 2000.

Associate Producer

Madame Curie, For Me and My Gal and *DuBarry Was a Lady*, MGM, 1943.

T V

Suspense, "The Case of Lady Sannox" and "Black Passage," 1949; as herself, *Stella Adler: Awake and Dream!*, 1989; as herself, *American Masters*, "Broadway's Dreamers: The Legacy of the Group Theatre," 1983.

TOM OPPENHEIM was born in 1959 in New York City. He studied acting with his grandmother, Stella Adler, and at the National Shakespeare Conservatory. He began teaching voice and speech at the Stella Adler Studio in 1990 and in 1995 took over as the Studio's artistic director.

Theater credits include Jambalaya's production of *Othello* as Iago, *Henry IV*, Part 1, and *Macbeth* at the New Jersey Shakespeare Festival, *Henry VI*, Parts 1, 2 and 3, at Theater for a New Audience, *Juana Queen of Spain* at Ensemble Studio Theatre, *Bound East for Cardiff* at the Provincetown Playhouse, *Romeo and Juliet* at Mint Theater Company, *Comparing Books* at the Producer's Club, and Jambalaya's production of *Featuring Loretta*. Film credits include Mike Nichols's *Wolf*, Art Jones's *Going Nomad* and *Dodgeball* and Deborah Kampmeier's *Worm in the Bottle/Man on the Moon* and *Virgin*. TV credits include Sidney Lumet's TV series *100 Centre Street*.

He has built on the quality of the Stella Adler Studio of Acting by engaging a faculty of national and international stature and developing a curriculum that renews the original spirit, intentions and ideals of Stella Adler, Harold Clurman and the Group Theatre, while maintaining palpable contact with the contemporary world. He has created a myriad of extracurricular programs, most of which are named in honor of Harold Clurman. They include the Harold Clurman Lecture Series, the Harold Clurman Poetry Reading Series, the Literate Actor Reading Series, the Harold Clurman Center for the Spoken Word, the Harold Clurman Center for New Work in Movement and Dance Theater and the Harold Clurman Laboratory Theater Company. Additionally, a venue has been developed for classical music and jazz. In 2003, Mr. Oppenheim initiated the Stella Adler Outreach Division for lower income youth in the tristate area, which provides the Adler brand of actor training, a training that believes growth as an actor and growth as a human being are synonymous.

MEISNER TECHNIQUE

Teaching the Work of Sanford Meisner

Victoria Hart

Acting is sourced in ancient ritual—the gathering of the tribe in an experience of the collective unconscious. This human connection to the shared feelings of the audience, generated by a commonality of gesture and language, is enhanced by the actor's deep connection to and faith in his imaginary circumstances. In simple terms, if the actor is living through the events of the play—feeling what the character is feeling and doing what the character does—the audience is drawn into and experiences the events and, in a real sense, becomes a participant in the drama. Neither the style, nor the period, nor the role the actor must embody alters this fundamental principle. The experience bypasses the intellect and goes straight to the heart. Empathy ensues.

THE REALITY OF DOING

There is a world of difference between the actor who is caused authentically to do what his character must do and the actor who only indicates or self-generates his actions. Meisner did not invent this concept, but it is the principle upon which his technique is based. The concept is simple, but to execute it effortlessly, to make it a part of one's acting reflexes, is more complex than one imagines at first encounter.

It is not my intention here to write a how-to on the teaching of the Meisner Technique. Much will be left out, and some important areas will be merely mentioned in passing. What follows, then, is my description of the process and the elements that distinguish Meisner's solutions for the training of actors.

The technique is often mistakenly identified exclusively by Meisner's signature repetition exercise. Repetition encompasses the basic principles of the technique and lays the foundation for the student's understanding of the Reality of Doing. However, it is only the beginning of a rich process, a complete technique of acting craft that is divided into two distinct phases.

The first-year curriculum addresses the basic issues of acting craft: the necessity for each actor to learn his own acting instrument, and how the actor functions in a theatrical reality as distinguished from his everyday use of himself. By the end of the first year of work, the actor will have addressed, drilled and made himself conscious of all the elements he encounters when working on a role, prior to the crafting of character. First-year actors have not yet learned to transform in order to serve a character, nor have they learned how to analyze and serve scripted material.

In the second year of training, the skills acquired in the first year are applied to the process of crafting a role. In the first year, the actor begins with himself—how *he* responds and behaves in an imaginary circumstance—but now he must begin with the play or its equivalent and the character (or role) he will be bringing to life, addressing the real work of the actor. As the curriculum progresses, it covers every basic skill the student must acquire to begin to master his acting instrument.

THE TECHNIQUE: FIRST YEAR

Meisner understood that when most actors are faced with a script, they immediately get a sense, a vision of how their role should come to fruition. They see and hear it and then rehearse to incorporate those visual and aural images in themselves. That is part of the actor's talent. However, this asset, the ability to envision a finished product, can become an obstacle to finding a really rich and authentic performance. An actor may use the script as a crutch, narrowing his interpretive choices and leading him to reciting and indicating a role, rather than bringing it to life.

It is useful to think of the whole first year as one exercise, the various components of which are incorporated one at a time. Even the scene work is part of this design. The process is quite specific and is designed to root the actor in the fundamental principles of acting. As each element is introduced, the actor is able to focus on it and make it part of his process, working in class with the teacher and in his rehearsals. Each new element builds on the preceding one, and each element has its own integrity, its particular role in the process of acting. There is no character work as such in the first year—the actor is always himself in an imaginary circumstance. The content of each exercise is improvised, not rehearsed, and never repeated. What *is* drilled and rehearsed is the process, and the elements that define the exercise. This trains the imagination and talent of the actor and becomes more complex as the year progresses.

REPETITION: THE EXERCISE

Meisner begins this process by removing the script, and with it, any necessity for the actor to achieve a predetermined result of any kind. The exercise starts with two actors standing facing each other, five or six feet apart.

Just Repeat

One actor starts the exercise by responding to something he sees, something tangible that is true and present about the other—nothing complex, just his open and honest observation. The other actor must listen and repeat exactly what he has heard.

Repeat Exactly What You Hear, and Tell the Truth!

In the beginning there is only the actor's statement: "You are wearing a red dress." The partner must simply repeat this. No lines to bring to life, no clever comments to improvise; she must simply listen and repeat exactly what her partner says back to her, *unless* it causes her to repeat something she believes to be untrue. So, she answers, "I'm wearing a red dress." By changing the pronoun, she has made a change in the repetition in order to keep the answer truthful from her point of view. As the repetition moves rapidly back and forth, back and forth, faster than you can think but no faster than you can hear, the actors begin to respond to one another. They are making real contact with one another, effortlessly, by the simple act of repeating exactly what they hear, listening and answering, responding through the repetitions.

Act Before You Think

The teacher makes this exchange move rapidly, forcing the actors to respond freely, before thinking, so they do not edit their responses. There is a lot of laughter and silliness at first, because people make verbal mistakes and then have to repeat them exactly. Before they know it, they stop paying attention to themselves, lose their self-consciousness, give up feeling awkward and begin to play.

Acting Is Reacting

As they work, students are guided by the teacher to respond to the exchange personally—to treat this as a reality—so that their acting circumstance becomes a new kind of awareness of the other. It all happens so rapidly that they cannot reflect, only respond. Their bodies start to loosen, their voices open, and they experience a kind of exhilaration. When you behave spontaneously, it is as if a muzzle has been removed from your very being; you feel free and energized. It is an extraordinarily liberating experience to act impulsively in every moment. Without that dynamic, acting becomes predictable and, in a very real sense, inhuman. For the time being then, the students' "acting is reacting." This is not Meisner's definition of acting, but it does accurately describe what the students are being asked to do. The Reality of Doing means that students are not *pretending* to listen and respond; the exercise requires them to truly do so.

Subtext

In these early exchanges, as partners give their full attention to each other, listening and answering, they are hearing more than the words. They are responding to the meaning expressed not just by what is said, but how it is said. We call this the *subtext*—the real meaning behind the words that surfaces in inflection and body language and the multiple nonverbal cues by which human beings communicate with each other. Learning how to listen and respond to this subtext, in every moment, is probably the most important skill the beginning actor can acquire.

Changes in the Repetition

In responding to this subtext, the students discover they are spontaneously making changes in the repetition. The actress repeats, "I have a red dress," and her partner says, "So, okay, you have a red dress," expressing his annoyance at having repeated this observation again. His irritation and his contact with his partner have led him to make a simple, organic change in the repetition. There are guiding rules that assist the actors in making these changes spontaneously, so they do not follow the conventions of everyday conversations as they practice this new method of communication.

The "River of Impulses"

The rapid-fire repetition creates a current between the two actors that generates spontaneous and authentic impulses in both. And because these feelings have not been predetermined or summoned, they reveal the actor's true feelings. Meisner calls this "riding the river of impulses." *Webster's New World Dictionary* defines an impulse as "an incitement to action arising from a state of mind or some external stimulus . . . a sudden inclination to act, without conscious thought . . . a motive or tendency coming from within." In other words, something one has not *thought* so much as *felt*. This is, as we shall see, a significant distinction!

Point of View

Our feelings signify what the world means to us, and the knowledge of how we feel about things—what outrages us, makes us laugh, cry, cower—is what we will ultimately draw on in acting. Students must learn what these feelings are, how to gain access to them and what to do with them. During this process they must be dedicated to finding their own truth in order to inhabit and serve the lives of the characters they will encounter in their work as actors.

This early work sets students on a course to understanding what it means to be truthful when living in the imaginary world. It establishes in them a deepened connection, both to themselves and to their acting partners. The work in this first year has to do with the actor experiencing over and over what it is to be in touch with his most truthful responses—his impulses—and allowing himself to freely respond from them.

Discovering What Is True

During this part of the process, the teacher must assist the students to experience and clarify the difference between what is a real impulse and what is simply a defensive—and therefore, not truthful—response. For example, they may be truly listening, but what they hear may cause them to defend themselves rather than experience hurt feelings, or they may respond sentimentally. To place oneself in real contact means to experience what is true, with no denial, no buffer of explanation that allows one to avoid the real meaning and its intent. In some sense all of these responses are *true*, but we are defining *true* to mean unmanaged, not filtered through the controls we acquire to maintain our equilibrium as social adult beings.

The actor must learn to recognize an acquired social response—one required of us in our everyday lives as adults, but often not expressive of our true feelings. We are used to answering content, following the rules of a logical conversation, not responding to the subtext that is often dismissed or buried in the exchange of information. The exercise is designed to assist the actor to hear and invite this subtext and to open himself to the experience in every moment.

Once the students have become comfortable with these new, lively exchanges and have incorporated the various rules for organic changes without having to think about them, a new piece of the exercise is introduced.

THE ACTIVITY

The activity presents new demands on the actor's concentration. As the exercise develops, the acting circumstance now has a more familiar reality. Instead of two actors facing off during the repetition, one actor will be in the room doing a task that we call an *activity*, and the other will enter the space.

The Reality of Doing: What Makes an Activity?

First, the activity must have a concrete problem or task that is very difficult to accomplish and, therefore, engages the actor's total attention—a cracked teacup that must be mended perfectly, a signature that must be forged, a torn canvas or garment to repair, a design to transfer. There must not be any gray area: the actor must be able to know in every moment whether he is accomplishing his task or failing. Having this *standard of perfection*, as it is called, keeps the actor honestly tied to real action. Without this, the Reality of Doing is not present.

Second, the actor must invent a circumstance that is *simple*, *specific*, *personal* and *imaginary* that justifies doing this activity, and which he can easily accept as his reality. It has never really happened, but he can accept that it could have personal meaning for him.

Third, the failure to accomplish the activity must have concrete consequences. "I will feel disappointed/scared/embarrassed/unhappy" is insufficient. It is not *specific*. It may be true, but it does not properly train the actor's thinking. When the actor is learning the meaning of specificity, he must determine what concrete thing will happen to him in his circumstance if he does not accomplish this task; e.g., he will lose his apartment, his job or his girlfriend. Can you see how this forces the actor to really "do" and not merely indicate; how the specific consequence makes for a specific and more personal response?

Actor's Faith

The ability to accept something that is imaginary and to respond to it as if it were real is part of the actor's talent. We call this *actor's faith* because of its similarity to religious faith. The actor accepts his circumstance as a reality before engaging in the exercise. This is his homework, and it is this that propels him to accomplish his activity. Often actors refer to this as their "motivation." In the exercise, the actor's ability to accept his imagined circumstance is part of the personal research of the first year's work that allows the actor to discover what he really cares about in his heart. Actors respond easily to what they truly care about. Obviously, for our purposes, it does not matter whether he solves his dilemma and accomplishes his task; what matters is what happens to him during the struggle to do so.

Coming to Life: "The Pinch and the Ouch"

The struggle to do the activity and the need to answer the repetition cause the actor to come to life and create his behavior. The frustration and distress that ensue are by-products of the reality of really doing—not pretending to do or trying to feel. Emotion that is caused to surface in the actor this way is affecting and moving, because the observer recognizes it as honest. Meisner teaches that good acting concerns itself with finding good "pinches." If we know in our heart why we are doing something, the act of doing occurs easily, naturally, without strain. Acting that does not embrace this human dynamic will not be truly alive. Meisner uses the concept of "the pinch and the ouch" to illustrate the role of cause and effect in the process of acting.

A Triangle of Attention

In the exercise, the necessity of listening and repeating at every moment remains the central element. Everything that has preceded the addition of the activity is retained, but now there is a triangle of attention. One actor is completely focused on accomplishing her activity, and thus her answers, her repetitions, are filtered through this struggle. Her partner, entering the room, is focused on her, and his repetitions are caused by what he experiences as he takes in and responds to her behavior. The exchange of impulses remains, but the subtext is now generated by a more complex circumstance, the addition of the activity.

TIME

Once the actor is using the activity well and crafting in a more sophisticated way, the element of time is introduced. This ingredient adds immediacy and so lifts the exercise to a heightened reality that the actor is now prepared to experience. He must craft this element specifically and truthfully, not simply hurry his work. He must determine exactly how much time is needed to accomplish his work and then digest this information so that he can fully accept it as a reality. He crafts this piece of the circumstance so specifically that he has just the right amount of time to accomplish his task—no extra minutes— so that his attention is total and he has no need to think, just to do.

As the actors work with this activity in the beginning weeks, their reasons for completing the task become more truthful and personal, and their investment in living in their imaginary circumstance deepens. Their experience of themselves becomes fuller, more interesting, often simpler, and always more expressive of who they really are.

Crafting the Circumstance: A Sense of Truth

In this first year of training, the actor is always himself in the imaginary circumstances. He may use real people in his life, but they too must remain who they really are—real people, now in imaginary circumstances. He can invent a girlfriend, a director, a waiter, as long as he can ultimately accept them as a reality. The events have never happened, but it is essential that they be easily accepted, not far-fetched, impossible daydreams (these are useful, and there is a place for them in the work later, but not here). Now he is learning what it means to accept a reality in the imaginary world he lives in when he acts.

The actor presents his invention to his imagination. As he begins to *take in* his idea, something inside him, what we call his "sense of truth," will either respond ("Yes, I can believe this is happening, I can accept that this could be true") or it will not. If it is a good, meaningful circumstance for him, some real feeling is stirred in him when he imagines it. Often this feeling is accompanied by behavior—he grins, he frowns, his hands shake or pound the table. This sense of truth, a kind of inner compass that guides the actor as he crafts his work, is engaged continuously throughout the training.

The actor's use of his imagination has been the subject of acting training throughout its history. Stanislavsky, inspired by his contemporaries and his own relentless search to find a reliable craft for actors, emphasized the actor's natural propensity to live in his imagination, believing that it is, in fact, the single most important part of his talent, without which he cannot begin to act. Meisner's process embraces fully the belief that the imagination, rather than one's retrieved past experiences, produces the most robust, interesting and reliable behavior.

Encouraging students to explore and use their imagination, rather than work from the limitations of their literal reality, is simultaneously liberating and demanding. And because the students are required to craft a new circumstance and activity each time they work, both in rehearsal and in class, they are strengthening and expanding their use of their imaginations and are challenged continually to think in these new terms.

ADDING THE ACTIVITY TO THE REPETITION

Adding the activity to the exercise guides the actors to a fuller experience of the Reality of Doing. If the actress, Jill, has included all the elements of the activity, her concentration will be deeply and easily engaged. Previous classes will have made repetition more reflexive, so that when she is struggling to do her very difficult task, answering her partner does not require her full attention. She has spent whatever time she needed to craft her activity and accept the reality of her circumstance. That is her personal and private work. She will bring this to class or to a rehearsal, and what happens will be lived through improvisation with her partner.

Endowing the Object

If, for example, Jill is not a capable seamstress and has found an inexpensive shawl with delicate embroidery that needs mending, she has the beginnings of a good object. Then she must craft a simple circumstance that fulfills the requirements discussed above. Why must she mend this? How did it become ripped? To whom does it belong? What will happen to her if she doesn't get it done by a specific time? The object must be able to hold the value she endows it with—her sense of truth will neither respond nor engage if it does not. She may get an idea quickly, or it might take her some time, but she will know she has invented a good circumstance, her reason for having to fix this shawl, when her idea stimulates a response that tells her, "If this were true, I would be compelled to fix this. I would really be in trouble, and I could not tolerate that. I would not have to pretend; I would really have to do it."

An Example: Living through the Exercise

Jill has put a lot of time into finding the perfect object, and she is excited by the circumstance she has crafted. Every time she thinks about the stupidity of "borrowing" without asking, and the possibility of losing her job and the money she was counting on to go to Paris with her boyfriend, the personal ramifications make her heart beat faster, and her sense of failure is palpable. She is fully connected and invested in her circumstance.

The Knock: A Surprise

A new element has recently been added to which Jill must respond—the knock. Now Joe knocks on her door, and she is obliged to respond directly to the knock and open the door. No "Hi, how are you?" chat. She must accept Joe as an uninvited and unanticipated interruption and honor all the rules of the repetition as she goes back to her activity, which requires her total attention and concentration. She must mend the shawl perfectly by 3:15 P.M. so that she can return it before its absence is noticed by her boss. The necessity to respond through the repetition is now filtered through the struggle to do her activity. At first, she seems to be doing two things at once, but, if she has done her homework correctly, she cannot do both. She has just enough time to must mend the shawl, and she must answer her partner in every moment, repeating responsively. The rules of the exercise must be honored. Each time her partner repeats and demands her response, the distraction causes her to lose concentration, and her stitching looks abysmal! The worse it looks, the more upset she becomes, and her partner, in turn, is upset as well, as he opens himself to the contact and responds to her behavior.

THE OBJECTIVE

Initially, the other actor simply knocked and entered, stood and worked off his partner, responding through the repetition. Now he also has a new element with which to work. Instead of simply beginning the contact with an arbitrary knock on the door, he gives himself a simple and specific reason for his visit. This is his *objective*. The objective is a basic and complex part of acting. At this stage of the exercise, the objective is there primarily to justify the initial contact. It does not have any active purpose in the contact. In our example, Joe must respond and use each moment in the repetition as it comes to him from Jill, continuing to take her personally and responding in kind.

While keeping the objective simple and specific, Joe must also include in its crafting the idea that Jill is the only person who possesses what he needs—something that is not easily given, i.e., the keys to her car or her family's cabin—and that he can't ask her for this later. Choosing an inventive objective, one that stimulates his imagination and engages his attention, keeps the actor from anticipating as he begins the exercise and enters the reality of the circumstance. It also helps to justify his remaining in contact when he encounters some resistance from his unhappy and unwilling host.

> What you do doesn't depend on you, it depends on the other fellow.
>
> —SANFORD MEISNER

Once Jill opens the door and responds, contact begins. If Joe is to be available to respond, intent on working off his partner, responding truthfully and spontaneously in every moment, he will need to keep all of his attention directed on Jill, not on his objective. "I do only what she makes me do." This means he must never *adjust* his honest response while in the exchange, even if his partner responds to his repetition by saying irritably, "You are interrupting me, be quiet!" In life he would try not to take her rude behavior personally. He might be puzzled and put off, but he would refrain from responding from his feelings, in order to get the keys he is hoping to borrow. So, while in real life he might leave his partner's room and come back another time, here the goal is to experience his partner's responses and behavior as the circumstance dictates and to express how he feels in return. The objective can justify his remaining when the contact begins to heat up and he feels uncomfortable, but it must never interfere or alter his honest response.

There Is No Right Response, Only Your Truthful Response

When Joe's partner, upset with the shawl and with Joe's constant interruption, tells him to "shut up and be quiet," and he repeats what she has said—"Shut up and be quiet"—he has an opportunity to make contact with her distressed response, and to experience and express in the next moment how it has made him feel. He may find himself shouting, apologizing or laughing. There is no right response, only his truthful response to what has happened in that moment. He must remain true to the principle of the exercise and do only what the other makes him do. He must learn how to evaluate what exists, learn how to take it in personally, so that he will come alive in the contact, not simply observe and comment or remain dispassionate. He is encouraged to use the repetition to seek his point of view and respond from it. Often, in life, we instinctively do the opposite.

What happens to Jill as the exercise progresses is inevitable: the necessity of completing the activity by a certain time, and the necessity of repeating responsively in every moment, cause Jill to become upset. Her feelings come to the surface as a by-product of the Reality of Doing. Joe may feel terrible and want to leave, or he may want to help, or he may become upset himself. Both partners must continue to respond to each moment through the repetition.

This exercise is about placing yourself in contact, in order to experience moment-to-moment how the other person is making you feel. That would be a crazy thing to do in life—you'd burn out pretty quickly—but it is necessary when every moment counts and must contribute to the whole, much as do the notes in a piece of music or each step in the choreography of a dance.

An ounce of behavior is worth a pound of words.

—SANFORD MEISNER

The actors are learning to use their imaginations to create human behavior. Jill must engage her sense of truth and confront the meaning of her circumstance in her heart, accepting this as a reality, or she will simply be thrown back to indicating behavior. If the information she gives herself does not ultimately result in clear and vivid behavior, it is of no value. The exercise will test this, but she must continually present information to her sense of truth as she crafts and prepares her activity at home.

As she works to craft these activities, she is discovering what she cares about, what has genuine meaning for her—not assumed meaning, theatrical meaning or big meaning, but human, truthful, personal meaning. She is discovering the material that will eventually serve her crafting of character, so that she may live through the experience of a play world as deeply as she does in these exercises.

Ending of Repetition

After weeks of working, as the students become more adept with these new elements, the necessity of repeating in every moment begins to interfere with the truthfulness of the exchange. It muffles the full experience of the other and does not permit the actor the time he needs to truthfully take in what is going on. When the repetition is slowed down, the exchanges become richer and deeper. The actors begin to craft on a personal level, becoming deeply affected by their circumstances and by each other in the exchange. They experience coming to life quite fully, let go of many of their inhibitions, and have a new and more fully realized sense of living truthfully under imaginary circumstances.

As the actors have become more skilled at hearing and responding to the subtext in their exchanges, they move almost intuitively, organically, to this next stage. Repetition's function was to create a new series of habits in the actor, and having embraced and drilled with these "training wheels," as one of my students put it, the actor can now maintain his concentration and the continuity of the contact without this demand. He retains the experience of the other in the contact, remaining available in every moment, taking his partner and her behavior personally and responding in kind.

Wait! Take In!

This part of the process requires the teacher to assist the student in waiting to speak until a significant impulse is present. After months of verbalizing every moment, the habit of repetition has become reflexive and is difficult to leave behind.

Joe must maintain contact and verbalize his response only when he *must* speak; when the moments in the contact add up to something he no longer can withhold, or a sudden change in the other's behavior causes him to respond spontaneously. Only when he does not know how he feels about something and feels it is necessary to understand the other's response does he use repetition—to make contact with the response and take it in a second time, so to speak.

The Triangle of Attention Retained

Jill is still engaged in doing an activity. She need only respond when truly distracted by her partner from doing her work. She will find that because they are not repeating in every moment, she has more sustained periods to do her work, so that her responses come more frequently from her struggle to do her activity and less frequently from the frustration of her partner's interruptions. Whether she continues with her activity or responds to her partner is dictated by their acting instincts, their sense of truth and their crafting.

EMOTIONAL PREPARATION

Emotional preparation provides the actor with a means of bringing full emotional life to the first moment of contact. This tool is one of the most important components of Meisner's teaching. Simply stated, it asks the actor to use the process of daydreaming to induce the emotional life the character requires prior to entering the scene.

This addition to the exercise is introduced in the first year, after the class has been working for weeks, laying the foundation for the more advanced, deeper work. It is a superb, valuable and essential element in the training.

The Daydream vs. Emotional Memory

Emotional memory refers to Stanislavsky's initial use of the recalling of details of actual events in the actor's life to produce authentic emotion. Meisner believed using one's imagination to invent circumstances allowed greater freedom and access to the actor's emotional life, and was healthier and more compatible with the artistic temperament. Imagined scenarios may be populated with real people, but the events have never actually occurred. They are not memories; rather, they are one's hopes and/or fears lived out in a daydream.

Daydreams vs. Night Dreams

Daydreaming is a process native to human beings. In life, it is often a discomfort or a heightened experience (or, conversely, a lack of sufficient stimulus) that triggers this process. It is a mental reshaping of reality that satisfies the needs or anxieties of the conscious mind, unlike our night dreams, which more often concern anxieties buried in our unconscious. This is at least one explanation of why we freely share our night dreams, but almost never expose our daydreams.

Daydreams are also distinguished from night dreams in the sense that they can be controlled—one can come out of a reverie at will. A horn is honked, a question posed, a subway destination reached, and the daydreamer comes back to what his day demands of him in the moment.

Daydreams vs. Thinking or Imagining

The daydreaming process is also different from thinking. When you are in a daydream, you lose conscious awareness of your surroundings, move into an altered state and—most helpful for the actor—respond emotionally to your subject as if the events were actually taking place. During a daydream, the nervous system actually responds. Behavior is produced: the heart beats faster, the palms perspire, the muscles tighten or expand, tears or laughter may result.

Daydreaming on Command

In our everyday life, daydreams and night dreams occur spontaneously, but the actor must learn to daydream at will to use it as part of his craft. The script dictates its specific needs—the character must enter the scene as if he has experienced the events that have occurred in his offstage life prior to that moment. When the scene requires a heightened emotional state, emotional preparation is a reliable tool.

Fantasy vs. Reality

Because the daydream's primary purpose is to induce a feeling, the actor is encouraged to allow these fantasies to include any area he has not been able or willing to explore in front of the class. He may feel that certain issues are too painful or embarrassing to discuss in a critique, or his sense of truth may tell him it won't work; he can't accept his daydream as a reality. At this point in the training, the actor may invite daydreams that belong to the realm of fantasy, areas we commonly refer to as wish fulfillment: winning Academy Awards or lotteries, sleeping with movie stars, flying to the moon, murdering enemies, battling monsters, saving the world, falling out of airplanes, riding naked on horseback . . . through the galaxy . . . with Sting! You get the picture.

Inviting the Daydream

Meisner cautions the actor that emotional preparation is perhaps the most delicate of all the actor's tools, and must be treated as such. Knowing that mastery in this area may take a long time allows the student to come to this part of the technique more gracefully. He will benefit from allowing these daydreams to come alive by invitation, so to speak, rather than by any forced demand. This is an adventure, an exploration, a tool to further assist his talent. He must learn to approach emotional preparation with a spirit of adventure, or the work will become dreary when it should be stimulating, exciting and transforming. There are actors who encounter this area of study with exuberance and others who are more cautious; some realize that they daydream all the time, and others claim they almost never do. In any case, this begins a deeper process of personal research that opens a new area of the imagination to be mined.

Secrets

The teacher tells the actor that he must never reveal his daydreams— not to his colleagues, not to his teacher, not to anyone. They are for his private creative process alone. Their power, in fact, is enhanced by this freedom of privacy. As he imagines his fantasy, his involvement deepens. He begins to actively live in the daydream; it takes on a life of its own, and he begins to respond.

Adding Emotional Preparation to the Exercise

The setup for the exercise changes to accommodate this new element. Now the actor will be living with his partner in the world of the exercise (just roommates, nothing more complex). The actor coming to the door (coming home) works with a circumstance that requires an emotional preparation. Alone, at home, when he has plenty of time and no pressure to produce, he prepares this circumstance and brings this research to class. If he wants to experience grief, he thinks of a circumstance that will upset him, such as the loss of a good friend. Outside of class, he practices, inviting the circumstance to come alive in himself little by little, through his actor's faith and his talent, and he permits himself to move from thinking to the daydream state, where the daydream begins to have a life of its own. In class, outside the door, he prepares, focusing on the part of the daydream that is most provocative. When he feels himself appropriately alive, he must come out of his reverie and relate himself fully to the reality of his circumstance and to "coming home." As he enters the room, he begins to change into his sweatpants, intending to go to bed. Suddenly, as he is taking off his boots, he finds himself crying quietly, then sobbing. His partner, already in the room, responds to this behavior. They may have an exchange that lasts for the remainder of the exercise, or one that lasts only a moment, with intermittent contact thereafter. The contact determines the content of the exercise and remains the most important part of the process. When this subsides, the actor continues to get ready for bed, or to pack to leave, or to do his schoolwork—whatever he has set up for himself so that he will never be in the position of acting his feelings, displaying his emotion, or seeking it!

Emotional Preparation Is for the First Moment

The emotional preparation acts as a filter through which the actor experiences the contact with his partner. He is now a sadder or happier person. Therefore, the impulses are often more intense, because the actor has been sensitized by the heightened emotion and circumstance. However, this emotional state must never override the principle of acting. He must learn how to shift his attention from himself to his partner, so that he can be open and available to receive her next response. That seems easy enough, but it is not our natural response in an agitated emotional state. In our everyday lives, when we feel deeply, when we are experiencing a heightened state, our attention remains on ourselves; we become as one, so to speak, with our happiness or distress. This is not helpful for our acting. Good acting has a constant give-and-take with the *other*, be it actor or object. The actor must always be available, receptive to this continual flow of cause and effect that creates the unbroken line leading the characters to the inevitabilities of beat, scene, act and concluding events.

The ability to remain available to a partner's responses when in this emotionally heightened state requires many months of practice in the gymnasium of acting class. With each new element added to the exercise, actors must go through a period of discomfort as they learn to process and integrate the information so that its value is experienced and their behavior is spontaneous. Emotional preparation is the least desirable way for the actor to come to life. Life that is generated by the combustion that takes place between the actor and his world as he lives through the events of the play is what people go to the theater and the movies to experience. But emotional preparation is a valuable tool, to be used selectively when it is necessary for the actor to bring himself, by himself, to a heightened state. It is also one of the more potent rehearsal tools for the actor as he works to craft a character and isolate moments in the script that he needs to address.

The Activity Expands

Now that the preparation has deepened and broadened the actor's personal research, the activity is adjusted to allow the actor to explore all areas of his temperament through the activity. He can engage his humor, his rage, his sweet and silly sides, his romantic or arrogant selves. As ever, the behavior must be the by-product of the doing. He must be inventive, bringing activities to class that will truly generate the behavior he has chosen to explore. Now the essential *standard of perfection* is often subjective. An activity must always contain a specific objective; a little struggle that guides the actor to specific behavior. For instance, if I am writing a eulogy for my friend, I know I will probably grieve, but the emotion of grief alone does not become useful to me as an actor until it is turned into a need to do something specific. I am trying to express what an amazing and beautiful person my friend truly was, so that everyone in the room, particularly his parents, will be soothed in their grief by my joy in his friendship. Can you see how my imagination will be stimulated, and my desire to do my activity better supported, when I express my objective specifically? This is what must hold my attention, not the idea of my grief. In fact, I must try not to let my grief impede my need to complete my task.

Acting Is Doing

Ultimately, acting is about what characters do, not what they feel. Feelings authenticate the actions and make them affecting, but they do not illuminate the character's journey, nor do they tell the playwright's story, which is, of course, every actor's ultimate goal. Emotional preparation is just that—a preparation. Emotion in acting is a by-product of contact with another actor and the things that are potent in his environment, be it a summer's night, a skull unearthed from the grave or a damaged shawl.

When the actor is required to literally enter laughing or weeping, or in some other heightened emotional state, he must find a way to bring himself to life. Emotional preparation, daydreaming, can assist him to this result. In effect, he is making contact with this imagination—*thinking* the events will not produce the desired behavior. A preparation need have nothing in common with the play's circumstance beyond the essential emotion and the desired behavior it produces. The actor's empathetic response to a character's plight will never be as deep and specific as the material that comes out of the actor's own psyche. But once the desired behavior is brought to the surface through the daydream, the actor must move his attention to the circumstance of the play. Think of a spaceship leaving behind the rocket that has fired it into orbit. The daydream is simply there to bring the actor's full emotional response to the surface.

It is essential that the actor come out of this reverie before entering the scene. The actor must practice shifting from his daydream to the reality of the play's circumstance at home, away from the rehearsal. He must have confidence in his ability to bring himself to full life through a personal daydream, but he also must have worked deeply enough on the character's circumstance to be able to shift his attention to what he is coming into the scene to do, and to be fully available to the demands of the first moment of contact. Over time, the association may recondition his response to the material, and eventually he may no longer require the original stimulus of the daydream.

The question of what makes an effective acting relationship is the final element addressed by and incorporated into the exercise. For the first time, the actors will have a shared circumstance—specific information they share prior to the exercise that will define their relationship.

Confronting the Circumstance

Unless they produce a response, the facts of the circumstance remain just that—information. The actor must always turn this information into meaning that produces communicable behavior. So, if my best friend has betrayed me with my boyfriend, I confront the circumstance to activate my true feelings and bring this hurt and anger alive in me. It is helpful in the beginning to find a potent, descriptive word or phrase that summons my full feelings about this situation. These feelings will not be polite or sophisticated, nor will my words be literary or attractive in this instance. They will be visceral and satisfying to my five-year-old psyche. I will not bother myself with any gray areas or obligations that might temper my response. I want one graphic label that says it all!

One Thing in the Heart at a Time

The actor is seeking a means of reducing a complex relationship to its essence. This may change in the next scene, the next beat, even the next moment, but he crafts one meaning at a time. This is what makes it possible to act complex characters such as Medea or Hamlet. The relationship is full of love; then something happens to change it radically. But there is one thing in the heart at a time.

Joanna crafts a circumstance and gives only the facts to her partner, Jill: Jill has betrayed Joanna's friendship. Jill must justify to herself why she has done this and how she feels about it now. Neither actress shares how she feels about the circumstance. Jill now takes this circumstance, confronts and digests it and makes it her own, much as we do with scripted material. She uses her daydreaming ability to help her live through the events that have been given to her, adding anything she needs to fill out the reality for herself. The circumstance must remain simple, with no complex plots that mask the real relationship. This is an acting exercise, not an exercise in playwriting. Jill imagines that the affair took place six months ago, and must give herself a good reason for having hidden her actions from Joanna: for example, the boyfriend agreed it was a terrible mistake, they were drunk, and that they would keep their affair a secret forever to avoid hurting Joanna. Jill then crafts an activity that has nothing to do with this event and puts her attention on whatever she has chosen to live though in the exercise. She is engaged and well occupied, her attention totally caught up in her efforts to do her activity, so that she will not anticipate Joanna.

In one form of this exercise, Joanna gives herself the circumstance of discovery (the boyfriend confessed), sets an emotional preparation to bring it alive, and, with this terrible distress, comes home. She must have in place something to come home to do, and what happens then is, as ever, dictated by the moment-to-moment life generated out of the contact.

These are very exciting exercises that train the actors' thinking, preparing them for bringing to life the relationships they will encounter in scripted material. Activating the relationship completes the exercise, bringing together all the ingredients that exist in a dramatic reality.

Scene Work

Throughout the first year, students work with scenes at critical junctures to clarify and apply the function of the exercise to a text. These scenes do not require crafting in the usual sense; there are no character considerations, no script analysis. The students are simply required to memorize a scene by rote so that they can express their impulses as in repetition, but now using the text in lieu of their own words. For now, only the actor's immediate personal response is wanted, whether or not it serves the scene. In this way, they are learning to really improvise, to work off their partners, moment by moment. The work of transforming responses to serve a character and the playwright's intent is the focus of the second year of training.

The first year is dedicated to providing actors with the opportunity to experience themselves fully and truthfully under imaginary circumstances. Removing all that the student previously associated with the act of acting, the technique isolates the most basic and significant element in the actor's process—the ability to create expressive and truthful behavior. Based on the principle of the Reality of Doing, the process develops the imagination and strengthens the students' connection both to themselves and to those they are acting with.

THE TECHNIQUE: SECOND YEAR

It was my original intention to begin this chapter with a discussion of the second year process, because this is where the technique finally functions. But it is in the first year that the vocabulary is introduced and the instrument trained, and I realized it was impossible to articulate the second-year curriculum without discussing the first. In the first year, students explore and experiment, through the exercise, to find their personal palettes, freeing their personality and imagination to a more developed understanding of how to function as actors in the imaginary world. They begin simply, with repetition, and throughout the year incorporate elements that address and strengthen the basic areas of acting craft and the process of improvisation—working off partners, learning how to use each moment, finding impulses and responding so that their behavior in the imaginary circumstance is authentic and spontaneous. There is a sense of competence and an exhilaration that is generated as the process becomes more reflexive and the actor begins to find a sense of ease. In the second year, the actor must begin with a character created through an author's imagination and a circumstance he has never encountered and learn how to do the detective work that will enable him to bring it to life through his instrument. And because actors must now learn how to serve the author, a whole new set of skills must be acquired. Here, in the second year, the actor and his character merge with the vision of the playwright and his director. The process is not graceful and the dynamic of the year is significantly different.

Scene One: A second-year acting class, October. Jill, the actress, slips into the chair next to her partner.

Jill is out of breath, having run from the subway without time to buy coffee. She has arrived just before the teacher and is distracted and anxious about her scene. It is not going well. The teacher keeps telling her that her preparation is not giving her the necessary emotion to bring the event to life. Their rehearsals for the scene from William Inge's *Picnic* feel wonderful. As Rosemary, the spinster schoolteacher, she ends the scene unraveled and begging Howard, the unglamorous, set-in-his-ways, good-old-boy owner of a hardware store in the next town, to marry her. But they never get past the first few beats in class. The teacher seems fixed on her preparation. She is feeling untalented, stupid and, what's more, guilty, because her partner never gets to show off his work.

"Okay—the teacher keeps telling us that emotional preparation is for the first moment and only for the first moment—that what happens thereafter must come out of the contact—that if we have really understood the circumstances and the relationships, we could begin to make a stab at living through the reality of our scene—and that our first-year work should have taught us how to work off our partner, so that *even without a good preparation* the contact will bring us to life! So why isn't she letting me get on with it?!"

Jill hears her name called, and her adrenaline level goes through the roof. "If I have to go through this one more time, I'll die. Why can't I get this deeply humiliated preparation! What is wrong with me?!"

She exits into the teacher's office to prepare. The door closes behind her, and for a moment she stares at the mess that looks more like a storage room than an office. She feels panicky and a little frantic. She sits on the worn settee rescued from some street corner and takes a deep breath. Her whole body responds, and she seems to let loose from some mooring tying her to her anxiety, the cramped office and the class on the other side of the door. She puts her head between her hands, closes her eyes and summons her daydream.

This scene should be familiar to anyone who has been in an ordinary scene-study class. The technical issues that the actress is being asked to address should be equally familiar. Every actor must address the events prior to his entrance in order to authenticate the life the playwright has written. What is particular to Meisner training are the tools she is being asked to use to bring this character's circumstance to vivid life, the degree of emphasis on each of the specific problem areas actors encounter, and the process used to solve each of these issues.

TRANSFORMING

In the beginning of the second year, several alterations are made to the exercise that introduce the process of *transforming* to character

73

work. I use two of these variations. The first teaches the actors how to research and justify a point of view that they do not subscribe to— e.g., bigoted or opposite feelings about a particular issue—and then incorporate it into the exercise, so that they begin to make it their own. This is a difficult but instructive addition that introduces the process referred to as transforming in acting. The second variation introduces the actors to the part of the acting process that requires them to create the illusion of behavior that must *not* be created authentically. We refer to these as *impediments*.

Impediments

An *impediment* is to an area of acting craft that must be created technically and expertly indicated, not lived through authentically. These include illnesses, from the common cold to consumption; physical problems, from rashes and sunburn to labor pains and gunshot wounds; environmental conditions such as heat and cold; accents and speech defects; and all altered states caused by alcohol or drugs—all physical disabilities or maladies that impede one's straight responses. This behavior must be specifically researched, independent of the emotional and psychological research normally associated with building a character.

Turning the Tables

This is a perfect encounter for students coming out of first-year work, where the emphasis has been on one's truthful emotional life. Suddenly they are being asked to create behavior that is not real, but that creates a perfect illusion, so that anyone observing will accept it as fully real and respond to it appropriately.

Of course, this will only be a part of their crafting of character. The scene is never solely about the impediment. For example, imagine a scene in which two people who happen to have English accents are sitting in a car, arguing. It is hot in their car, the man is smoking a joint; and then the woman goes into labor. The crafting includes all the essential character and relationship work, and its meaning must be authentic; the contact must be sustained, with the objectives informing each moment. However, those accents, that heat, the joint and the labor pains are not real. The actors must address these issues before and away from the rehearsal. They must bring in their solutions, fully crafted and in their control, so that the director can do his work. They must not be thinking about how they sound, playing at being stoned or improvising the labor. This must be quite specifically worked out and carefully scored to support the text. Anything that is not expertly created, any behavior that does not ring true or have the right rhythm or patterns, will break the illusion and bring the audience's attention to their fabrication. The behavior must become reflexive, so that they can remain in good contact and put their attention where it needs to be—on what is happening between them as the scene unfolds from moment to moment.

Once the students understand that they must strive for a professionally acceptable level of execution, they encounter a new area of training that is significant beyond the issue of impediments. The physical demands of impediment work reveal to each actor a part of his talent that he may or may not be able to access easily. It becomes important to his training that he acquire physical and vocal flexibility and control. When impediments are executed well, the body responds and experiences sensory memory that produces richer behavior, heightening both the actor's and the audience's faith in his reality. In the following weeks actors have the opportunity to incorporate impediments into their scene work. Working with an accent or a painful ulcer, simulating being drunk or stoned or having the flu, they begin to see how essential this information is to creating a character's reality.

The First Scene: Round One

Now begins the real process of crafting a role. The students learn how to take the skills acquired in the first year and begin the slow process of applying them to their real purpose—serving the playwright's vision and his words, and the director's intentions to communicate a specific experience to an audience.

What Elia Kazan said about directing can also be said of acting: "It is turning psychology into behavior."

Scene Two: The teacher's office, several minutes into Jill's daydream for the character, Rosemary.

"Dammit, I'm not supposed to be crying! Rosemary's distress does not lead her to tears. She feels humiliated and cheated, yes, but she is angry. I know this. I have worked to understand this. *I* would cry; *she* becomes a tornado, demanding and threatening. If I cry, I won't be able to do what I need to do as Rosemary to make Howard promise to marry me!"

In her daydream, she begins to move her attention to her imaginary life in the circumstance. She thinks of Howard and his clumsy lovemaking, the smell of whiskey and the matter-of-fact way he behaved as they returned to the car. She sees him sharing his night with his buddy, a wink, a slap on the back, and the anger begins to swell inside her and transform her tears into a very particular kind of rage. "Yes," she thinks, "this is better; this feels right."

She needs to be fully in the reality of her circumstance, and to move into the contact only when she is ready to respond, available to her partner and their first moment together. She stays with her circumstance, living in it now quite deeply. Eyes still closed, she feels him opening the car door and imagines staying in the seat, holding her purse so tightly to keep from throwing it that her hands begin to tremble. When she opens her eyes, she finds herself smoothing her skirt, throwing her head back in an automatic defiance that is not studied or planned but a clear consequence of her interior turmoil. She picks up her bag and opens the office door that now leads into her imagined backyard. As she enters, her partner moves to her to take her and guide her by her elbow, back, back, back to her life as Rosemary, to leave her there, to abandon her to her pallid and passionless existence as the scene begins.

Crafting a Role: Turning Psychology into Behavior

The playwright provides a kind of blueprint—the words he leaves on the page that he has imagined and then determined his characters will speak. This blueprint is the equivalent of the things we say spontaneously when living through an exercise. Once a circumstance has been crafted and accepted, what happens spontaneously in the contact, what we are caused to say to one another, comes from who we are—our character.

Now we find we must craft in the reverse order from our process in the first year. We begin the process by identifying with the character in our script. We read the script and learn how to ask the questions that guide us to an understanding of why the character says what is written. We learn to decipher what he wants and what causes him to do the things he does. Now we must decipher the character's psychology in order to create his behavior.

An Acting Score

The students learn to identify the information and to create what we call a score. Becoming conscious of what the character does and discovering what he needs from the other characters as he lives through the writer's circumstance is a new and complex area. The smaller units that make up each scene, often called beats, allow us to examine this little by little as we apply our newly acquired tools to building our character. At first, doing this work does not seem to be the road to spontaneity—everything begins to feel structured, methodical and technical as the process is taken apart once again and examined and drilled, one element at a time.

First Read of the Scene

The students read the play as many times as they wish, but they must first read it as an audience would experience it, all at once. They read to take in, to make contact with the material, the images, the language, the world of this play, making no judgments. Then they read it again from their character's point of view. They gather as much information as they can, enabling them to discuss the scene knowledgeably in class with the teacher. Then they bring their scene to class, to work with their partners for the first time.

Contact

The actor is encouraged to work off her partner—to allow her scene partner to affect her, to take him personally—much as she did in the first-year scenes. However, in the first year the scenes were memorized by rote, to allow the actors to use the text to express any meaning coming from the partner. Now the process begins with script in hand, and the actor needs to be able to look up from the page so that she can take in her partner's responses, not just hear him but see him as they lift the words from the page and turn them into responses. She must not keep her head in the script, going cue to cue, but must remain alert and curious, making discoveries and asking the questions that the remaining rehearsals will be devoted to answering.

Rehearsals Are Not Performances

At this beginning stage, the actors use their experience of good contact to discover the other actor in this new circumstance. They are guided away from conventional line readings that do not reveal anything human or particular about the character beyond the literal. They do not attempt a performance. They are making contact with the material and must remain open to its mysteries. They must trust their instincts and their talent, and allow themselves to be present to the text as it plays itself out between them. As they begin to immerse themselves in their new life, they are working very personally, listening and responding, seeing what falls into place and what does not. The students have had some experience of this in the first-year scenes, learning to let the contact inform how the lines emerge and not the other way around. Their sense of truth now knows the difference between *indicating* and *accepting* this new reality, and they will work to deepen this connection organically as they rehearse.

Improvising—Staying Alive!

Really listening to the other actor and taking him in personally, responding with the text, feels new, because the actor is now taking her time to feel her way through the scene, but it is essentially the same evaluative process she experienced in the first-year exercises and scenes. Now, in the early stages of rehearsal, as she works off her scene partner, she may find herself responding in ways that serve neither the character nor the intent of the playwright. Her honest responses are now discoveries signaling areas that must be personalized, meanings that must be transformed in her homework, as we will discuss below. The actor may respond fully or simply remain curious in the first few readings of the scene. She must remain true to the principle of acting that says, "I (really) do only what something (really) makes me do." She must remain vigilant. She has devoted a year of rigorous training to acquiring the skills that will lead her away from an indicated and superficial approach to a text. Second-year students are gathering essential information, learning how to ask the questions that will stimulate the creative process of bringing a character to life.

Technique Serves Talent

The actor is encouraged to follow every impulse as it comes to her from the other in the circumstance, to discover the relationships and the subtext buried in meanings she has yet to explore. In the first reading, actors often find themselves living a scene so fully that they spend the next weeks trying to achieve consciously what they found so effortlessly and spontaneously at first. In point of fact, this is precisely what craft serves—the need to capture these wonderful improvisational discoveries and experience them freshly each time. Just as in a good exercise, the actor is riding on the "river of impulses," only now with script in hand. As the actor begins his investigation of his character, his personal research is informed by work in the rehearsals.

Homework

When the actor's personal response does not serve the character, or when he is unable to decipher what his response should be, he works on this alone, at home, and brings the results of this private work to be tested in the following rehearsals. Working this way allows his instincts and his intuition to contribute to the rehearsal in a nonintellectual, lively way. The necessary thinking and analyzing can assist him more productively when he is alone at home. Rehearsals are for dancing together.

Meanings

After the first read-through, the first assignment concerns identifying the character's essential point of view—how he feels about everything he talks about and everything that other people tell us about him. First, we identify those facts that are clearly stated in the text and are not debatable. Then, as we explore the text, we uncover those meanings that are implied, inferred or interpreted by the director and actor. However it comes to him, the actor must identify deeply and personally with these core meanings. It is useful for the actor, in establishing his preparation, to determine the character's immediate preceding circumstance. This is part of the first homework assignment, so that he may bring active behavior to his first moments of contact. This use of preparation is invaluable in supporting the actor's faith in his new circumstance and enriching his exchange with the other actors in these initial rehearsals at the table.

Character: Transforming

Now we begin the process of transforming our personal response to serve the character. There are two major ways to make this connection, this bridge between the actor and the character. They are inextricably bound for the actor, and make up the lion's share of the basic work on any role. One way is to identify what the character is doing, as you understand it from the blueprint of the script—here she *demands*; here he *refuses*; here she *threatens*; here he *gives up*. Second, to achieve empathy with the character, to feel what she feels, we use the process of particularization.

Particularizations

Particularizations are emotional metaphors that help us to understand something in the script we do not personally identify with, respond to or know much about. Using the daydreaming process and connecting it with something personal inside you, something you do know a lot about, will help you to experience this meaning in an active way. When you have personalized what you cannot relate to by finding its particular meaning, behavior will be stimulated that will signify the desired response. Does this sound familiar? It is not unlike the kind of research we do when hunting for emotional preparation material.

Finding the "As If"

When we particularize, we look for our personal "as if." For instance, in life I adore kids, but my character detests them the way I detest cockroaches. So, I need to transform my personal response. This is the first step. The actor knows what behavior she must produce when she is around the children in the play; finding the right particularization (e.g., roaches) will help her to do so.

Activating the "As If"

Next, the actor must daydream, bringing the meaning of this particularization alive so that it creates the appropriate behavior to connect to the material in the script. Peter Brook likens this aspect of the rehearsal process to the dyeing of cloth: each time the cloth is dipped, the color deepens. It is a conditioning process that ultimately allows the actor to transform her responses. These are real feelings, mind you, transferred from the actor's natural response to a new stimulus.

Actions: Acting Is Doing

The predominant focus of the second-year work lies in training the actors to understand and work with actions—what they are, how to identify them and how to turn them into spontaneous behavior to serve the character and the play through the Reality of Doing.

Feelings authenticate the behavior, but it is what I *do* because of these feelings that makes my acting clear. Actors struggle with this. It feels so good to feel deeply that it is always difficult to put emotion in its proper place. As we learned working with activities and preparations, emotion is always a by-product of doing.

Actions Give Form to Emotion

The action acts as a conduit. Like a straw dipped into your drink, it pulls the emotion to the surface. As the actor responds in the moments, his feelings travel through his actions. We create a score of these actions, a series of notations that assist us during the rehearsal period, when we are working out our performance. It is like inner choreography. It cannot determine how affecting our acting will be to an audience, but it will always help clarify the character's behavior and journey.

Identifying the actions specifically, then finding the best way to express the action so that it stimulates the appropriate behavior in the world of the play, is difficult to put into practice. Ultimately, it is what acting is all about; what constitutes the performance seen by an audience. We spend the rest of the second year addressing this in all its ramifications.

What Makes an Action

The first thing we work to decipher is what makes an action—what determines that it is *actable*. For example, I can embarrass someone (objective) by making a joke (action). To joke is an actable action; to embarrass is not. I cannot *embarrass* someone without *doing* something that will fulfill that objective. Clarifying the difference between meanings, objectives and actions may seem at first to be an academic concern, but this process of demystification yields a freedom that, even during this early encounter, produces richer and more sophisticated work. The actor's instincts are supported consciously, providing him with a new kind of confidence—concrete tools that address concrete problems he can begin to identify and solve in his acting.

Character Actions

As the year progresses, the actors learn how to state these actable actions in less dry and general ways. If you find, for example, a way to articulate what your character's action is with language and imagery that he might use, it can suggest something to the imagination that will result in behavior more specific to his character. Instead of just *to joke*, I *screw around*, which might be useful to a character in a play like Bogosian's *SubUrbia* but not for Mercutio in Shakespeare's *Romeo and Juliet*, who might *taunt*. To suggest this action to myself in this way does not separate me from my character or place me outside and in judgment of his behavior, and it makes my choices more specific and stimulating.

Character Objectives

Every character has a dominating psychological need that informs his life's goals, usually referred to as a *super-objective*. In acting, as in life, an objective is something that informs a person's behavior. In order to create a true identification with my character, I must understand why she does the things the writer has her do. For instance, because she wants to impress her boss, a person might make him a wonderful gourmet dinner, stay late at the office and walk his dog. Why she is ambitious in this way is part of the actor's investigation of her character.

The work of the first year was devoted to the experience of being caused to do things, as opposed to pretending or indicating. The actor was required to craft reasons that had real meaning and would propel his need to do his activity. He was required to practice crafting reasons for coming to knock on his partner's door and, later, to justify a full emotional life. What occurred in the contact, the things that he did and said because of these reasons, happened spontaneously. Now the actor must consciously craft the impulses and objectives that will inform his character's actions. The objective informs the action; it is the motivation, the pinch. I can indicate an action, but only actions that are genuinely caused create a performance that is truly lived through and will touch the heart of the audience.

The objective must always be present in acting, in every single moment. Without this, the actor is not tied to needing the other. It is what makes living moment-to-moment possible. An action without an acting object (a person, place or thing) is not an action. It is just recitation.

On Its Feet: Place

At the table, the actors working on the scene from *Picnic* have rehearsed the first beat of the scene over and over. They know how they feel about every moment. They have particularized all of these meanings in order to create an active identification with this character, this circumstance. Every relationship has been boiled down to a simple, potent word or phrase and activated in their homework. While still at the table, the teacher has continued to probe those moments that have been glib, indicated or ignored.

As the scene is brought to life with behavior more authentic and consistent, the actors move away from the table to incorporate the reality of their environment. They established in their homework what their relationship is to the backyard, and they have made that meaning active. Now they must deal with their physical life in the space. Incorporating work discovered organically at the table is exciting but unsettling, particularly without a director. The teacher cautions them to take it easy at the beginning, to work only one or two beats at a time as they incorporate these new elements into their score.

After weeks of working on this scene, they are beginning to use the actions and particularizations to good effect. As they move from the table work, they are encouraged to be more specific in the way they live in the space, to bring in whatever they need to stimulate their faith in the physical reality of their world, and to be as specific and conscious about choosing these elements as they have been about their table work. Also, if they have not already done so, the teacher suggests that they think about wearing more character-appropriate clothes to help them find a more specific physical life. These are not costumes, as such, but clothes that support whatever behavior needs extending for their personal sensory investigation. This is not to create *business*, but to keep finding ways to communicate the characters and how they feel about themselves in this circumstance, in this moment—her dress too tight or losing a button, his tie loosened, the shoes too tight, the jacket off and folded over an arm because the actor has decided his character is feeling hot. This investigation provides the actors with another means of building their bridge to the characters.

THE SPOON RIVER MONOLOGUES

Scene 3: An actor, Joe, in a bookstore.

Joe turns the purple paperback over and reads the written comments. "*Spoon River Anthology*, by Edgar Lee Masters. Hmm. 1915? Dead people? 'Scandals and tragedies, corruption and murder'? Sounds good." He flips open to the middle of the book and reads. "'Edmund Pollard.' Sounds old." He scans the first few lines:

> I would I had thrust my hands of flesh
> Into the disk-flowers bee-invested,
> Into the mirror-like core of fire
> Of the light of life, the sun of delight.

"Oh, great. Great. What is he talking about?!"

The assignment was simple enough: to read through the poems and to pick a few that he found himself responding to personally, and to bring this list to class. He is not to practice reading the poems, not to do anything but make choices. It was nice to have this assignment just now. He felt relaxed and not stressed. He was delighted to be able to work alone for the first time. "No more scheduling issues, no more hysterical partners to deal with—just me and the material. Perfect!"

The extraordinary material that this collection of poetry provides is a most fortunate choice for this next step in the actor's process. He has just experienced his first attempts to make conscious use of actions and objectives; to apply his inner research to serve another human being's point of view and life. The chosen scenes allow for an identification that is not too removed from each actor's sensibilities; his own psychology can easily embrace these character elements. Now he is given material that will include heightened language, the language of poetry, with its particular intensity and economy of images and circumstances that make new demands on his use of the technique and his ability to craft interesting and vivid characters.

While an obvious value of these poetic portraits is to give the actor a means of approaching monologue material, that is not the main objective. The curricular focus continues to be on actions. Now, however, the actor will focus on a smaller, more contained piece of text. And because it is poetry, this text is loaded with meanings to decipher and particularize. He will work on these as he would on a beat in a scene, as a response to the imaginary events preceding this text. He will examine each thought, each phrase, each if, and or but to understand the way Masters has put this text together to serve his character. He will learn how to translate this into a full, living portrait of the character in action in the world of Spoon River.

The class is excited. They have each come in with their favorite choices and are eager to begin. The teacher calls for volunteers, and Joe raises his hand, with his elbow still remaining on the arm of the chair. He is not sure he wants to be first. The teacher catches his eye and calls his name to begin.

He moves to face the class, sits as instructed by the teacher and reads his list of titles aloud. The teacher tells him to pick one and simply read it, allowing himself to make contact with the piece as he reads, but not to act anything, not to try to do some kind of oral interpretation. Just read. He begins with "Edmund Pollard" and finds himself becoming moved as he reads aloud:

I would I had thrust my hands of flesh
Into the disk-flowers bee-invested,
Into the mirror-like core of fire
Of the light of life, the sun of delight.
For what are anthers worth or petals
Or halo-rays? Mockeries, shadows
Of the heart of the flower, the central flame!
All is yours, young passer-by;
Enter the banquet room with the thought;
Don't sidle in as if you were doubtful
Whether you're welcome—the feast is yours!
Nor take but a little, refusing more
With a bashful "Thank you," when you're hungry.
Is your soul alive? Then let it feed!
Leave no balconies where you can climb;
Nor milk-white bosoms where you can rest;
Nor golden heads with pillows to share;
Nor wine cups while the wine is sweet;
Nor ecstasies of body or soul,
You will die, no doubt, but die while living
In depths of azure, rapt and mated,
Kissing the queen-bee, Life!

One Action, One Objective

Once the piece is chosen, the teacher takes the student through the text one thought or line at a time, and they talk about its meaning. The student is asked to articulate what he thinks the character is trying to say, what the piece is all about, in simple, actor-friendly language. So, one piece is about revenge, one about lost opportunity, one about life's triumphs, one about regret, or loneliness—what might have been or should have been, or what really was!

As with the process of working on the scene, the actor deals first with the facts the written material presents to him; the circumstances for these people who are speaking from the grave. In each instance, they are sharing the most significant parts of their lives, but they are describing how they feel about it now, in this miraculous time that has been given to them to speak.

In previous scene work, students had the benefit of the whole play, other scenes, other characters giving them information about who they were prior to the events of the play, and they could imagine living through the scenes that led up to their circumstances. Now, students have only a few stanzas that express the summation of a character's whole life! The actor must honor that.

Choosing the Preparation

The first thing to determine is the character's point of view, how this character feels about his life as revealed in his epitaph—joyous, embittered, embarrassed, regretful, giddy and so forth. In this circumstance the character's life has been stripped down to one vivid meaning. The actor must identify the essential meaning at the core of this text. A full preparation is a kind of heartbeat that helps the actor's journey as he merges his life with the character.

The Actor's Paraphrase

The first assignment for the student is to make the text his own by means of something we call an actor's paraphrase. This is another way to particularize—out loud! This is not something the actor writes down and memorizes. It is a way to improvise, alone and out loud, with the events, the life circumstance of the character—in effect, to build a series of associations, memories and daydreams that help the actor to acquire his new life. He begins to follow the blueprint Masters has so eloquently given, thought by thought, working his way through the entire piece, improvising as he makes contact with the character's living epitaph and enters his life.

He takes the first thing the character says and puts it into his own words. This is not an intellectual, literary exercise. He is attempting to understand the meaning behind the imagery and to let it suggest a lot of detail, let his imagination be stimulated by the poem's language, so that his talent opens to meet these meanings. As he works his way through the whole piece, he will need many more words than he will eventually use when he has returned to Masters's text. He need not worry about being literate. His job is to make this deep connection to the material.

He brings this paraphrase to class, so that the teacher can follow the direction of his homework and help him to an exploration of text that is far deeper and more specific than the prior text work. When it becomes apparent that the actor has matched the intensity of the language with active meanings, he begins to bring Masters's text back, a little at a time, paraphrasing whenever he senses he is being glib with the text.

Living Through the Paraphrase

Scene 4: The classroom—the teacher, Joe, Jill and classmates. Joe is not happy.

"She's talking about the exclamation points, for Christ's sake! And the dash? I thought we weren't supposed to pay any attention to punctuation. I thought punctuation was the writer's means of communicating with the reader, not the actor! We were supposed to ignore all of that. 'The actor's punctuation is created by the impulses as he lives through the text'—I loved that idea! What's the deal here?" He takes a breath and looks down at the text, left upside-down on his seat next to his old scene partner. Jill picks it up and hands it to him, and their eyes meet in the camaraderie of the now all-too-familiar frustration that seems to accompany every new thing this damn technique demands!

The teacher tells him that his preparation was quite nice, but he is leaving out several significant things. Because this is poetry, she explains, he must turn it into dialogue, treating this text in much the same way he would begin with Shakespeare. The exclamation point is there to reveal a sense of immediacy and enthusiasm; the dash is an extension of this enthusiasm, this exhortation. This must inform his actor's paraphrase.

"Back to the homework! Figure out why you don't seem to embrace these meanings in your paraphrase. The line about indulging in the feast of life was glib. You only talked about it. Talking is not acting. Just saying the words in a different way is not paraphrasing in any useful way for an actor. How in God's name are you going to get to a glorious moment that allows you to say, 'Is your soul alive? Then let it feed!' if you don't discover the whole image of the feast that leads up to that? You don't have that in there at all. You're so eager to get to the section about 'milk-white bosoms' that you leave that out. But you change the whole piece if you do that, don't you see? You've got to find in yourself the necessity to talk about life as a feast you are entitled to gorge on! Indulge yourself. This guy feels he missed his life. He probably read a lot of books on bee-keeping and flowers instead of sleeping with women and enjoying his own lusty nature. You begin the piece so alive, and then it deteriorates because you don't really do what you say you're doing. Preparation is still and forever for the first moment of contact. You can't spend the rest of the piece hunting for or hanging onto emotion. It's unaesthetic and contrary to everything you've been taught. If

'Edmund' reminds you of how you were at his age, and you have worked to make that a reality for yourself in your crafting, why isn't he touching you more? It's all still a notion, an idea you have. Until you find a way to really connect your idea with a particularization, it will just do zip for you, my friend!"

"Great. Just great. I have no idea what I'm doing. She thinks I'm a washout and is giving up on me." Joe sits down and prays that the break will come soon, so he can go downstairs and get some air.

"This *Spoon River*—not for the constitutionally weak-spirited," Jill jokes as they take hands and rush down the stairs. "Omigod, you were terrific up there."

They laugh, and the moment of crisis is absorbed by the reality of their mutual super-objective: to become wonderfully competent actors, unafraid and eager for the high-wire life they will soon be entering. No time for indulgent self-pity. Onward and upward! Back to the drawing board. The lesson for the day is now already being addressed in his imagination; he finds himself muttering, "Edmund, I thank you."

Finding the Action

In working with the paraphrase, as the meanings are particularized and behavior and impulses emerge, the actor must identify the action. Now that he knows how he feels about everything he is saying, now that he has a visceral response, he must put this in service to the action. In other words, he must ask, "What am I doing because of what I am feeling?" The teacher guides the actor to determine the strongest choice. The meanings have been transformed and particularized and are now, once again, elicited through the Reality of Doing.

The Acting Object and the Objective

Once we have identified the action, we must identify with whom we are speaking and what we need from them: justice, approval, release, revenge, etc. Remember, every action has an implied objective, and if this is not implicit in the actor's score, he will not be in true contact with this imagined partner. In every moment there must be something that binds the actor to the other's response, makes us need to know how the other is responding to what he is doing and saying. This is what keeps the actor in the moment, and what repetition trained him to do.

Endowing the Audience

When an actor is doing a monologue, his partner exists in his mind's eye. He must activate his relationship to this partner as specifically as he would if she were physically present. When he knows who this person is, specifically, she begins to take on a life of her own, and he actually experiences her response to him in much the same way as when he is walking down the street and anticipating a meeting with an old friend or enemy.

Because the actor knows how his character feels in every moment, and because he knows what he wants from this person, He feels the responses coming from his imagined partner much as he would know the responses from another character in a scene. He knows his response, but seeks it freshly each time. In so doing, he sets himself to receive the pinches he needs to cause his action in every moment. Again, he does not *think* these responses; he rehearses sufficiently so that they occur spontaneously. In this way he is continually in contact and his acting remains improvisational and alive.

The How of the Action

As the actor works to find his character and identify with his circumstance, the actions inherent in the text reveal themselves. He must make choices that he feels best serve the piece. A young, flirty character will plead for her life very differently than an old drunk, *and* an old drunk might plead for his life like a young, flirty character. These choices are what make character work so exciting. *How* you do what you do reveals more specifically who you are, and is often the distinguishing factor that lifts a particular performance, making it truly memorable.

Character Ideas

As the actor gains competence with his piece and is living through the events of his character's journey, fully connected to these things we have discussed, he is encouraged to add some special character adjustment that will further serve his portrait, making it more specific and interesting. Sometimes an impediment lends itself nicely to enrich the piece and helps to transform the actor further—an accent, a stutter, a limp to help suggest some interesting behavior to the actor. He may choose to do his piece as if drunk or drugged; he may alter his physical bearing or work with an image inspired from a painting, novel or object. This is a significant and wonderfully rich part of the process of acting, and it can illuminate and inspire the actor's choices as he brings his unique vision to creating the character.

The Tools

Just as in the first-year exercise, each element—identifying circumstance and relationships, emotional preparation and particularizing meanings, the actor's paraphrase, actions and objectives and, finally, character—is focused and worked on so that the actor does not substitute one for the other. Each part has its own function and integrity, and each part serves the whole. And each time the actor works on material, these ingredients must be crafted, either intuitively or consciously. Ultimately, no one cares how you get there—these elements are simply what must be present when good acting is happening.

As students work with the *Spoon River* pieces, trying to create behavior by extracting information from the richly condensed text, the emphasis remains on actions and particularized meanings. They have moved beyond their straight responses, transforming them to serve their characters. The more students are asked to depart from their natural responses in a fictional circumstance, the more difficult and challenging the work of the actor becomes.

NURSERY RHYMES

Using Mother Goose nursery rhymes as a text, the actors are given a new assignment. They are asked to choose a rhyme and justify its text with three different circumstances. They must treat this assignment as if they were isolating and working on a beat from a scene. Each line of the text must be approached with the tools the actors have been given thus far in order to create clear and truthful behavior—who, what, why, when and where. In order to accomplish this they will have to make many character considerations and time and place adjustments so that the text does not sound out of tune with their circumstance. They can break up the sentences any way they wish, but they must not change any of the text or the order of the words or assign words a meaning they cannot hold. But they are encouraged to make use of homonyms (e.g., one/won) to open their thinking to a more imaginative use of the material! The text must be transformed into truthful and justified dialogue with the same cause-and-effect sense of any scene. They may cast anyone in the class willing to rehearse with them, and use any costumes and objects needed to turn this beat into a clear piece of acting. After a brief demonstration in class, they are off to struggle with this new exercise.

This is a delicious opportunity for actors to come up with inventive acting ideas, and to cast themselves in roles they have been eager to play but have not tried. Courtroom dramas, high romance, criminal adventure—sadistic characters, troubled victims, older, younger, stupid, greedy, horny, mentally deficient, paranoid, elegant, heroic, seductive. This exercise works the imagination because it is not easy to justify three versions of the same rhyme. Actors find themselves taking risks, trying on characters and circumstances and using language more creatively.

Acting Ideas

In crafting, we talk a great deal about how to pin down our acting ideas—to make these decisions that have, perhaps, been an intuitive and unconscious part of the actor's talent. The exercise drills the notion that behind every action there must be an idea, a way of doing that reveals the character through the actor's personal lens.

For example, in attempting to articulate a more specific action, actors often add adverbs—"I will plead humbly." This can lead to a rather general and indicated result. But if the actor suggests to himself that he will plead *as if* he were talking to God, he has used the action to serve character more specifically, and stimulated behavior that is more interesting and that will easily become part of his acting score.

SECOND ROUND: THE CHARACTER SCENE

The second round of scenes encompasses all of these issues and provides the next level of challenge for the actors through more complex characters and circumstances. Students are assigned material that is not easily within their range, with characters that require crafting beyond the particularizing of broad emotional colors and relationships and the identification of appropriate actions.

Here begins the most interesting and rewarding part of the process—learning how to apply the technique to more advanced material. The process encompasses all the information students have worked with, now in the service of more complex acting issues. Students work slowly and deeply now to integrate all this information, spending as long as eight weeks on the second scene.

THIRD ROUND: THE STYLE SCENE

Finally, the students are given scenes written in a style or language they have not yet encountered, i.e., by writers such as Wilde, Pinter, Molière, Shepard and Shakespeare. These scenes demonstrate how the basic tools can be applied to any demand the actor will encounter after leaving the classroom to pursue his professional training. At NYU, much of the advanced work of the third round is covered in a curricular production rehearsed over the semester, outside the classroom work, to help the students to apply the work to the rehearsal process through performance. When preparing the final third-round scene for class, the students are now able to work on their own with more confidence. Their understanding of the process is now informed by the long rehearsal project and the experience of performance. It is a rewarding conclusion to the two-year process, both for the actors and for the teacher.

There is a part of the acting experience, this journey to acquire skill and craft, that is so delicate and personal that it does not ever become part of an actor's consciousness. The student leaves the training period and, at first, tries religiously to do what he has learned he must do. As he separates from his training and enters the profession, the areas of craft that he has studied begin to merge with his instincts and become a part of his acting process.

What is true about relationships between people is equally true of one's relationship to an acting technique: as you enter a romantic relationship and begin to sense that it is the right one for you, you fall in love. As you enter deeper and deeper into the relationship, it is all you care about and all you feel you will ever want or need. It becomes, of necessity, quite exclusive as you explore all the details, all the parts of this person. You feel complete, needing nothing additional—you have found the answer to your dreams. Then, after you have lived in the relationship long enough to feel secure, you are able to take in the world around you again, and you find you have additional needs this one person cannot possibly fulfill.

In the life of an actor, craft is something that will be continuously addressed. With each new role, many of the same acting problems surface; however, it is equally true that, with each new role, the actor will find himself entering the relationship a somewhat different person. He brings his life, as it evolves, to every role, and each time he has had new experiences, relationships and ideas that specifically alter how he will understand this next encounter. New material may expose areas in his technique that need to be stimulated or understood differently. He may seek additional training with a master teacher or work on his voice or his physical restrictions to expand the range of his talent.

For the teacher of any craft, as his relationship with the various parts of his subject becomes more intimate, he too begins to feel needs beyond the scope of his particular technique. In the realm of art there are no boundaries—there must never be. A technique is simply a jumping-off place, a way of addressing what is truly beyond our ability to acquire or define—talent—and assisting it to its fulfillment.

ENDNOTES/SOURCES

Epigraphs:
(Page 61) Meisner, Sanford, and Dennis Longwell, *Sanford Meisner on Acting*, New York: Vintage, 1987, p. 52.
(Page 63) Ibid., p. 4.

RECOMMENDED READING LIST

Theater, formerly *Yale/Theatre*, vol. 8, nos. 2–3, Spring 1977, "The American Actor."
A marvelous compilation of articles and interviews with Meisner, Adler, Strasberg and others.

Clurman, Harold, *The Fervent Years: The Group Theatre & the '30s*, New York: Knopf, 1945; Da Capo Press, 1983.
Clurman's impassioned opus describes the history of the Group Theatre and the many personalities and forces that made it work.

Cole, Toby, ed., *Acting: A Handbook of the Stanislavski Method*, Three Rivers Press, 1947.
This book contains two articles—"The Work of the Actor," by I. Rapoport, and "The Creative Process," by I. Sudakov—that were cited as influential by Meisner, especially regarding the Reality of Doing.

Doob, Nick, dir., *Sanford Meisner: The American Theatre's Best-Kept Secret*, Princeton: Films for the Humanities & Sciences, 1985.
This wonderful film, often aired on PBS, shows Meisner teaching in the classroom and working with some of the issues discussed in the chapter. The film includes well-known actors and directors talking about their experience with Meisner and with the technique.

Gray, Paul, "The Reality of Doing," *Tulane Drama Review*, Fall 1964.
This article is cited on page 10 of a special edition of Meisner's book, *Sanford Meisner on Acting*, in a chapter that discusses "Stanislavsky in America."

Meisner, Sanford and Dennis Longwell, *Sanford Meisner on Acting*, New York: Vintage, 1987.
This is undoubtedly the most significant Meisner book. You will get a sense not only of his teaching, but also of the man in the classroom.

Smith, Wendy, *Real Life Drama: The Group Theatre and America, 1931–1940*, New York: Knopf, 1990; Grove/Atlantic, 1992.
An excellent, detailed account of the history of the Group Theatre.

SANFORD MEISNER was born in Brooklyn, New York, on August 31, 1905. He attended Erasmus Hall High School and then the Damrosch Institute of Music, intending to pursue a career as a concert pianist. He had, however, always been drawn to the theater, even creating plays with his cousins when he was younger, and he dropped his music studies when he found an opportunity to act with the Theatre Guild. The play was Sidney Howard's *They Knew What They Wanted*, and in her meticulous history of the Group Theatre, *Real Life Drama: The Group Theatre and America, 1931–1940* (New York: Knopf, 1962, p.11), Wendy Smith notes, "Watching the intense, naturalistic performance of Pauline Lord . . . he began to realize that 'acting which really dug at me was what I was looking for.'" In *Theater* magazine ("The American Actor," vol. 8, nos. 2–3, Spring 1977, p. 40), Meisner recalled, "I liked all the actors who were emotionally alive." Meisner had befriended Harold Clurman, and they spent hours sharing their ideas and passion about the state of the theater. Meisner invited his friend to come to see him in his first good role at the Guild, in Pirandello's *Right You Are if You Think You Are*. Also in the cast was the man with whom Meisner and Clurman would be connected for the rest of their lives: Lee Strasberg.

When the Moscow Art Theatre came to New York in 1923, it brought the extraordinary awareness that a system of craft was available to assist actors to a more authentic use of themselves onstage. In 1928, Strasberg and Clurman were among the first to attempt to create a new kind of theater company for a new generation of actors, and Meisner was, in Smith's words, "their first disciple." He was seventeen when he first studied with Strasberg at the Chrystie Street Settlement House, and while he grew to disagree deeply with much of Strasberg's teaching, in Suzanne Shepherd's interview in *Theater* magazine, he acknowledged that "the biggest single influence in my life was Strasberg." In 1930, Meisner became a member of the Group Theatre, participating both as an actor and, later, as a director. He acted in many of Clifford Odets's plays during his time with the Group, including the legendary first production of *Waiting for Lefty*, which Odets directed himself. He remained a member of the Group throughout its existence, but ultimately found his true calling as a teacher, saying (*Theater*, p. 39), "The best part of me comes alive when I'm teaching." When Stella Adler returned from her now famous visit and tutorials with Stanislavsky, Meisner was amongst those in the Group who were inspired by the clarity of the new information.

For many years, the Neighborhood Playhouse School of the Theatre provided Meisner with the opportunity to teach. In 1935, he became head of its drama department, and it was there that he developed his exercises. In the interview with Shepherd (*Theater*, p. 43), he said, "I knew what I wanted and I poked around after it . . . all my exercises were designed to strengthen the guiding principle that I learned forcefully in the Group—that art expressed human experience—which principle I have never and will never give up." Meisner left the Playhouse for five years to become director of the new talent division of Twentieth Century Fox, and while there he starred in several movies, including *Tender is the Night* and Odets's *The Story on Page One*. In 1962, he became director of the acting department at the new American Musical Theater Academy. He returned to the Playhouse and remained head of its drama department from 1964 to 1990. In 1985, Meisner cofounded the Meisner/Carville School of Acting with James Carville on the island of Bequia, in the West Indies, and also in Hollywood, California, where it continues to exist. In 1995, a theater was added to the school, forming what is now the Sanford Meisner Center for the Arts.

Sanford Meisner died on February 2, 1997.

VICTORIA HART was born in New York City and raised on Long Island. She studied dance with Anna Sokolow at the Henry Street Settlement, where, as a teenager, she took her first acting classes. She graduated from Western Reserve University (now Case Western) with a BA in theater, and earned a Masters in educational theater from New York University while teaching a drama program she created for elementary school children in the South Bronx. She attended classes at HB Studio, first with William Hickey and Stephen Strimpell and later with Uta Hagen. She taught acting at Rutgers University for twenty-two years. During her Rutgers tenure, William Esper became the head of the newly formed Mason Gross School of the Arts. Hart studied with Mr. Esper, a former student of Sanford Meisner, and later trained to teach the Meisner Technique under his guidance. Alongside Esper's graduate program, she headed the BFA acting program at Rutgers, developing an introductory curriculum to prepare undergraduates for the two-year Meisner program. As part of this curriculum, she began directing, in order to bring the classroom process through to rehearsal and performance. During this time, she also taught the two-year Meisner curriculum to aspiring professionals at the William Esper Studio in Manhattan. In 1995, after leaving Rutgers, Ms. Hart was invited to teach and direct as a guest artist at North Carolina School of the Arts by director and dean Gerald Freedman. She taught and directed there over a four-year period, while continuing to teach at the Esper Studio in New York. In 1998, she joined the drama department faculty at New York University's Tisch School of the Arts, where she is the director of the Meisner Extension. Her husband, Joseph Hart, who continues to teach at Rutgers, is a playwright and the creator and artistic director of the much-loved Shoestring Players. They have two daughters, Rebecca and Megan, to whom she dedicates this chapter.

BEYOND MICHAEL CHEKHOV TECHNIQUE

Continuing the Exploration through the Mask

Per Brahe

In August 1932, Michael Chekhov and his second wife, Xenia, arrived in Lithuania, a few miles from the Russian border. For the first time since his enforced exile from Russia five years earlier, he was finally able to teach, act and direct in his native language. He had discovered the magical quality he called "It"—the highest level of artistic inspiration and super-consciousness—one night during a performance in Berlin, and he discussed the pursuit of It in his first lecture at Lithuania's National Theatre (now the Kaunas State Academic Drama Theatre): "Every time I teach actors, I ask myself, Will something special happen inside this room today? Together, will we find the It that I am always searching for, both in my material and with my colleagues when performing onstage, but never can find? Will I find the secret today in our work? Will our work reveal the It of the actor's precious dignity? Will the new theater be revealed here, now, today?"[1]

Chekhov brought that question to the Lithuanian stage, where he ambitiously directed Shakespeare's *Hamlet* and *Twelfth Night*, Gogol's *The Inspector-General* and Richard Wagner's opera *Parsifal*. Audience response to his productions was ecstatic. The success of his work and his teachings told him he was on to something. Unfortunately, the Bolshevik politicians grew wary of Chekhov's influence. As a result, his life in Lithuania quickly became a nightmare.

Chekhov's notes from this period show him in physical and intellectual transition. His experience in Lithuania opened a new door in his quest to define It and learn to summon It at will. How does one bring It to the stage? How does one keep It present? He would spend the next twenty-three years developing the tools to accomplish this on a regular basis.

Despite his long life as an actor with a brilliant understanding of creating expressive characters, there still remained much to be discovered through his work as a teacher and director. Near the end of his life, Chekhov began work on a book for writers and directors that would follow his first book, *To the Actor*. Although Chekhov died before finishing this project, his materials were compiled and the book completed by Charles Leonard. The book, *To the Director and Playwright*, remains a testament to Chekhov's career as an actor and teacher and is his legacy to the next generation of actors, directors and playwrights. The most striking text in the book was transcribed from a lecture delivered in 1955. It was to be the curtain call of his long journey discovering compassion for the craft of acting:

> The true professional loves everything in [the theater], of course. Why? Primarily because he loves the wonderful world that is opened up to him though that magic of make-believe, which is acting. "Acting" is the key word. The playwright at work is mentally acting all the characters of his play; the director vicariously sees himself acting all the roles in the play while he is rehearsing it; the actor enjoys the pleasure of transforming himself into every character he plays and expressing himself through their masks or personalities.[2]

In this last lecture, he sensed that there was a hidden resource available to the actor, but he could explain it only through instinct, and he merely mentioned the key word—*mask*.

Speaking over the phone for the last time to his longtime secretary, Deirdre Hurst du Prey, from his hospital bed in Hollywood, where he was recuperating from a heart ailment, Chekhov said, "Mama, Mama, I am lying here and am thinking it all over again and again. And if I can, when I get out of the hospital, I will work more with masks, because I am sure there is more in the masks I need to know."[3] A few months later, Michael Chekhov died at home of a heart attack, never having the opportunity to follow his inspiration. Had he been able to work with masks as he planned, perhaps he would have found a way to achieve the elusive It.

Stanislavsky used psychology, Meyerhold used the physical body, and Chekhov united the two. But Chekhov had come to realize that the material he had been using his whole life was not enough to reach full power and truth for the actor. I believe the missing link to the truth for which they all were searching is in the mask.

MY FIRST ENCOUNTER WITH MICHAEL CHEKHOV, AND THE LINKING OF CHEKHOV TECHNIQUE WITH THE MASK

During the latter part of his term in office, Soviet Premier Mikhail Gorbachev was encouraging a gradual opening of Russian politics and culture. As such, he was open to a challenge from Scandinavian countries to share artistic performance theories and ideologies through a cultural exchange called Next Stop Soviet. I was asked to participate in this exchange festival at the GITIS institute, Moscow's oldest and largest theater school.

The cultural exchange was to be between nine Danish and nine Russian acting students. While planning the visit to Russia, my Danish students decided that they did not want to take with them any material representing traditional Danish theater. I had the idea to travel to Bali, Indonesia, and have the world-famous mask-maker, Mr. Ida Bagus Anom, create eighteen masks for the special cultural exchange. At that time, mask work was not offered in the actor's training curriculum at GITIS in Moscow. In fact, it was not allowed, though we were able to get special permission from the dean to work with masks because of the unique nature of the artistic exchange.

I had met Anom once before, and was excited by the opportunity to commission him for the masks. I wrote to him and tried calling several times, but at that time, communication to Bali was less than dependable, and he never received my letter. When I arrived in Bali, he was surprised but gracious. I told him that I had come to have him make eighteen masks. After a brief silence, he replied, "Why eighteen masks?" Confused and extremely jet-lagged, I asked if there was anything wrong. He replied that there was nothing wrong; he was struck by the fact that, when you add the digits in the number 18, the result is 9, a special number in Bali. He took this as a sign that the project was going to be a great success, and he wanted to get started right away. This turned out to be the first of our many projects together.

On September 9, 1989, I left Denmark for Moscow, bringing the special collection of eighteen hand-carved wooden masks to an old, impoverished stage in the middle of Moscow, far away from the colorful tropical island of Bali. This would be my attempt to break down the language barriers existing between the students, allowing the Danes and Russians an opportunity to improvise and act together. In the course of the following three weeks, my life would be forever changed by the experience of teaching Russian acting students the joy of working with masks.

During the first week of the festival's acting workshops, rumors were flying concerning my eighteen masks, and most of the comments were negative. So, when permission was given for me to begin and the time came to launch my *mask energy*, I was more than ready to start. It was my first time teaching outside of Denmark, and I was a bit apprehensive working with first-rate Russian acting students who had trained under a very different structure than that of the clean and cozy traditions of Denmark.

To my amazement, there were no professors present at the beginning of my first mask class. I waited for what seemed to be an eternity, but finally, to maintain my nerves and sanity, I began the class without the other professors present. The class began without resistance from either camp of students, and after the thirty-minute warm-up, the professors arrived. The students had just begun to glide into the energy of the masks, becoming freer and more expressive in their movements and voices. Upon seeing this, the professors picked up their notebooks and began archiving, without showing any emotion or connection to the students' work. Shaking the walls of the old-fashioned Russian training room, the chaos, joy and freedom that came out of the students' mask work was thrilling. It shocked the professors to see how far the masks were able to take the Russian students in such a short time. Immediately following the first class, Russian professors Natasha Zwerev and Oleg Khuraschov briefly conferred and then said to me, "Do you know that your masks release work like that of the best students of Michael Chekhov?"

Before that moment, I didn't know anything about Michael Chekhov. I had written his name in my sketchbook when it had been mentioned during exercises that first week, but none of my work was in direct relation to his material. The Russian professors were amazed and frustrated by my ignorance of what Michael Chekhov had done for the Russian actor. They explained to me Chekhov's use of staccato, legato, center, feeling of ease, imagination, incorporation, inhaling, exhaling, creative individuality, form, beauty and atmosphere.

In that moment began the amalgamation of the work released from my Balinese masks and the work of Michael Chekhov. It was pure spiritual alchemy. Coincidentally, the marriage of these ideas was occurring in a building situated between Chekhov's house in Arbat Square and the Moscow Art Theatre. The Russian professors invited me to return the following year to direct various August Strindberg texts. They promised to carefully teach me Michael Chekhov's material.

My powerful initiation at GITIS energized my spirit and inspired a dramatic change in my life as well as in my art in the theater. It afforded a perspective that allowed me to plunge deeply into Chekhov's material through masks.

The next year, I worked in Moscow for two months, and when I returned to the public theater school in Denmark, I realized the new information I had acquired was too progressive for the Danish school's traditional training. In 1991, exactly 100 years after Chekhov's birth, my own Michael Chekhov Studio became a reality. It was the first introduction of Michael Chekhov material to the Danish theater, and the first Danish theater school that made his work a foundation to actor training. I was able to create an ideal training and working environment, free from the commercial pressure for success; a studio filled with young and excited students eager to experiment and grow artistically. This gave us the freedom of letting our material cultivate and mature into clearly crafted artistic works.

The combination of mask work and Chekhov exercises took the training to another level. It was like two circles overlapping one another, and where they overlapped, a new life and inspiration flew into the training room. We created a huge library using material we had compiled from English, Russian and German books containing Chekhov exercises. We attended international conferences to compare our translations, adaptations and applications of the material to the work of other Chekhov teachers.

After the first two years of my Michael Chekhov Studio, I had gained sufficient international recognition to allow me to spend more time out of Denmark. In 1998, I received an invitation to teach at the Eugene O'Neill Theater Center in Connecticut as part of the International Michael Chekhov Conference.

My first meeting with American actors showed me how deep mask and Michael Chekhov work could go. For the first time in my life, I worked with actors who had an open will to enter deeply into my material with respect, joy and love. In six days, I had received numerous invitations to teach in the United States, and I decided to move to America, where I still live and will remain until my last curtain call.

THE ACTOR'S STILL LIFE AND
THE BALINESE DANCE

To support the kind of physical responsibility required of his body, the actor must train with specific exercises so that his body develops a confident vocabulary of specificity. This provides an ongoing foundation of craft for his journey as an artist on the stage. Michael Chekhov's collected exercises—specifically, the nine exercises appearing in the beginning of his book *To the Actor*—provide a clear way into developing this new language for the actor's physical body. In my years of training professional actors, I have not known any other material that provides an actor with better essential tools.

As a painter works on his still life so he or she can understand and master the painting skills of stabilizing light, creating forms and shadows, composition, colors and space, so too must the actor practice exercises that hone his or her own Actor's Still Life.

The first nine exercises Michael Chekhov describes in *To the Actor*, which I call "The Actor's Still Life," are as follows:

1. Open, broad, simple movements
2. The ideal center in the chest
3. Molding
4. Floating
5. Flying
6. Fire/radiating movements
7. Ease of form
8. Beauty
9. Feeling of wholeness when crossing the threshold

It must first be understood that most of Michael Chekhov's material in *To The Actor* is comprised of exercises developed to keep the actor's body and imagination energetically balanced. Before the development of these exercises, Michael Chekhov became hugely successful as an actor, and lost the balance of his own physical energy due to the abuse of alcohol. Success can be a double-edged sword if the body and the mind do not maintain their balance. Chekhov, like many other actors of his time, had the misfortune of combining work, fame and alcohol.

Once, when Chekhov was performing onstage to a full house, he broke character and began laughing hysterically. His friends noted that his success and imagination were rapidly spiraling downward. While attempting to control his imagination and physically ground himself, Chekhov first explored Hinduism, and later the anthroposophical work of Austrian philosopher Rudolf Steiner. Inspiration from both of these sources saved Chekhov's mind. He was so moved by Steiner's work that when he took over the Moscow Art Theatre's second studio, after the early death of Yevgeny Bagrationovich Vakhtangov in 1922, he started incorporating Steiner's work into the training. It caused a huge controversy among the actors in the Second Studio, and his Russian colleagues, with the help of the Bolsheviks, forced Chekhov to leave Russia. He never returned.

During the run of a show, the greatest difficulty and challenge for an actor is to sustain a believable moment-to-moment life within the atmosphere of the play, fulfilling the demands of the playwright, director and character without becoming mechanical and uninteresting through dull and routine expressions. The actor and his body must be constantly alert, ready to receive and change according to the rhythm and tempo of the world of the play. Moreover, the actor's body must be able to maintain a feeling of ease while the expressions of his voice move with the emotions of joy, hope, sorrow and anger, creating a unique piece of art. The actor must be able to sharpen his or her inspiration and imagination. Behind all of that there is a complete human body that requires nourishment and rest.

Once he begins working with Michael Chekhov's material, the actor realizes that not only does the depth of his work become more enriched, but there is also a change in the way he operates in the world on a day-to-day basis. This is because, like the gestures of the Balinese dance, these exercises are universal and are already implanted in the human being. Rudolf Steiner felt that the human being is a free individual with huge resources. These exercises come from the same resources incorporated in the Eastern martial arts and dance forms.

Each Michael Chekhov exercise must be incorporated piece by piece. The actor must approach Chekhov's material with the mindfulness of a serious practitioner, understanding that it is an ever-growing process. The actor will have many moments of achievement, but these moments are only small steps forward into the evolving material.

To ease the mind of those young actors searching for rewards in their training, I turn to a philosophical quotation that helps them to have more confidence while approaching the material step by step:

> Everything has already been accomplished, and so, having overcome the sickness of effort, one finds oneself in the self-perfected state. That is contemplation.
>
> —CHÖGYAL NAMKHAI NORBU

From my experiences as a director and a teacher, I have found that the best entrance into the world of Michael Chekhov exercises is through a *sensation of ease*. While watching a ceremonial dance in Bali, I was able to draw a connection between Michael Chekhov's exercises dealing with "feeling of ease" and the seamless beauty of the traditional Balinese dance, which is generated from the dancer's role as a joyful and loving servant to the spirits and the audience. Chekhov's idea of acting is the same. No moment onstage must be filled with tension. Even if an actor is going to play a "heavy" or evil character, he must perform with the greatest sensation of ease. Heaviness leads to a lack of creativity, and it can, in the worst cases, depress or repulse an audience.

Many actors confuse the word *ease* with relaxation. Sensation of ease is not to be used as a means of relaxation, but to provide an energized quality within the ease of one's movements. Even the actor who is playing Hamlet must move with a sensation of ease and beauty while engaged in choreographed stage combat. As soon as an actor understands sensation of ease, his body begins to radiate another quality—the sensation of beauty. In fact, not only will sensation of ease inspire the actor in his performance onstage, it will also affect both the person behind the character and the audience.

With the help of a sensation of ease and beauty, the body is ready to incorporate the Five Qualities of Movement: molding, floating, flying, fire and radiation. These can stimulate and increase the dynamics of an actor's physical vocabulary in the craft of acting, leading directly to the expression and understanding of humanity. During these exercises, intellectually driven students often panic, thinking that Chekhov was a mysterious alchemist. He was not. The body naturally embraces these Five Qualities.

THE IMAGES

Start by moving with legato movements, as if you are *molding* through clay. Register the sensations. Monitor your physical control. This is the beginning of understanding earth-like movements. Once you have worked with earth, then you move on to the sensation of *flying*, the sensation of not being able to keep your feet on the ground, or *floating* gently in water. Finally, use staccato movements and imagine you send out *flames* in all directions.

ETHER BODY

Using the Five Qualities leads us into an area where the masks open inspiration. There is no doubt that the essential preparation for the masks is through training the body using the Five Qualities. Coincidentally, my masks are predominately painted in colors that symbolize the Five Qualities.

You may be asking, "Are there five natural qualities or four?" We are most familiar with the four elements of earth, wind, water, and fire. But there is also a fifth, which the Greeks called the *ether body*. It is an energy spontaneously awakened by the masks and generated by this kind of theater training. The ether body awakens after the body's release of the first four images. Some people can see it, many more feel it; very few use it onstage. But as soon as it loses its abstract nature and becomes a desired quality, the actor will realize that the ether body begins to develop itself in the actor on its own and becomes an expressive energy that an actor can command and radiate onstage.

In my mask work, the fifth element is present as soon as the fire energy is awakened in the body. As soon as the actor incorporates the image of the mask into his imagination, the body's transformation takes place, and the ether body begins to take shape. Even after the mask is off, the ether body maintains the quality of the image of the mask, and it takes a few moments for the actor to process the experience and then take on his own ether body. This is the beginning of understanding real *transformation*.

Moving with the help of the ether body offers an actor a way into sensation of ease. In my work as a theater director, I ask actors to imagine that their ether body moves before they do—standing up, jumping over something or up onto a table.

Actors using these elements will soon feel that they are able to radiate certain qualities. Chekhov talks about radiation as a means of giving or sending out. Its counterpart is to receive. True acting is a constant exchange of the two. The more you radiate, the more you receive, not only from the ensemble but also from the audience.

One of the joyful side dishes in mask work is the freedom the actor gains. It has nothing to do with the "freedom" associated with the ancient tradition of Mardi Gras, or the carnival in Venetia from which it is derived. This is an internal freedom, an inner liberty that comes from tapping into all of the inner qualities of one's self.

When working with Michael Chekhov's material, the physical body will begin to gain a freedom for which it has been longing since it was introduced to language. Words disrupt the body if they are not learned through physical incorporation. This is the beginning of the controlling mind's attempt to dominate the free physical expression of the body. The controlling mind is like a serpent, ready to strike when one gets bored. And one does get bored! When this happens, the actor begins to blame every external stimulus nearby—the teacher, the technique, himself, other students, Michael Chekhov, blah, blah, blah! Hang in there; it is all part of the wonderful process of being an artist. Do not feed the snake of the controlling mind; embrace it and enjoy the battle of discovering and deciphering one's self, moving back and forth from the controlling mind to one's *higher creative self*. Judgment is physical tension. Surrender to ease. One can always climb the mountain, but one cannot complain about the mountain's nature on the way up. One's higher creative self is much stronger than one's controlling mind. As the student works with Chekhov's material, the controlling mind will begin to silence itself.

The classroom can be like a battleground between the student's judgmental mind and the teacher's process and technique, but if the teacher is savvy enough to understand that this battle is also a part of the process, the war will end in the classroom with the liberation of the student's imagination. There are teachers who say, If it isn't fun, it isn't Michael Chekhov. I counter by saying that learning to master any skill is seldom fun, and truly mastering Michael Chekhov's material, really discovering one's own personal power, can be very scary and not at all fun.

In my training, the bridge between the first nine exercises and the essential character work begins with balancing the body and releasing the tensions that it may still be storing.

THINKING, FEELING AND WILL

Balancing thinking, feeling and will is the foundation for an actor's complete transformation. Without these elements to stimulate form, the body cannot achieve the right balance. It is also the foundation for mask work, and it is essential for an actor approaching Chekhov's material.

To stimulate the body in thinking/feeling/willing, I ask my students to center themselves, standing upright, and to take one step in each of the eight available directions, paying close attention to coming back to the center before stepping in another direction. The center position, or ninth position, represents the body as being in the center of the universe.

The body must move with three different qualities at the same time:

1. Thinking: the actors imagine that they move like a walking stick, stiffly and rigidly.
2. Feeling: The actors move the body with an image of a veil, focusing on the breath.
3. Willing: Focusing on the feet, as if the actor were a marching soldier stomping on the floor.

The second pillar in the bridge to the essential character work is what Chekhov called the "seaweed exercise," in which the actor must imagine he is seaweed, fixed to a stone and swaying back and forth, moving the body in many different directions. This loosens up any blocked energies in the joints, and most importantly, it activates the energy of the spine. The spine is the central highway for incorporation and imagination, which is the key to creating characters.

The image of a mask enters the body via the energy of the nervous system. When the actor holds the mask in front of him, he does not try to predetermine what he sees or how to act the mask, because the mask is not a character, but a pure image. A body that is blocked by tension around the spine has greater difficulty incorporating and using an image than a body with an open and flexible spine. In my work, actors imagine that the image has moved into their spines, allowing its inspiration to flow from the top and back down to the lowest part, generating the image's information throughout all of the body.

When the actor's balance is established and the spine is opened, the physical body and the mental body are now ready to explore creating a character.

THE ART OF THE CHARACTER
AND WORKING GESTURE:
THE SECOND STEP TOWARD THE TRUTH

There is a famous story about the student Michael Chekhov being praised by his teacher, Konstantin Stanislavsky, for presenting a truthful and heartfelt scene concerning his character's dead father. Chekhov's work pleased and moved Stanislavsky, who went on to affirm Chekhov's crafting of character and implementation of the Stanislavsky system. Stanislavsky said it was so nice to see an actor thoroughly applying his own experience of his real father's death to the text of the scene. Chekhov replied by saying that his father was not dead—he had just used his imagination. Upon hearing this, Stanislavsky expelled Chekhov from his class for fourteen days.

Michael Chekhov found Stanislavsky's insistence on being "true to life" limiting, so he explored the uses of imagination and theatricality that he learned from Vakhtangov and Vsevolod Emilievich Meyerhold. Chekhov's concept of character was quite different from Stanislavsky's. Chekhov disagreed with Stanislavsky's emphasis on the actor's ego. Under Stanislavsky's method, if an actor played a character whose child was ill, the actor imagined that his own child was ill and responded with truthful emotions, movements and facial expressions, resulting in an artistic creation that expressed the playwright's intentions. Regarding this difference, Chekhov states, "The difference is that, with Stanislavsky's method, the character's child becomes the actor's focal point, since the actor must see only the things seen by the character residing within him. With my understanding of Character work, the character becomes the focal point, which of all is the actor's true object, and through the character the actor is able to feel so much more of what the father feels for the child than he could possibly be capable on his own, by doing it for the father as it were . . . That was the gist of what we discussed: the supremacy of the character's ego (me) against the actor's ego (Stanislavsky) and I must confess that neither of us convinced the other."[4]

The need for more artistic inspiration in his own work drove Michael Chekhov's search for a better and more fruitful way of creating a character and satisfying his need to transform. The central question that guided Chekhov in his methodical research was, How does the artist reach a level of artistic inspiration? Is this a matter of chance, or can it be maintained continuously through methodical application? He recognized that everyday consciousness was of no help in the creative process. He described analytical, intellectual reasoning as a murder of art. The creative process is not achieved by regimenting thinking, but rather by transforming thought into imaginative thinking. In my opinion, the masks validate Chekhov's argument of how to approach character over Stanislavsky's.

THE FOUR STAGES OF TRANSFORMATION USING THE MASK

When I teach actors the art of transformation in a mask class, I begin by explaining the four stages of transformation: concentration, imagination, incorporation and inspiration. The actor focuses on the mask, which he holds up in front of him. I call this *concentration*. At this moment, the actor begins to imagine that the mask either talks to him or looks at him. That is *imagination*. Then he puts on the mask, which is *incorporation*. He allows the mask to enter deep into his body and take him into his *inspiration*. The transformation occasioned by the mask is present when the actor begins to generate sounds that are indicative of the physical center of the mask, rather than the actor's own idiosyncrasies.

It is at this point that the mask takes over and does what it wants. The mask will keep going with the inspiration and the creativity, letting the character find his objectives in as many free, expressive moments as are available. There are no judgments, and this opens up the actor's ability to listen. It becomes pure inspiration.

Now put the dying child about whom Stanislavsky and Chekhov were debating in front of the mask, and you will see that the mask knows exactly how to respond. It is all imagination and inspiration from an incorporated image. This is what makes actors artists and not psychiatrists!

The mask's atmosphere radiates from the body and fills the entire training room. I then instruct the actor to remove the mask while still incorporating the image, which activates the ether body. The power is not as aggressive as when the mask is on, but the actor's choices have the same specificity as when he was wearing the mask, and it is both easier for the actor to control the atmosphere and less intimidating for an audience.

All of the elements of transformation in Chekhov's exercises are present in just one experience in my mask class. Masks represent the thinking, feeling, and will qualities of characters—similar to the characteristics Ibsen used to distinguish the characters in his plays, whom he identified as "idealists, compromisers and realists."

An actor whose body is out of balance will not be able to overcome habitual behavior and master these subtleties. If the will is not stimulated, his character work will be overly emotional and sentimental. A thinking actor will judge himself and will almost never find the character, and an actor with an overpowering will is like a bull in a glass menagerie, unable to be sensitive to the world of the play. Understanding the thinking, feeling and will elements of the body allows the actor to fully enjoy and navigate through the experience of transformation.

It is important that all of this material be developed in the actor at a gentle pace. If an actor rockets from his usual way of working into his inspiration, he can be overwhelmed when he feels that he is losing his connection to his controlling mind.

Combining mask work with Michael Chekhov technique creates a huge freedom in the body, but after the first breakthrough, the controlling mind begins to take over, judging the actor's newfound freedom. Then the battle begins! When this happens, it is important to stimulate the thinking, feeling and will of the actor's body.

It is also important to note that the controlling mind is always present. The actor must not try to *destroy* it, but rather to embrace it. It is through understanding the controlling mind's function that the actor gains compassion for it. There are many examples of artists who are not able to balance themselves between their controlling mind and their inspiration, leading them down the path of a destructive lifestyle. This often happens when a child is forced to stay in his world of inspiration by an ambitious parent, as in the case of Mozart. His father kept him in his "wonder child" state of inspiration, and Mozart had difficulties operating in the real world. He lived and died in his inspiration. The enormous impact the mask has on the body will take the actor into a world of high inspiration, but in an environment that will allow the actor to come back and properly file the experience, so that it can be used whenever he needs it. It is unbelievable what the body can do when it is in a state of inspiration.

The argument between Chekhov and Stanislavsky about the character's objective can be settled through mask work. I have proven in my work that an actor must navigate through the character's ego in order to understand his objectives in a scene, and this comes from the inspiration of an incorporated image. The sharp image of the mask provides inspiration after inspiration to the actor, so swiftly that it often leaves the actor speechless when he realizes how accessible and available his impulses and imagination are when he allowed to create in a training environment where "No" does not exist. This is the formula for inspiration!

If the actor takes the visual image of the mask and tries to act or imagine how the character performs, as in Stanislavsky's understanding of character development, the actor will be exhausted, frustrated and angry within minutes. This is because he is acting an idea, which does not allow contact with his inspiration. His work will be filled with judgment and tension, because the image of the mask will want to take the actor in a specific direction, but the actor's controlling mind gets in the way, causing exhaustion and emotional response. A major goal of the mask work is to teach the actor to trust the unknown of his inspiration. When we allow ourselves to make immortally creative choices, our work becomes timeless.

A deeper way to understand the power of an image devoid of judgment is to put a mask on an actor without allowing him to look at it first. This forces the actor to listen to his inspiration, because he does not have any preconceived identification of the image. This technique now involves more than just the actor; it includes the spectators and other actors in the ensemble. Because the actor wearing the mask does not know what mask he has on his face, he is forced to trust the inspiration that is coming from within and above, and he must rely on his audience or fellow actors to function as a mirror. Human beings communicate on another level, where they inform each other of their identities through the images of their faces. In this sense, ritual is brought back into the theater. On a deep level, the actor begins to realize that acting and character are not in his control, but rather in the control of a universal nature. He begins to nurture those around him with the power of his transformation and his deep connection to his imagination. The image of the mask has penetrated the actor's inspiration.

During the mask work, the spine begins to get warm, sometimes hot, and there is an area right behind the shoulder blades where an actor will burn if he has a physical or emotional resistance to the mask's image. Having another person touch the palm of his hand to this area of the actor's back, where the shoulders meet the spine, can allow a release of energy and help the actor to go deeper into the experience of the mask/character. The energy travels down the spine and back up to the crown of the head, all the while generating heat to the top of the head—the gateway to the actor's inspiration. If I place my hand directly on top of the head, the inspiration lessens. It is important that the will force be active in this case, because the actor must always have a connection to the earth, even though he is moving freely through his inspiration. If the will is not activated, there can be a sensation of a lost connection to the lower half of the body. This can be ameliorated by merely focusing on the heels of the feet and their connection to the floor.

CENTERS

Michael Chekhov talks about different centers within the body from which an actor chooses to let a character emerge, centers that can help the actor create a character fully or stimulate him in different situations. The source of this idea is not clear from the material I have, but the mask works from this same concept of physical centers. And no matter where I go around the world, whether it is America, Russia, Australia or Scandinavia, a single mask stimulates the same physical behavior in any language. I have masks that affect different centers, inside the body or externally—for example, a mask centered in the nose causes clownish movements and behavior.

In addition to a fixed center for a character, an actor can also add a movable center. As you are reading this, imagine there is a little fast-moving planet orbiting your head. After doing this for a while, you should feel dizzy, even drunk. Now add a color to the image that is circling your head. What new qualities have you noticed in your body and imagination?

Centers in the body are also connected to nationalities. The Danes, after the loss of all their international properties, have developed a center in their knees. The French, with their love of kissing, eating, smoking and drinking, incorporated with their guttural language, have their centers in their mouths. The Spaniards have a strong center in the sternum, and Italian centers are in the constant movement of their hands and arms. The Lowlanders, such as the Dutch, who have an extremely strong will force, have their center under the ground. To survive and dodge the rush-hour traffic on Fifth Avenue in New York City, move your center into the hips, the rhythm of the City.

PSYCHOLOGICAL GESTURE: THE TOOL TO REPLACE THE CONTROLLING MIND

As soon as character is in place, it is time for the actor to incorporate *psychological gesture*. Psychological gesture is Michael Chekhov's trademark technique. Because of its popularity, it is also his most abused and misunderstood theory. Psychological gesture is effective and simple, and the inspiration and creative outcome produced by the actor who uses it are fabulous. The best way to approach psychological gesture is to be brave enough to think simply.

Some actors have difficulty understanding and embracing the combination of the two words "psychological" and "gesture" as one concept—psychology, having solely to do with the mental and emotional mind, coupled with gesture, a purely physical abstraction. This confusion creates chaos for the heady or intellectual student. Some students even take it to a deeper fear, by assuming the combination of psychological insight and gesture will open doors into their personal lives, revealing secrets they do not wish to share with the rest of the world. To alleviate this confusion, as a teacher and director I use the term *working gesture*, which was Vakhtangov's term for his concept of the physical body informing the emotional constitution. It is important to note that the work of Vakhtangov, Meyerhold and Stanislavsky inspired the foundation of Michael Chekhov's material, and specifically his use of the term *psychological gesture*.

Psychological gesture is a human faculty that, when understood properly, can be transformed to a powerful tool—working gesture—for an actor onstage and in film. For example, everyone who rides a New York subway uses psychological gesture to navigate through a subway car while avoiding physical contact with strangers. If a threatening individual approaches, the body contracts and immediately imagines itself pushing or pressing the menacing person away to a comfortable distance. Pushing and pressing are among the elements of psychological gesture known as *archetypal gestures*, which include pushing, pulling, throwing, pressing and lifting. If the dangerous-looking person continues to approach, without responding to the contraction and pushing, the body transforms the process into a physical action—running! The body can also do the opposite: it can expand and push or throw its energy to the person before he gets any closer. In real life, of course, if you intuitively feel that there is danger, you should not attempt to push the person away, rather, you should move to a place where you feel safe. However, in the controlled environment of theater and film, you have the freedom to experiment with gestures without the fear of being hurt.

If the scene just described took place on a stage or in front of the camera, the psychological gesture would be vague and lacking in power. That is why it must be boiled down into a specific gesture in which you radiate and incorporate its qualities. This is how a working gesture works, for both theater and film.

ANCIENT KNOWLEDGE

The understanding and knowledge that the body is guided or stimulated by a series of gestures did not originate with Michael Chekhov. It can be found in Tibet in the old Buddhist thangkas (Tibetan spiritual art). The thangkas represent wisdom, compassion and death. Thangka art is comprised of a series of iconic mandala images—circular designs containing concentric geometric forms, images of deities, etc., and symbolizing the universe, totality or wholeness in Hinduism and Buddhism. For example, often male and female characters embrace each other at the center of the thangka, the male figure representing fatherhood and compassion and the female figure signifying motherhood and wisdom. Over the shoulders of the male character hangs an image of an elephant skin, signifying the remembrance of the past, the challenge of human transcendence. The Tibetans say that we as human beings carry our past lives like the heavy skins of elephants, and in order to achieve enlightenment, human beings must move through life without the weight of the past hindering our movements. The image of the elephant skin exists as an archetypical psychological gesture. First it was an image, then it became a body expression, and then written words, which Chekhov describes as "a character entirely attached to an earthly kind of life."

Thangka paintings also contain other human iconographic images, representing attachment, fear of death, jealousy, pride, mental obscuration, greed and anger. These, too, have their own distinct gestures that actors can access when developing a role. Michael Chekhov's work leads to a deep understanding of oneself, because images that can be transformed into gestures exist in the thangkas. I want the next generation of actors to know that in the end, we get to a point in our work where we increase our wisdom and compassion. An actor will find that he is on the path to a deeper incorporation of the character's life if he starts to work with the compassion for his character.

EXPANSION AND CONTRACTION:
THE MOST COMMON AND USEFUL GESTURES

To understand the power of the working gesture, begin with the simple gestures of expansion and contraction, both important exercises for the body's preparation for the stage. In my work, I call expansion an *open gesture* and contraction a *closed gesture*. For the contraction, imagine walking down the street and suddenly running into a person to whom you have owed money for months. The closed gesture that your body takes on is a contraction. On the other hand, imagine that you meet an old friend whom you haven't seen in years. Your body will then take on an expansion, opening up with a light vulnerability.

HURD HATFIELD ON PSYCHOLOGICAL GESTURE

Hurd Hatfield (1917–1998), a famous student of Michael Chekhov, demonstrated psychological gesture at a Michael Chekhov conference in Riga, Latvia, in 1996. Encouraging his students to use as much of the space around them as possible, he said, "Do variations of wide, expressive, simple movements . . . Make them clear and reach out without any tension in your muscles."

Hatfield started to show the power of his gestures, and immediately changed from a frail old man to an energetic, alive character. His eyes radiated youth and passion. Then he spoke of creating what he also called an "open gesture." "Open yourself to an extreme gesture, spreading your arms and your legs wide, and imagine that your body becomes larger and larger . . . and your mind becomes bigger and bigger." He then asked the students to find a neutral position for their bodies. "Do it a couple of times or more, so you start to sense that it works for you. Every time you must put more of your inner being into the open gesture, so you start to understand and sense the *expansion* in your body." At the same time, he inspired his students by also doing the exercise himself. He demonstrated for all of us in his class that age is merely a physical center. The physical body can be marked by the years, but deep inside us dwells life.

Then Hatfield closed himself, crossing his arms across his chest, and knelt down, bending his head down low. He asked his students to imagine that they could become smaller and smaller, like a spiral moving more tightly inside itself until it totally disappears, while the space around them was shrinking as well. He said to use opposite images from those used for the expansion. Then he slowly opened himself up and followed the movement, step by step, until he stood upright in a total expansion. He then advised his students to do it all over again. That was the simplest and easiest step toward understanding working gesture. Actors must practice this exercise often in order to truly be able to utilize its power onstage.

I begin teaching working gesture by asking students to first work outwardly, with the gesture, and then add their text. I then ask the actors to incorporate the sensation of the gesture, but in a neutral body, imagining it ten times stronger than when they did it physically. Then they add their text again. Finally, I ask them to improvise a simple situation with a conflict, or just let the working gestures, contraction and expansion, guide them into actions and conflicts.

OVERALL GESTURE

The *overall gesture* is the gesture you create for the character's objective in the play. Each character has a goal. If the character does not fulfill his objective, he is considered a character in a tragedy; if he succeeds at achieving his objective, the play will have a happy ending. In Ibsen's *A Doll's House*, Nora could have the gesture of trying to get out of a bodysuit of plastic wrap that her husband has wrapped around her since their marriage. Overall gestures turn an intellectual understanding of the character in the play to a direct physical sensation that stirs up the character's actions. Imagine that you have to rush out of your office door, but your boss needs you to take a message immediately. You can't show your boss your frustration, but you are still being motivated by the need to get out of the door. Your overall gesture is heading for the door. Your boss is the obstacle, and your actions in dealing with the obstacle are colored by your overall gesture.

These simple gestures keep your body, and *not* your brain, busy, and the actor who keeps rehearsing with these gestures outwardly will also develop a strong, sensitive body and begin to open up to the understanding of space and time. First, practice these archetypal gestures physically; then, playing with them vocally with text, incorporate both into your character development.

THE ART OF ATMOSPHERE

Step by step, I have described the entrance into the imagination and inspiration. All the preparation in the exercises leads to the final experience, which is often indescribable *atmosphere* and the art of the ensemble.

In his lectures at the Kaunas State Academic Drama Theatre, Chekhov described a significant experience that led to his understanding of atmosphere. Chekhov gave an account of himself as a 40-year-old artist, discovering a new element of theater. Following harsh times in Berlin, Vienna and Paris in 1932–1933, years that included successes and fiascos, Chekhov began working in Berlin with the great German director Max Reinhardt—ironically, one of Chekhov's most unpleasant experiences.

Performances of *Hamlet* were to take place in Vienna, but Max Reinhardt had not scheduled enough rehearsal time, so he assigned Chekhov to perform in a George Abbott and Philip Dunning play, *Broadway* (called *Artists* in Europe), in the role of the husband, Skid. Despite Chekhov's dislike of the rehearsal process, this role was a huge success for him.

In his book *Mikhail Chekhov as Actor, Director, and Teacher,* Lendley C. Black describes an event in Chekhov's performance that drew him further into his search for truth in acting. During a long monologue in the third act of *Artists,* Chekhov was surprised to find that his consciousness was separating from that of the character. He was both performing the character and observing it from the outside. Chekhov, the actor, was personally at ease, while the character, Skid, was experiencing pain. The audience was spellbound, and the other actors were relating to Chekhov more openly than they had in rehearsals. Chekhov watched and gave commands to his character while another part of his consciousness performed as the character. He had complete control over the performance. He also realized his consciousness was influencing the audience. As a result of this split consciousness, both Michael Chekhov's and Skid's entire beings were filled with an incredible power, mesmerizing the audience.

From the Lithuanian lectures we learn that Chekhov was enlightened by his experience. In Lithuania, where he could use his native language and work with students and friends from Moscow, he talked about that brilliant night in Vienna and about the essence of the experience and the power of atmosphere.

In a memorandum written to a student at the Lithuanian State Theatre, Chekhov wrote:

> There exist soulless human beings with cold unexpressive eyes and lifeless facial expressions. They are not present to their surroundings. We only speak to this kind of human being if it is necessary. We do not love them; they are not attractive to us. It is the same with many plays; they are cold, soulless and do not move the audience.

The mechanization of art has been plaguing the theater for generations. The dilemma between the playwright, the director, and the actor consists of a system of training actors and directors to produce a product based on the limitations of psychological time—past and future. The human body and the body of a play both have very specific souls, and in order to reach the complexity of humanity, the artist must not identify with the psychological limitations of the mind. Only then can an artist truly work from his inspiration.[5]

The previous exercises lead an actor into the world of atmosphere. It is, in practice, an image that is incorporated into the body and mind. Technically, an incorporated image starts to create different tensions in the muscles that radiate this special *energy* we call atmosphere.

If a space has been abandoned by human beings for a long time, it is cold and without any atmosphere. A long time ago, I was walking around in a little village in Rumania and suddenly stood in front of an empty building, more or less a ruin. It was not possible to enter, but looking through a little hole in the door, I could see the damaged interior. It was an old synagogue, unused for decades, which had been destroyed by the Communists. It was cold and without any kind of atmosphere.

If I could have entered into the space with my image of the building incorporated inside me, I would have taken over the atmosphere of the room by painting it with my own atmosphere of sorrow and fear. We as human beings paint spaces with our energetic atmosphere, and the more we become aware of painting a space with our personal atmosphere, the stronger we may feel the room or area.

Chekhov continues:

How often do human beings, under influence of atmosphere, act or use words that they bitterly regret afterwards? How often do human beings praise others for their beauty and noble acts? And how often do instant heroes dismiss their actions due to the circumstances of the atmosphere working through them?

The answers to these questions relate not only to life but to the stage as well. Stage Atmosphere is a valuable source of real inspiration for the actor. The actor becomes more expressive, realistic, heartbreaking, and even more wise if he acts in a play where he lets the Atmosphere make the rules of his actions. The Atmosphere inspires the actor; it gives the actor unpredicted color, intonations, movements and feelings.

An actor cannot get closer to accomplishing his or her character without focusing on the atmosphere of the play. No other source can give the actor the full experience of the character except through the use of Atmosphere. If he neglects atmosphere, the actor separates himself from his greatest teacher and the creative process.

The power of using Atmosphere can be deeply experienced for an actor as soon as he realizes that "the Atmosphere has its power to change the content in the words and the mise-en-scène."

When a moment of atmosphere appears in my class or onstage, it won't take long before "something special happens inside the room." We find It together in our work; a curtain is drawn away, and we look through a big window into the future of our art. We look into the new theater. Atmosphere isn't It. Atmosphere is the key into It. During such moments, I have experienced an actual change in the light of the room. With me, the students have been lifted out of their mundane realities. They are no longer students or actors; I am no longer a teacher or inspirer. It is not clear to any of us who is observing whom. Even though a single actor can create It, a strong ensemble can amplify It. The way into It is generated from the Actor's Still Life, characterization and working gesture into atmosphere, and with the help of mask work.

In world theater, the place to find It visualized is in the Balinese dance. Balinese dance exemplifies the maximum gestures a body can utilize to realize the flow of energy that is part of It. In Bali, Michael Chekhov's It is called *Taksu*. Let me attempt to further define It by describing Taksu.

TAKSU AND THE BALINESE EGOLESS THEATRE

In Bali, Taksu can be present in dance, masks or painting. I believe there is no accurate translation of *Taksu*, no Western words that can describe its meaning. The first western visitors who experienced Taksu through Balinese mask work called it "charisma," but this is incorrect. The dictionary definition of "charisma"—"a divinely bestowed power or talent"[6]—does not suggest the sudden flow of ease and light that radiates from the body when Taksu is present. Taksu is not a trance or an altered state of consciousness, but a heightened awareness to form. Like Chekhov, I believe this experience is beyond words.

The recorded lecture of Michael Chekhov's last six-hour master class, *Michael Chekhov: On Theatre and the Art of Acting*, reveals that he too understood that there is a quality in performance, a hidden power in us that we do not embrace: "Deep within ourselves are buried tremendous creative powers and abilities. But they remain unused so long as we do not know about them, so long as we deny them. Although they are beautiful, powerful and wonderful, we are—and this is a disease of our time—we are ashamed of them. And thus, they often remain ignored and lie forever dormant because we do not open the doors to our hidden vaults and fearlessly bring them to the surface."[7]

Antonin Artaud was fascinated by the same hidden power when he saw the Balinese dancers in Paris in 1931. He wrote, "It is certain that this aspect of pure theater, this physics of absolute gesture which is the idea itself and which transforms the mind's conceptions into events perceptible through the labyrinths and fibrous interlacing of matter, gives us a new idea of what belongs by nature to the domain of forms and manifested matter."[8]

In my eighteen years of travel to Bali I have witnessed the phenomenon of Taksu twice. The first occasion was during a shadow-puppet performance by I Wayan Wija and Ida Bagus Anom, who were improvising to entertain some guests in Anom's home. The second occasion was during a visit to Bali's most famous painter, Ida Bagus Made, when he revealed one of his masterpieces, which he had secretly hidden behind an unpainted canvas. My desire to catch more of this rare and beautiful spectacle is one major reason I return to Bali year after year hoping that one day I can bring Taksu into the western theater, with the help of the Balinese masks.

The first time that I experienced what I now understand as Taksu was during a rehearsal of Theatre du Soleil's adaptation of Klaus Mann's novel *Mephisto*. The famous Danish actor Jens Joern Spottag, playing the role of Hendrik Höfgen, gave me my first experience of this great power. In the scene where Hendrik Höfgen takes dancing lessons from his black German lover, there was a moment where Jens's compassion for his character and the other actress, combined with his concentration and precision, allowed him to radiate a sublime energy or quality that made me cry during the rest of the rehearsal. In that moment I felt a release like one feels after a heavy burden has been taken away. That was the only time I had this experience during the rehearsal—although the scene reached perfection of form and timing, it never appeared again. By the time the audience appeared, the actors' good timing and use of legato and staccato produced good performance energy, but there was never Taksu. In that one moment, watching the rehearsal, my artistic instinct told me that this was what I missed in theater and what I would search for until I could incorporate it in my own directing.

When I was directing in Denmark, I referred to Taksu as "energy." I was constantly searching for ways to train my actors to maintain this "energy" for every performance. During rehearsals, I was successful at sustaining this energy, but when the audiences showed up, the actors' lower egos dictated the performances. The "sugar" of the audience fed their egos well, and the more praise they received, the less energy they generated.

Taksu appears spontaneously through any number of rituals. In Bali we see it in religious offerings, which also provide a fantastic atmosphere. Masks and atmosphere complement one another: the stronger the shape and design of the mask, the stronger the impact on our imagination. I have seen pictures of the masks used in the Paris exhibition, and those images were much stronger than the masks used in Bali today. There are only a handful of mask-makers whose handicraft equals that of their ancestors who performed for Artaud. Ida Bagus Anom is one of them. I asked Anom if he did any ceremonies or put any magic in the masks he created for me, and he said that he did not—he believes that his religion and beliefs are not to be exploited by Western intrigue. He said, "I focus on the *art* of the mask, not the magic!" This exchange helped me understand where the strong impact of the masks comes from.

In many cases, the image of the mask replaces the actor's pedestrian self-image with stronger, freeing images. In this sense, the masks "clean the house": they break through the actor's judgmental mind and create an opening for inspiration and imagination. As actors work with these strong images, Taksu may appear.

The Western burden of being raised to value individuality highly creates a huge ego that challenges work with the masks. In the mask work, the ego is knocked down, but it will strike back again and again in its effort to maintain control over the body. There is an aspect of surrender in the image/mask work.

What does Taksu mean for a Balinese dancer? When I spoke to Anom about it, he said that it is sometimes there and sometimes not.

In many dances performed for tourists, there are no signs of Taksu. There is beauty and charm, yes, but not the sublime dance that Artaud had witnessed. What did Artaud see in Paris in 1931? He had his first experience of beauty and form observing a performance exhibition for the gods. He saw ancient metaphysical gestures incorporated into a dance for Balinese deities. He was stunned, unable to decipher the secret behind what he was observing.

This non-individual education of the dancer was unknown to Artaud. The Balinese dancer does not add anything to his ancestors' dance tradition. In fact, the teaching of the special Baris Dance to a little boy can only take place if the boy stands on his father's or teacher's feet, following the traditional dance moves. The small boy's body can barely do what is required, but after many years he will be able to perform even the most complicated details of the dance. Only in this way can Taksu appear in the dance—not through individual artistic expression, for the Balinese believe that everything has already been accomplished by the spirits, so being original does not exist. More expressively, Taksu is found in the Balinese dance exemplifying the maximum movements for the energy of the body, which is the ultimate gesture. The longer the dancer allows himself to move in the dance with the precision of each choreographed posture, the more energy he will gain, until a moment is reached when he begins to radiate the sublime. This is Taksu.

The best artists all have a deep awareness of precision, specificity and form. It is through these qualities that Taksu begins to appear. None of these artists relies on an audience. I recently asked Jens Joern Spottag if he remembered the special rehearsal of *Mephisto*, and he was blank—he did not! The moment-to-moment precision of art is the most important vehicle for the artist, not the benefits or rewards of the product. When the Balinese dancer is finished with his ceremonial dance, he does not bow for the audience, and the audience gives no applause. In Bali, the applause is received from the spirits. The dance is a matter of stamina and spirituality, which leaves no room for egotism. This is also the challenge in the conceptualization of Michael Chekhov's material. It all boils down to understanding form and gesture, qualities, atmosphere and the lower ego.

Michael Chekhov's first nine exercises are all incorporated in this ancient dance, almost as if Chekhov took the dance and separated its movements into nine exercises. Michael Chekhov's work is universal, and does not belong to any specific master teacher, establishment or estate. It belongs to the body.

ENDNOTES/SOURCES

Epigraph:
(Page 104) Norbu, Chögyal Namkhai, *Dzogchen: The Self-Perfected State*, Adriano Clemente, ed., John Shane, trans., Ithaca, NY: Snow Lion Publications, 2000.

1. *Michael Chekhov's Lectures at the Kaunas State Academic Drama Theatre, 1932*, Moscow: GITIS, 1989. Translated by the author.
2. Chekhov, Michael, *To the Director and Playwright*, Charles Leonard and Xenia Chekhov, eds., New York: Harper & Row, 1963; Limelight Editions, 1984, p.14.
3. Author's notes from Deirdre Hurst du Prey master class at the Eugene O'Neill Theater Center, June 1, 1999.
4. Black, Lendley C., *Michael Chekhov as Actor, Director, and Teacher*, Ann Arbor, MI: UMI Research Press, 1987.
5. *Michael Chekhov Lectures at the Kaunas State Academic Drama Theatre*. Translated by the author.
6. *The Collins English Dictionary*, London: HarperCollins UK, 2000.
7. *Michael Chekhov: On Theatre and the Art of Acting*, New York: Applause, 2004.
8. Artaud, Anton, *The Theatre and Its Double*, New York: Grove Press, 1966, p. 62.

RECOMMENDED READING LIST

Black, Lendley C., *Mikhail Chekhov as Actor, Director, and Teacher*, Ann Arbor, MI: UMI Research Press, 1987.

Chekhov, Michael, *Michael Chekhov: Lessons for Teachers of his Acting Technique*, transcribed by Deirdre Hurst du Prey, Ottawa: Dovehouse Editions, 2000. A transcription of eighteen lessons Chekhov gave to du Prey and Beatrice Straight in 1936.

————, *On the Technique of Acting*, Mel Gordon, ed., New York: Harper-Collins, 1991.
This is a new edition of *To the Actor*, with additional material from Mala Powers and an introduction by Gordon.

————, *On Theatre and the Art of Acting*, New York: Applause, 2004.
CD recordings and a companion booklet of six hours of Chekhov's lectures to actors, given in 1955.

————, *To the Actor*, New York: Routledge, 2002.

———, *To the Director and Playwright*, Charles Leonard & Xenia Chekhov, eds., New York: Harper & Row, 1963; Limelight Editions, 1984.

MICHAEL CHEKHOV's American Years: 1935–1955. In 1934, Michael Chekhov arrived in America and spent time in New York, Philadelphia and Boston. In February 1935, he appeared onstage with other Russian emigrant actors. They were announced as the "First American Repertory Season of Modern Soviet Plays and Russian Classics," and renamed the Moscow Art Players by their impresario, Sol Hurok, who hoped they would be mistaken for the original Moscow Art Theatre. The performances were presented over a period of four weeks in New York's Majestic Theatre.

They performed a repertoire of seven plays in Russian. Chekhov performed in Gogol's *The Inspector-General* and *Marriage*, Ostrovsky's *Poverty Is No Crime*, Shkvarkin's *Strange Child*, Bulgakov's *The White Guard* and an Anton Chekhov sketch, *I Forgot*. These productions were extremely successful.

At this same time, Beatrice Straight was looking for someone to create a theater program at Dartington Hall in Devonshire, England. Together with Deirdre Hurst de Prey, Straight had been touring the United States, searching for the right teacher. After they saw Michael Chekhov perform in *The Inspector-General* and Anton Chekhov's one acts, they were convinced that he was the person they needed.

The Chekhov Theatre Studio opened at Dartington Hall on October 5, 1936. There, Chekhov found a place free of commercial pressure where he could develop his technique.

Chekhov's second opportunity to influence American theater came in 1938, after several young male members of the studio joined the British armed forces, and the shadow of war began confusing the atmosphere at Dartington Hall. The students voted to relocate the studio to the United States for the duration of the war. Chekhov intended to bring the studio back to Europe after the war, but he never succeeded.

In January 1939, Chekhov's studio relocated to Ridgefield, Connecticut. The site included one hundred and fifty acres of land with a building large enough to supply large studios, a library, recreation rooms, dormitory rooms for students and a theater. It replicated the beautiful rural setting of the Dartington Hall studio, and was only fifty-five miles from New York City.

The Chekhov Studio's first major production opened on October 24, 1939, at Broadway's Lyceum Theatre. It was an adaptation of Dostoyevsky's *The Possessed*, written and codirected by George Shdanoff, Chekhov's assistant.

After the studio disbanded, Michael Chekhov completed his 1942 version of *To the Actor* with the assistance of Deirdre Hurst du Prey. She had become his personal secretary during their years at Dartington Hall, and had taken notes on every class and lecture at the studio to aid Chekhov as he prepared the book.

Michael Chekhov's last appearance on a New York stage occurred in September 1942. He played in a series of one-acts based on stories by Anton Chekhov, including *The Witch* and *I Forgot*, which he had performed in his American theater debut in 1935.

On October 2, 1942, Chekhov permanently relocated from New York to Hollywood. In 1943, Chekhov played the village patriarch in Metro-Goldwyn-Mayer's *Song of Russia*, directed by Gregory Ratoff, who had persuaded Chekhov to move to Hollywood. The film was released in December of 1944 alongside another Chekhov film, *In Our Time*. Chekhov's next film, *Spellbound*, directed by Alfred Hitchcock, brought him an Academy nomination for best supporting actor.

Among the actors he taught in Hollywood were Ingrid Bergman, James Dean, Gregory Peck, Marilyn Monroe and Yul Brynner.

After his second heart attack, in 1954, Chekhov stopped acting in films but continued to lecture and teach. In 1952, with the assistance of Charles Leonard, Chekhov revised and condensed his original text for *To the Actor*. Harper and Row published it in 1953. On September 30, 1955, Michael Chekhov died of a heart attack at his home in Hollywood.

PER BRAHE is the artistic director of Studio 5. He has been a professional director, writer, actor, teacher and painter since 1967, and has directed more than eighty-five plays throughout the world. He is an internationally known mask teacher and master teacher of Michael Chekhov technique, and an expert in Balinese Mask. He taught at GITIS in Moscow and at the International Summer School in Irkusk, Siberia, and has been an invited master teacher at the Moscow Art Theatre. After teaching and directing throughout Europe and Asia, he discovered a new understanding of mask work, which he has put to dramatic use in his productions and master classes. He is the founding member of the International Michael Chekhov Association. He is an associate teacher at New York University's Tisch School of the Arts, Yale School of Drama and The Actors Center, and has taught at the National Theatre Institute, the New York School for Film and Television and the Bill Esper Studio. In 1991, he founded the Michael Chekhov Studio in Aarhus, Denmark, and in 2000 he was the artistic director for the Michael Chekhov Conference in Siberia. He is the artistic director for the Bali Acting Conservatory.

UTA HAGEN'S TECHNIQUE

Carol Rosenfeld

Aspiring to a "condition of complete simplicity costing
no less than everything."

—T. S. ELIOT, "LITTLE GIDDING"

Uta Hagen's death in 2004 at the age of 84 marked the end of an
era in American theater history. For seventy years, her acting,
teaching and writing inspired friends, fellow actors, audiences and
students. Refusing to compromise in the commercial world, she
demanded respect for the theater and for the art of acting.

Uta Hagen started creating her exercises in the 1940s and '50s
because she wanted to isolate and avoid the pitfalls she encountered
in performance. The '50s were a time when many actors relied on,
and audiences accepted, artificial stage behavior and easily learned
theatrical tricks. Hagen developed a technique that kept her performances spontaneous, always growing and alive. Anyone who had
the opportunity to see her perform the same role more than once
would see a different performance each time. Her performances
always improved over the course of a play's run. Believing that what
she had learned could benefit other actors, she developed and refined
a set of exercises throughout her years of teaching at the HB Studio,
the acting school founded by her husband Herbert Berghof in 1945.

Hagen's technique grew out of three firm principles, which she
outlined in her book *A Challenge for the Actor*: first, "that the basic
components of the characters we play are somewhere within ourselves"; second, "that voice and speech, the soul and the mind, are

not separate from the body but originate from it, emanate through it"; third, that the actor's work must always find its way into action; and fourth, "that everything we do is conditioned by our expectations, and that what actually happens is never totally in tune with them."[1] Most important, she knew that when you have made every detail in the play as specific as it can be, you can let the circumstances of the play *happen to you* and propel you into action. You will have given yourself the necessary belief to be truly alive onstage.

For Hagen, acting was the exploration and discovery of the mysteries that make us human. She challenged herself, as well as her students and fellow actors the world over, to always strive to create characters who were living, thinking human beings with hearts and souls. She required students to fearlessly open their senses to all external stimuli that "induce in us everything from spiritual ecstasy to excruciating pain." To Hagen the five senses were the pathways to the body, mind, heart and soul.

From the moment Hagen's book *Respect for Acting* was published in 1953, it was used far and wide as a basic training text for actors. However, over time she was disappointed in the work of many of the students who had used this text. Hagen's frustration drove her to probe further to correct the misconceptions these actors had distilled from the book and then brought onstage. This led to *A Challenge for the Actor*, a book which really shows the actor *how* to use himself and, at the same time, make the crucial distinction between truth in art and truth in life. Because the technique emphasizes the actor's use of himself, it is essential to stress that this work does not encourage *naturalistic* acting—being "natural" onstage is not the goal of the technique. I mention this because so many students mistake being "natural" for being truthful. They strive to bring the ordinary, irrelevant, trivial and habitual aspects of themselves to their work, when, in fact, truth without meaning has no place onstage. Hagen taught that "reality is theatrical, in the very best sense of the word," and that "there is nothing larger than life."[2] As we are socialized to accommodate the environment in which we are raised, some of us lose our bodies, voices and individuality. We cease to surprise ourselves. Yet when we witness extreme or unusual behavior, we find ourselves saying, "If we saw that onstage, we wouldn't believe it." How sad. What does this say about what we expect to see onstage and our understanding of human behavior? In Hagen's view, "Realism entails a search for *selected* behavior pertinent to the character's needs within the prescribed circumstances of the dramatist."[3] In this collaborative art form called theater, everyone involved—director, playwright, designer and actor—selects what will happen onstage. Naturalistic acting, therefore, is anathema to the art of acting.

Hagen taught that "the theater should contribute to the spiritual life of a nation."[4] For an actor striving to breathe life into every character, shortcuts, tricks and easy answers won't replace dedication to understanding the human condition and human behavior. An actor must have craft and technique. As actors develop their craft, they open their senses, which is the only way they can connect to their physical and psychological perceptions and experiences. Hagen's technique provides the bridge to producing sensations at will in the service of a character onstage.[5]

The six steps and the ten exercises found in Hagen's book *A Challenge for the Actor* form the core of her technique.[6] I hope to entice the reader to study her definitive, articulate book, watch her at work in *Uta Hagen's Acting Class*, and then find a class where the exercises can be practiced. They are incredibly practical and will enrich an actor's work at any level. Beginning actors will be surprised and motivated by how much they learn about themselves, and about human behavior in general, as their powers of self-observation increase. Experienced actors will deeply appreciate how much the exercises stimulate their creative juices when they are working on a specific role or in a classroom situation, and studying the exercises will enable them to practice their craft when they are not working.

I will discuss Hagen's six steps and outline the purpose, preparation, execution and practical application of each exercise. Then I will present guidelines garnered from years of dealing with my students' experiences working on the exercises. I will talk to you, dear reader, as if you were going to be doing the exercises for a class that you are taking.

The following "six steps" can lead you into the world of any scene or play. Eventually, these questions become a part of your being and the basis of your craft. They also provide the structure for Hagen's exercises.

THE SIX STEPS

STEP I: WHO AM I?

Acting students can apply this question to themselves or to their characters in a play.

What is my present state of being? You may be agitated, rushed, energized, exhausted, calm, feeling sorry for yourself, bored, concerned about a friend or your job, lonely, etc. Your present state of being is always the result of the things that are happening in your life and the people with whom you are involved. Your state of being will always be informed by the elements you choose to focus on when you work with the other steps.

I can't count the number of times my students have responded to a critique by saying, "That's the way I am," or, "That's what I do," or, "I wouldn't do that." All three statements close the door to possibility, to surprise and to the discovery of new behavior, and they reveal a total misunderstanding of what it means to use yourself as you try to find identification with a role. All three statements also reflect faulty thinking, because no one acts in a single way at all times, and no one can predict how he or she will behave in the future!

A student who makes such a statement demonstrates a lack of skill in self-observation. I hope that, as you work with the six steps and apply them to Hagen's exercises, you will become more aware of the things that trigger your own behavior. As a human being, you may not realize what you are capable of until life or a role presents you with circumstances that give you the opportunity to learn more about yourself. It stands to reason that, when you have to do things in a play that you have not yet done in the course of your own life, you might feel ill at ease, uncomfortable or downright blocked. When this happens, it is a signal that you have identified the work you have to do.

Self-knowledge is the work of the actor. Acting gives you the opportunity to shed the social mask you wear every day in order to protect yourself as you make your way in the world. In some ways, the work you do on yourself, your instrument, is like peeling an onion, layer by layer. As you remove each layer, you can't help but become more honest with yourself in recognizing and accepting your strengths as well as your weaknesses, imperfections and idiosyncrasies.

Every now and then, stop and ask yourself, "Who am I?" Don't settle for just any off-the-cuff answer. You might close the door on change and growth.

How do I perceive myself? Depending upon your circumstances, you may see yourself as a victim of some situation, as the luckiest person in the world, as misunderstood, or as a great Shakespearean actor. You may think you will never get another job, or that you are cursed, or that you are fat and ugly. You may feel deliciously sexy, or like the loser of all time. You may feel as though you are on your deathbed. Although your perceptions of yourself seem true at the time, they are usually transitory and can vanish in an instant.

What am I wearing? Factors such as the time of day, day of the week and season of the year, where you have come from and where you are going, and your present state of being will determine what you are wearing. What you are wearing also gives you information about your "Who am I?" and how you perceive yourself.

STEP 2: WHAT ARE THE CIRCUMSTANCES?

What time is it? (The year, the season, the day?) Time rules our lives more than anything else. An actor develops a special sensitivity to time, and becomes aware of just how strongly it affects all aspects of life. When researching the era, decade and year in which a play is set, you enter the wondrous worlds of history, geography, science, music, literature, art, politics, social systems, religion and business. This is one reason the world of theater can claim to be the great liberal art that it is.

Answering the following questions will reveal just how crucial time is in influencing human behavior, and how it relates directly to every character you will ever play:

- ☐ What year is it? What decade? What month of the year is it? What season of the year? What is the weather like?
- ☐ What day of the week is it? Is it a holiday?
- ☐ What hour of the day is it?

Playing a character from a time period other than your own is the closest you can come to time travel—moving into the realm of other dimensions, transporting yourself and the audience into some time in the past or the future.

As you enter the world created by the playwright and director, the *given* element of time determines much of the following:

- ☐ Your age and your background
- ☐ Your social status
- ☐ The weather
- ☐ Elements of your physical surroundings (such as whether a room is hot, cold, dark, quiet, stuffy, bright, etc.)

- What you wear
- Your hairstyle
- How you express yourself
- Your vocabulary
- The books you read
- The kind of music you listen to
- Your attitudes toward sex and courtship
- The dances you do
- Your relationships
- Your emotional state of being
- Your physical state of being
- What you have been doing up to this moment
- What you are doing in the immediate present
- Your future plans.

At what time does my selected life begin? This question helps you pinpoint the exact moment your exercise begins, and overlaps with defining your immediate circumstances.

Where am I? In what city, neighborhood, building and room—or outdoor setting—do I find myself?

What surrounds me? What is the immediate landscape, the weather, the condition of the place and the nature of the objects in it?

Place is an essential, far-reaching part of Hagen's technique, because the environment and surroundings in which we find ourselves affect our bodies whether or not we are conscious of it. You can think of time and place as a sensory repository. As your awareness of and sensitivity to the role of time and place in your own daily life grows, it becomes obvious that you must incorporate these elements in your work, because they play the same role in the lives of the characters you create.

Working on place is also one very concrete way of creating a productive rehearsal environment. It does require a willingness to schlep props to class, work out a logical floor plan, and push furniture around when setting up an exercise or scene to present in class. Unfortunately, too many actors skip this work, as if it is incidental or something to address later in their process. It should be one of the first things you establish. As you work on all the exercises, you become adept at setting up your own environment, using the objects that you bring to class as well as those already in the classroom. We emphasize this because, when you are rehearsing a scene or play, *specific* surroundings will feed your senses as you get on your feet.

Remember, human beings do not live in a vacuum. At any given moment, every person on this planet is somewhere specific, surrounded by a multitude of objects. Go to any museum and you find that this has been true since the beginning of mankind.

What are the immediate circumstances? What has just happened, and what is happening? What do I expect or plan to happen next, or later on? You cannot be too specific when creating your immediate preceding circumstances. Make personally meaningful choices. They serve you by giving you an inner occupation that connects you to your past and brings you into the present as you begin any scene or exercise. You may also have an inner occupation related to your future circumstances. When creating your circumstances, be sure that your present always has an immediate, detailed past that you really relate to, and an immediate or not-too-distant future that is also meaningful to you.

STEP 3: WHAT ARE MY RELATIONSHIPS?

How do I stand in relationship to the circumstances, the place, the objects and the other people related to my circumstances? We have a point of view, opinion or feeling about almost everything. Becoming conscious of how you stand in relationship to the circumstances and places in which you find yourself helps you make choices for the situations you create for your exercises. Circumstances may make you feel unsure of yourself, extremely self-confident or deeply disturbed. You may detest the situation you are in, or it could make you feel totally safe and protected. Circumstances can throw you off-guard, make you crazy or energize you. You may be in an environment that you know very well and that holds wonderful or sad memories. You might be somewhere that is new, strange, off-putting, cold, intimidating or foreboding. Becoming conscious of how you stand in relationship to the objects (foreign or familiar) in your surroundings, as well as your own possessions, increases your sensory and emotional connection to every object you handle. Becoming more conscious of the cast of characters in your life and how your relationships affect your behavior helps you become more honest and personal in your work.

STEP 4: WHAT DO I WANT?

What is my main objective? What is my immediate need? Steps 4, 5 and 6 are all related. In fact, all the questions overlap. The consequences of asking one question will have a rippling effect in your work, and lead you to ten more. Remember that, as soon as you define an objective, you must ask yourself what is at stake if you don't achieve it. Decide what stands in your way, and what you have to do to get what you want or need.

STEP 5: WHAT IS MY OBSTACLE?

What stands in the way of what I want? How do I overcome it? Although beginning students often have a hard time identifying obstacles, as you study your own life, you will see that you encounter obstacles all the time—some more difficult to overcome than others. When you encounter obstacles you become animated, physically and emotionally. Your verbal will—your need to speak—increases. Obstacles take many forms; they can come from within yourself or from without. Obstacles cause you to do the many things you do.

Obstacles from Within

- ☐ Your thoughts or ways of thinking, the way you phrase a thought
- ☐ Your habits or obsessions
- ☐ Your personality traits
- ☐ The assumptions you make
- ☐ Your wants and needs
- ☐ Your fears
- ☐ Physical impediments or disabilities; illnesses
- ☐ Mental or emotional disabilities.

Obstacles from Without

- ☐ Things you can't control (people, places and things fall into this category)
- ☐ Natural forces
- ☐ Circumstances or situations in which you find yourself.

An object may have an obstacle built into it (a pen that is out of ink, a pencil with a broken point, a cup of tea too hot to drink, etc.). Other people's resistance, or their pursuit of what they want, can get in the way of what you want. Your own desires and needs, or your own relationship to what you want, can be an obstacle, too. Your very state of being may be an obstacle. A time element may be an obstacle as well.

STEP 6: WHAT DO I DO TO GET WHAT I WANT?

How can I achieve my objective? What's my behavior? What are my actions? Since taking action is at the heart of all acting, the sooner you become oriented to *thinking* in terms of actions, the better. This should become second nature to you. Every time you wonder what you think the character should be feeling, replace that speculation with the question, "What am I *doing* here?" Begin to build your own vocabulary of verbs. Your vocabulary of transitive verbs (verbs that signal some action performed on an object) will become richer and richer. Because your relationship to language is highly subjective, your personal relationship to individual words is a vital ingredient in your selection.

Learn to recognize the difference between the sensations you have when you are sending an action and the sensations you have when you are holding onto an emotion. Never evaluate an action's effectiveness while you are sending it. Always send an action with an expectation of what it will do to the other person and how that person will respond. Any action you send will have been evoked by what has just been done to you by your fellow actor.

When you find that you want to feel something but cannot, you can be sure that you are focusing incorrectly and that you have not found an action to play. Doing is acting. Acting is doing.

During this phase of the work you will undoubtedly become more aware of the actions you habitually choose in your day-to-day life. As an actor you will always be testing new actions—actions that you may never have played or have always dreamed of playing.

At this point, I'd like you to reflect on how fascinating human beings are. We are capable of wondrous and staggeringly beautiful, as well as horrific and unconscionable, deeds. As a student of the craft of acting, you are given the chance to find, create and build both your voice and your body and to use them well. You have the opportunity to discover the glory of language, from Shakespeare to rap, and the breadth of the human condition. You have the chance to find your own humanity.

THE TEN EXERCISES

The ten exercises in *A Challenge for the Actor* are as satisfying and necessary for the actor as scales are for the musician or barre work is for the dancer. Each exercise presents a technique that addresses common, recurring problems you encounter when developing a role or in performance.

When you have done all ten, you can combine them to create more challenging exercises of your own design. This will stretch your imagination and increase your agility.

EXERCISE I: PHYSICAL DESTINATION

It's easy to walk and move like a person when you know where you are, what you want, why you want it, and why you are doing what you are doing. It is easy to talk like a person when you are really in your body.

Purpose

Physical destination refers to every move you make from the moment you come onstage to the moment you leave the stage. It is the exploration of those things that send you from one place to another and determine the logic of your physical life. This exercise provides the foundation for your life onstage, as you discover how your surroundings determine and affect your behavior. With physical destination you establish the roots through which your psychological, physical and verbal life can flourish and become manifest.

Remember that "physical destination" refers to more than where you are going at the end of the exercise. It is not about completing or concentrating intently on an activity.

What You Do

You choose a familiar situation involving familiar objectives such as getting ready for work, for bed or for company, or for going to the gym, the store, or on a date. You could also be coming home from work, shopping or a date. Your objectives may involve morning, evening or weekend routines, or special activities such as wrapping a birthday present, giving yourself a facial, cleaning out and organizing your briefcase, preparing your child's breakfast and lunch box, packing for a weekend trip, mending a garment or mailing out your photo and résumé. Choose a situation in which you pursue that specific objective at a specific time and place for a specific reason. Then select a three-minute section to present in class.

You begin by making an entrance from offstage. You also give yourself a reason to exit briefly and then return to continue what you were doing. The first entrance from offstage requires a specific preparation, so that you can come from your imagined past reality into your created reality onstage.

Planning

I repeat: you cannot have authentic physical destination when you don't know where you are and what time it is. Therefore, use a room in your apartment, dormitory or office as the basis for the floor plan for your scene. On any given day, you use and handle countless objects that end up in various and sundry places in your home or office. What occurred in the day or two prior to your scene to determine where your selected objects are located when you begin? The more detailed and personal you are in setting up your environment, the easier it will be for you to follow through when pursuing your objectives. Once you have selected your objective and planned the surrounding circumstances, be sure to create obstacles you must overcome. If necessary, add and adjust them as you rehearse.

Preparing for any of these exercises involves planning, rehearsal, final selection and testing your work in class. Use the six steps mentioned earlier, and plan ahead. Draw a floor plan of your rehearsal space to take to class to make your setup move smoothly. Bring in as many objects as you need to connect your senses to the space you wish to create. Select those items that you need to pursue your objective, as well as those items that will give you a *sense* of the particular day and hour, and what you have been doing leading up to this moment in time. These items will trigger your faith in your "selected" circumstances.

Clarification: What Actually Happened vs. "Selected" Life

You may think that you are supposed to re-create three minutes of your life exactly as they originally happened. That is not the case.

This exercise is *not* about re-creating anything that has happened to you. Instead, you *use* things that happen or have happened to you as the basis for your exercise, because you can pinpoint, dissect and specifically *know* all the elements you need as you proceed through the six steps. From the moment you decide on the circumstances of your exercise, it will never play the same way twice. As you rehearse, you may have to add an obstacle that didn't exist in your actual life experience. Something else may happen that you decide to include in your surrounding circumstances. Don't try to control your thought process, and you will experience your exercise as if it were happening now for the first time. Your objective and your sense of what is at stake will always keep you on track.

It is normal to have little, if any, awareness of the things you do in everyday life. Your mind is always active, and your waking hours are filled with concerns, thoughts and plans that come out of your past or your anticipated future. Your physical life requires little thought. However, as you work through the exercises, you become more aware and observant of what is normally unconscious behavior. As you rehearse, you will learn to trust the life you have selected, and you will be free to keep the concerns, thoughts or plans related to your given circumstances in your mind.

Rehearsal

The logic of physical action is automatic in your own life, because you are always somewhere specific, amidst specific objects, and you know how long it will take to perform a task or reach a destination. In rehearsing your exercise, experiment with keeping your selected life totally organic within the three-minute limit. By organic, I mean that you don't edit out moments of behavior that are true to what you are doing. For instance, if you want hot water, you may have to stand at the sink for the few seconds it takes for the water to get hot.

You may find that your first rehearsal lasts twenty minutes. After you make a decision about the moments within those twenty minutes when your exercise begins and ends, it may last only five minutes. Eventually, after working on physical destination in class several times, you will learn how to arrive at an organic three-minute scene. Be careful not to try to squeeze what would normally take you twenty minutes to do at home into a three-minute exercise for class. Even if you create a circumstance in which you are in a hurry, you won't be able to reduce twenty minutes into three. The three-minute limit is an important factor, as it intensifies your experience and insight into each exercise.

Practical Application

As you work on physical destination, as your consciousness of your own behavior grows, and as you start to understand what animates your body, you become skillful at sourcing and motivating truthful behavior onstage. You will be able to justify, motivate and fulfill a director's direction. You will have a technique that helps you solve the problems that arise in rehearsal.

EXERCISE 2: THE FOURTH SIDE

Some people mistakenly think that the fourth side, or fourth wall, is something that separates the actor from the audience. But Hagen taught that "ideal communication between actor and audience occurs when the actor is intensely alive, physically and psychologically involved in fulfilling his character's needs, in action—*within* the magic circle of his playing area."[7] Since the actor's super-objective is communication, having a wall—even an imaginary one—between the actor and the audience would be absurd and counterproductive.

Purpose

This exercise gives you the ability to remain focused and involved in the circumstances of the play, yet completely open to the audience. You extend your faith in your environment to include the area in the theater where the audience is sitting. Since you will be talking in this exercise, you must deal with verbal actions, your verbal will, and the process of sending and receiving.

What You Do

You create circumstances in which your main objective comes from a phone call that you either make or receive. You have a meaningful need for being on the phone, and *you* have the primary objective, even if you are receiving the call. You are the leader of the scene. You may need to vent about some recent experience, get reassurance from someone close to you, make arrangements with a manipulative relative, complete a business transaction to your satisfaction, call your mom to wish her a happy birthday, gossip with a friend, console your cousin after the death of her father, etc. You will find it easier to identify your obstacles as you work on this exercise.

Practice this exercise until you experience the exhilarating freedom this technique provides.

Planning

Plan your environment with the same detail you used in the physical destination exercise. Once you decide which wall in your room will serve as your fourth side, indicate it by noting where your teacher and class sit on your floor plan. Create complete surrounding circumstances that may or may not be related to the phone call.

Use your personal phone calls as research: be mindful of your own behavior during every actual phone call you make or receive during the week before you take your exercise to class. At first, practicing and making adjustments so that you can rest your eyes on the fourth side will feel artificial and unnatural. You will have some moments when you don't hear what the person on the other end of the phone is saying, because you will be abnormally self-aware, thinking about the fourth side exercise. You will also discover that, during a normal phone call, you rarely notice your behavior (unconsciously doodling, sipping a beverage or fiddling with objects that are near you), because your attention is on hearing the other person's voice and contributing to the conversation. Little by little, you will become accustomed to giving your undivided attention to the phone call itself, while using the fourth side subliminally.

This exercise is as much about listening as it is about talking. Remember: you listen and receive what is being said in relation to what is going on in your own life at the time. Your responses are triggered by what the person on the other end of the phone says or does. Your responses will also be a result of feelings triggered by the subject matter, what you are trying to achieve and the obstacles you encounter. As you talk, you will be seeing your surroundings subliminally, and you will handle objects with minimal awareness of what you are doing.

Rehearsal

Once you have chosen your circumstances, unplug or turn off your telephone and rehearse with the dead receiver. As you practice, keep the image of the person you are talking to in your mind. Hear the voice in your mind's ear. Don't try to hear every word said to you. Instead, listen for the content and intent behind the words. Be open to what the person is *doing* to you (the tone of voice will affect you), and let yourself respond freely.

Be truthful about your side of the conversation. Don't add or repeat information in order to make your conversation clear to the audience. They will draw their own conclusions about the subject matter from your behavior.

Don't script or memorize your conversation. If you know what you want to achieve, your objective will keep you on track while you remain verbally improvisational. Avoid saying the same things in the same way every time you practice.

The key to executing this exercise successfully is *the position of your body*, because it will determine your ability to use the fourth side *effortlessly*. Dealing with the fourth side (the area where the audience sits) will be an adjustment for you. Therefore, as you rehearse, pay attention to the position of your body when you are sitting or standing. Obviously, if you bend over, you will see the floor, patterns on the rug, etc. If you sit back in a chair, you will look straight ahead and see photos and pictures hanging on the wall. If you lie on your back, you will see the light fixture and water stains on the ceiling. You want to find physicality that makes it *inevitable* for your eyes to land on objects on the fourth side.

If you find yourself concentrating on the fourth side excessively, or making the slightest effort to look in that direction, temporarily *disoblige* yourself from using it.

In Class

Be sure that your phone call is thoroughly rehearsed.

After you have set up your environment, take the time to set up your fourth side in your classroom or theater by mentally anchoring your imagined objects on the back wall *behind* the audience. Anchor your imagined objects on actual parts of the walls that you can easily see in your classroom or theater. These might be exit signs, pipes, the light booth, etc. Do this even if the wall you are using in your apartment is only two feet or less from where you are sitting. *Do not* place your fourth side in the air or space between the stage and the audience. If you do that, you eliminate having concrete objects upon which your eyes can *rest*. If you can't rest your eyes on fixed objects, you will not be *grounded* or *in your body*. Using the wall behind the audience provides an actual surface upon which to hang your imagined objects. Assume that your selected objects *are* where you have mentally anchored them and you will instantaneously experience the sensation of being in your own home. Just *knowing* where your objects are is sufficient. When one object flashes in your mind's eye, the whole wall will fall into place.

Also, give yourself more than one imagined object, so that you don't fixate on any single spot on the fourth side. Do this exercise until you feel you have experienced the ease of being open and private onstage. Remember not to *make* yourself look out at the fourth side. The slightest effort coming from trying to use the fourth side becomes a *forced moment*. Play your actions as if you were at home, and if you don't use the fourth side during your exercise, so be it. You will the next time.

Practical Application

Apply this exercise to all your scene work by setting up your fourth side before you begin every scene. Also, when you have a phone call in a play, remember to be as specific as you are in your own life. Make the person on the other end of the phone someone you know. Craft what the other person is saying so that it motivates the lines the playwright has given you.

If you are directed to *open out* to the audience, using the fourth side correctly will also prevent you from cliché posing. Most importantly, extending the reality of place to include the audience will allow you to be free, open and involved, and when you are, you invite the audience to enter the world of the play.

EXERCISE 3: CHANGES OF SELF, PART ONE

Purpose

This exercise is an almost foolproof and exhilarating way to learn more about the variety and sources of your own behavior, and to see how quickly you can change or tap into a different side of yourself. You will become acutely aware that you treat people differently depending on who they are, your history with them, how they are treating you, what you want from them and what else is going on in your life. You will have a more penetrating sense of your relationships, and you will also discover that no relationship is ever in a state of stasis.

What You Do

In this exercise, you make or receive three phone calls to or from three different people. Choose three people who cause your behavior to change drastically when they interact with you. Your selected circumstances should be unrelated to the phone calls. Make sure the changes that happen to you are because of the person and not the situation. You could be calling your father to ask him for money, but first have to deal with your five-year-old nephew because he answers the phone; then, while you are talking to your father, your girlfriend calls you on your cell phone. You could be calling your agent to find out why you haven't been sent up for a particular role, but have to talk to his secretary first; you might then call your best friend to tell him what happened. Regardless of whether you succeed or fail, really know what you want to achieve when you speak to each person, and determine whether you are the leader or follower during each call. The three-minute time frame forces you to select circumstances through which you will experience just how varied your own actions can be. Do this exercise many times, to explore the relationships in your life and build a stockpile of potential transferences to use in building your future characters' relationships.

One student who was working on this exercise created circumstances in which he had just received good news. As he talked on the phone, he had the same attitude with all three people. He wasn't enthusiastic, and his behavior didn't change when he spoke with each person. During the critique, he explained that in his life, when he received good news, he tried to stay cool and not get too excited. He had made a generalization about himself and his behavior, and his choice of staying cool had made it impossible for impulses to manifest in action, verbally or physically. He would have had much more fun if he had crafted such good news that he simply couldn't contain himself. Then, his enthusiasm would have been a helpful obstacle. My student needed to create more imaginative personal circumstances with more at stake. He needed to choose three people who affected his own behavior in different ways. He might have had a friend with whom he was completely open and free, whom he knew would be thrilled with his news because he had shared all the events leading up to this moment. He could then have received a call from a fellow student who had upset him by canceling too many previous rehearsals. He could have then called his father, who never liked to talk about anything personal. My student had instead settled for an *unchallenged idea* that he had about himself.

I hope that this story illustrates how the concept of using self in one's work can lead to serious confusion in the student actor. The confusion stems from the fact that most of us start with, and often hold on to, a rather narrow perception of ourselves. Using yourself doesn't mean that you remain true to *uninvestigated* or *unchallenged* ideas of who you think you are. Nor does it eliminate the use of your *imagination*. As an actor, you must relish imagining yourself in hundreds of situations that you may not have actually experienced. It is inevitable that the circumstances in the wide range of plays that you encounter will push you into areas of behavior that you have never experienced before. You must crave living through the experiences that any play provides and have the courage to discover your latent, or not-so-hidden, desires, drives and needs.

Practical Application

Through this exercise you learn how quickly your actions can change, and also see how your interactions with people strongly determine what actions you play. This exercise is a good way to begin developing a treasure chest of endowments for future use when creating relationships in a scene or play. So, what is an endowment?

ENDOWMENT: THE MAGIC "AS IF"

We begin endowing people at a very early age, and will probably continue to do so even after we become more mindful of this unconscious habitual activity. An endowment is the investment of an object with a quality that it does not possess. In other words, you treat the object "as if" it did possess that quality. You see a person and you jump to a conclusion about him because of his appearance or his behavior. Your conclusion deepens or shifts when you hear his voice, his speech or his accent. As you become more familiar with the person, depending upon who you are, what you want and the situation you are in, you may hold on to your first impression. It may get stronger, or it may vanish. These impressions will generate a whole set of expectations whenever you hear about or have to be with that person. In everyday life, our opinions, the assumptions we make, the suspicions we have about other people, or the circumstances in which we find ourselves determine our expectations.

Endowments of people fall into six categories: fact, opinion (which we often hold as fact), suspicion, speculation, assumption and expectation.

- Opinion: *That man is really stupid.* _____ *is a fantastic actor.*
- Fact (as you perceive it): *The speaker had a fabulous sense of humor and was very self-assured. The man sitting next to me has bad breath.*
- Suspicion: *I think my friend is on the verge of a nervous breakdown.*
- Speculation: *I might be able to convince my husband to go with me, even though he doesn't want to.*
- Assumption: *You think I am wrong. You want me to back down.*
- Expectation: *My boss is going to have a fit when I get to work late again. The party is going to be dreadful.*

Isn't your mind filled with these types of thoughts? Can you see how they affect your relationships? Your feelings about someone you know, someone you want to know, or someone you have known can totally determine how you see that person and then, consequently and most importantly, how you behave when you are with that person.

Endowment is a powerful tool for the actor. It is a way of getting your attention off of yourself and onto your fellow actors. You can use this tool to develop your relationship to each character in a play. It will strengthen your emotional connection to things you see, hear, touch, smell and taste. It will free you into action.

Try experimenting with endowments when you want to:

- Strengthen some aspect of a relationship
- Have a more specific emotional connection to your partner
- Motivate your actions.

Slowly but surely you will find endowments that engage you, that *affect* you. Finding endowments that have meaning for you will enrich your work as an actor.

EXERCISE 3: CHANGES OF SELF, PART TWO

By the time you come to this exercise, you will be using yourself more fully and fearlessly. Your insights will be sharp, clear and stimulating. You will be making choices that you are eager to test.

Purpose

Changes of Self—Part Two is about how clothing can affect a real change of self. You continue discovering and revealing different sides of yourself. You will see that you role-play all the time.

You instinctively select what you wear depending upon how you want others to perceive you or what you want to accomplish. Your clothes have an impact on how you feel about yourself and how you move. Your sense of touch—your skin—will be the conduit through which your physical and psychological perceptions lead to very specific behavior.

What You Do

In this exercise, you are almost finished getting dressed for an event. You could be going to an important audition, a formal dinner party, a Fourth of July cookout, a fancy dress ball, a rehearsal or your weekend soccer game. You could be getting ready to go to the theater, getting ready for a hot date, preparing for a cozy evening at home with a good book after a hard day at work or getting dressed to go jogging.

Planning and Rehearsal

Make sure your goals are clear and personal, so that you have motivated your need for the particular garments and accessories you select—shoes, underwear, jewelry, etc. Notice how your shoes change how you walk. How will you wear your hair? See which outfit pulls everything together for you and gives you the feeling and *look* you set out to achieve—your change of self.

You may not be happy with the result, because you may feel unattractive or less than perfect. These are sides of yourself as well. You should avoid using a mirror as the primary source for measuring your success, since it allows your eyes to dominate and makes you step out of your body to evaluate your achievement with too much objectivity. You want your body to feel and respond to the clothing you are wearing. Evaluate your progress by *sensing* how the garments affect you physically and psychologically.

Practical Application

Working on this exercise will make you more responsive to the costumes you are given when you are working on a role. Train yourself to think of the garments that you wear in a play not as costumes, but as your character's clothing. Since it is your responsibility to be able to wear all types of clothing, be aware of the texture, weight and color of the fabrics from which the garments are made. Then see how you move in them and how they make you feel. Your goal is to wear your costumes in a play as freely and specifically as you do your own clothing.

EXERCISE 4: MOMENT TO MOMENT

Purpose

With this exercise, you probe your emotional life and learn to trust the sources of your emotions. Emotion fluctuates wildly and is a consequence of the circumstances in which you find yourself. You don't plan when you are going to get angry, cry, laugh or scream, nor do you plan how long those feelings will last. You get emotional when circumstances come together in very specific, meaningful ways, and your expectations are either realized or not realized.

What You Do

For this exercise, you create circumstances during which you have an immediate need to search for a lost or misplaced object. This can be any object you frequently misplace—your keys, paychecks, checkbook, credit cards, eyeglasses, pieces of jewelry, a phone card, driving directions, addresses, phone numbers, theater tickets, airplane tickets, etc. But it must be one of great value to you, and/or one that you need in order to follow through with your immediate plans. Not being able to find this object will evoke strong emotions. What is at stake if you don't find it? Make sure that you know what consequences you face if you don't find the lost object within the next few minutes, and how you feel about them. As always, the time limit on the exercise illuminates your behavior under duress.

Rehearsal

As you rehearse your exercise, keep the image of the object in your mind. Really look in each place where you think it may be. Have at least five specific places where the object should or could be. Discover how something in one moment leads you to the next moment. Even on the way to looking in one place, you may change your mind and look somewhere else first. You have to bring enough materials to class that you can execute this exercise with total faith. For instance, if one of the places you are going to look for the lost object is in a drawer, you should plan to fill the drawer with the things you have in that drawer at home. If you don't, when you open the drawer, find it empty, and wave your hand around in it, you will merely be illustrating looking for something. If you have your own objects in the drawer, you can *really* look for the object with the expectation of finding it, and have an outlet for the impulses that move in on you when the object isn't there. Real physical obstacles and actions trigger real emotional responses.

Here is an example: you are ordering theater tickets on the phone and need to give your credit card number to the person taking your order. You go to get the card out of your wallet, only to discover that it isn't there. Your anxiety level skyrockets as you jump to imagining the worst—some stranger is on a spending spree with your card! You ask the agent to hold on, and you go to the sweater you wore the day before yesterday. You vaguely remember wearing it when you last used your card. You let out a groan, because your life has been crazy the last few days, and the sweater is under a pile of clothes that have been accumulating on your floor. You pick up the sweater, reach into one pocket—no card. You reach into the other pocket—no card. You moan and then curse as you drop the sweater back onto the floor, and your mind is already directing you back to your wallet, because that is where the card *should* be. It still isn't there. You realize the person is still on the phone, but who cares about theater tickets—you have to find your card, or make sure no one uses it! You go to back to the phone, cancel your order and slam the phone down. All you can think of is how this is going to inconvenience you, just when you don't need one more inconvenience in your life. You go to your backpack and dump everything out, search every pocket and then go to your day planner to get the phone number of the credit card company. You plop down on the chair and, as you reach for the phone, you see the credit card sitting on top of a stack of papers, where you had put it to have it ready when you purchased your tickets. With a sigh, you pick up the phone to call Telecharge again.

Remember, your faith in your imaginary circumstances is greatest at the moment you take an action. Therefore, if you really look for the object with the expectation of finding it in each place it could be, you will believe that it is lost.

Practical Application

This exercise will train you to think in terms of your *doings*, your *actions*, as opposed to your *feelings*. We usually remember how we felt during important events, but can't recall the specific things we *did*. My students are happy when they *feel* something onstage and often think (until shown otherwise) that those feelings were the be-all and end-all of their work. They then try to *hold on to* those same sensations again and again. Remember that the actor's work must always find its way into action. So focus on what you *did*, not on what you *felt*. It is imperative that you learn how to keep your emotional life free and moving forward. This is scary, because there is always the possibility that sensations won't move in on you in the same degree of intensity at the same moment every time. Be aware that when you try to repeat an emotion you experienced in a real event or rehearsal, having that same emotion becomes your objective and prevents you from playing actions in the immediate present. While working on this exercise, you will discover the kinds of choices that have meaning for you. You will also learn how to stay in the moment, trusting that you don't have to anticipate or think about the next moment, or feel the need to *set* or *push* for any degree of emotion. You will find that, every time you rehearse, you will be alive to the impulses that move in on you, and your work will be lively and fresh.

EXERCISE 5: RE-CREATING PHYSICAL SENSATIONS, PART ONE — ENDOWING OBJECTS

Purpose

This exercise leads you to a detailed sensory exploration of objects and sharpens your reflexes and physical agility. Through it you learn to set expectations that keep you from anticipating what is coming next. Remember, an endowment is the investment of an object with a property that it does not possess. In this exercise, you practice endowing inanimate objects, which, if real, could control you onstage. Before you select the particular qualities you are endowing, you will have to explore all the ways in which the object can impact your senses and affect your behavior.

What You Do

For this sensory exploration exercise, choose five objects to endow. You can choose mind- and body-altering substances such as alcoholic beverages (ginger ale for champagne, tea for scotch, water for gin and vodka, etc.), drugs and the paraphernalia that goes with them (oregano for marijuana, etc.) or medications (little candies for pills, cranberry juice for cough syrup, etc.). You can endow objects found in the kitchen, like water for oil; you can endow a dull knife with sharpness and pretend to cut yourself. You can endow seeing and killing cockroaches, flies or mosquitoes that aren't really in your space. You can endow easy-to-open jars with stuck lids, light suitcases with heavy contents, an empty vase with water that you spill, or dry umbrellas and clothing with rainwater. Once again, the list you can choose from is quite extensive.

Do this exercise until you can endow objects with total faith. Then apply the technique to your scene work.

Planning and Rehearsal

You are also practicing how not to anticipate by giving yourself a series of ordinary sensory expectations. For instance, if you are going to be endowing sour milk, you assume that it is perfectly fine and treat the action of getting the milk out of the fridge, pouring it and then drinking as you normally would. Practice until you are genuinely preoccupied with thoughts or images coming from your surrounding circumstances. If your expectation is that the milk is fine, and your thoughts are on other things, you will be surprised by the horrid taste and spit it out immediately, or hold the sour milk in your mouth as you to rush over to the sink. As you spit it out, you see a centipede in your sink and reach for a paper towel so that you can squash it. You might then have the lingering discomfort from the taste as you empty the carton into the sink and toss it into the trash can. You might even brush your teeth to get the nasty taste out of your mouth. Make sure that you can follow through on all your physical actions.

Practical Application

Certain events that take place in a play should not be real. Think about the times you have been in a theater when there was real running water onstage, or bacon was really being cooked, and you could smell it. What happened? You became occupied with wondering how they got the water to come out of the faucet, or your sense of smell took over and you didn't hear what the actors were saying. This is why the skill of re-creating physical sensations is important: it allows the actor to perform using objects that, if real, would have the potential to interrupt the action of the play or distract the audience.

EXERCISE 5: RE-CREATING PHYSICAL SENSATIONS, PART TWO — CONDITIONING FORCES AND PHYSICAL STATES OF BEING

Purpose

Conditioning forces are those sensory conditions that naturally come from a specific time and a specific place. We respond to these conditions reflexively and they affect us physically and psychologically. You must learn how to imagine and incorporate conditions that a playwright might require in a scene, such as darkness, quiet, stuffiness, extreme cold, etc.

Playwrights call for *physical states of being* as well, and you will have roles that require you to be drunk, hot, cold, nauseous, sweaty, dirty or tired. You may also have an ailment, such as the flu, a hangover, a headache, etc. Working on this exercise will help you find the physical adjustments you have to make to accommodate these physical states.

What You Do

You create total surrounding circumstances where there are three conditions that influence your behavior. For example, you could choose such conditions as quiet, a cold room, and a sprained ankle as part of your circumstances.

Planning

These steps may help you develop a physical state of being:

1. Remember the last time you experienced the condition.
2. Was it pleasurable or painful? Write a paragraph describing it in as much detail and as vividly as possible. Sometimes graphic images from TV commercials

can be helpful, such as a hammer pounding the actor's head to indicate an excruciating headache or a rope snapping to show tension.

3. Pinpoint the exact location of the physical condition. If you feel it in different parts of your body or if it is an overall sensation, pinpoint the area from which it emanates. For instance, if you are tired, perhaps your eyelids feel like heavy weights. From there you might feel it in your shoulders or your arms, and later in the stiffness in your neck.

4. What do you do to relieve the condition? Internally, do you contract into it, pull away from it, try to get over it or under it? Externally, do you make a cup of coffee to wake yourself up, splash cold water on your face, massage your temples?

Planning and Rehearsal

Create normal surrounding circumstances in which you have three conditions that affect the way you pursue your objective. After you have chosen the conditions for your exercise, practice by giving yourself the conditions at different times during the normal course of your day. Give yourself each condition when you are making your bed, taking a shower, standing in line at the grocery store or riding on the subway. As you work with one condition at a time, break it down to see what happens to you when you bend over, turn quickly, try to pick something up or sit down. What adjustments do you have to make to overcome the obstacles created by your selected condition?

After you have meticulously explored the conditions, set up the circumstances for your exercise. Begin with the condition that is the easiest for you; in this case, that could be the cold room. Then add the next (your sprained ankle) and, finally, the third (quiet). Do not try to hold on to all three simultaneously. Because the brain can only receive one message at a time, let your attention flow from your surrounding circumstances to the different sensations and thoughts coming from your choices. Make sure you give yourself maximum obstacles. For instance, if you have a sprained ankle, don't simply sit with your foot elevated during your entire exercise. If your objective doesn't require physical destination, you won't really be able to test having a sprained ankle. As you rehearse, create a circumstance where you get distracted by something else, forget about your foot, and then put your weight on it. You then reflexively scream and curse, as you shift your weight to your good leg to release the pressure and shooting pain around your ankle.

Practical Application

When you are working on a play that calls for a condition of any kind, begin working with it as soon as possible. If the writer has done his job, the text will *only* make sense with the condition as part of the circumstances. You may also intuitively feel that your character could have a condition not specified in the text that will strengthen your involvement in the circumstances of a particular scene.

EXERCISE 6: BRINGING THE OUTDOORS ONSTAGE

Purpose

Many plays are set outdoors or contain scenes that take place outdoors. With this exercise, you practice the technique of creating behavior that automatically occurs as a result of being outdoors. You apply sensory recall to provide the elements of nature that cannot be provided by the set designer.

What You Do

You set up a physical destination exercise which may take place on a front or back porch, in a yard, on a street corner, in a parking lot or a park, on a beach or a mountaintop, etc. You must have some purpose for being where you are. For instance, you may go to the park to do the Sunday *Times* crossword puzzle on a warm spring day. You have a carryall with a thermos of coffee, the newspaper, your puzzle dictionary, a pencil case with some pencils, an eraser and a pencil sharpener, a blanket and suntan lotion just in case the sun is strong enough for sunbathing. In the park, you encounter damp grass, lumpy ground under your blanket, and a cool, gentle breeze.

    I recommend that you go to a real location to *research* your place. With this exercise in mind, you will see many more details in the environment. What is overhead? What is underfoot? What is directly before you? What do you see in the distance? How far can you see? What is to your right and left? What is behind you?

When you go to your class, be sure to set up four "fourth sides" by anchoring the fixed elements in your selected surroundings (trees, the sun, clouds, moon, stars, paths, buildings and so on) on the fixed elements on the walls of your studio or theater. Endow all the other elements of your selected surroundings, such as hot sand, rocky soil, soft grass, a damp bench or muddy ground. The time will influence the weather and temperature in your given circumstances. It may be cold, chilly, windy, bright and sunny or hot and humid. Depending upon these conditions, you may be shivering or perspiring. You may have to deal with a persistent mosquito, ants or a bee.

Make choices that really affect your behavior, so that you can discover how nature moves in on you and what you do when it does. Once again, you will discover that you believe you are outside when you find your actions. Make sure you rehearse being outdoors *indoors* before you bring your exercise to class.

Practical Application

Apply what you learn as you do this exercise to the scenes and plays that take place outdoors.

EXERCISE 7: FINDING OCCUPATION WHILE WAITING

Purpose

Since so many plays do not use completely realistic settings, the actor must have a technique that gives him faith in his environment even when he is on an empty stage. You do not need furniture or many objects surrounding you to be fully occupied with forward-moving inner life coming from your given circumstances. You won't be stranded in limbo on an empty stage once you have mastered this technique.

What You Do

In this exercise, your immediate objective is waiting for a subway, bus, train, or maybe a friend. You set your exercise in a subway or train station, at a bus stop, or at an appointed meeting place, and you create four fourth sides, anchoring objects from your selected environment on fixed elements in your classroom or theater. You know what is behind you, to your right, to your left, and in front of you. You give yourself a strong preceding or future circumstance, so that you know where you are coming from and where you are going. Your immediate preceding circumstance could be that you just had a lousy audition, you were treated rudely when you went to your agent's office, you ran into someone you haven't seen in a year, you just bought a dress on your credit card that you shouldn't have, and so on. When you present this exercise in class, you will have the sense of really being where you say you are, and your faith in your circumstances will be strong.

Planning

Practice this exercise in the same way that you practiced the outdoors exercise. Paying close attention to the details of your surroundings, go to a real location to do your research. Throughout the week, observe your behavior while you are waiting for a bus, train or friend. Notice the pattern of your thought process and how your attention moves from outer to inner objects.

Rehearsal

Even though waiting is your main objective, your inner occupation will give you a forward-moving life strong enough to prevent the audience from intruding on your privacy. Your clothing and your inner objects will provide you with the means for staying active and alive. You might notice a piece of lint on your coat and remove it, step to the curb to see if the bus is coming, reach in your pocket for a handkerchief, check your watch to see what time it is and wonder if you should call ahead. As you work on this exercise, you will see how you are rarely alone—in your mind, that is. You are always thinking about something or someone—resolving an argument, thinking of what you should have said to a friend who has a problem, or reviewing a funny story you just heard. You might notice that your feet hurt, or that the sky is beautiful, or you might have a hunger pang and remember that you haven't eaten recently.

Practical Application

Once you have done this exercise, you will understand how essential it is not to set your thought process when you are working on a script. You have to keep developing and personalizing the meaning of your circumstances—past, present and future. When you successfully complete this exercise, you discover that you could be onstage indefinitely and the audience would never get ahead of you.

Purpose

There are so many plays, contemporary and classical, in which a character stands alone onstage, talking to himself. The actor must find the character's need and purpose for talking to himself. Before you apply this exercise to text, you should find out when and why you talk to yourself when you are alone. Even if you think you don't talk to yourself, you will begin to do so once you start working on this exercise!

What You Do

Hagen breaks down the ways you talk to yourself, explaining in detail how the underlying reason for talking out loud when you are alone is to gain control over something that is going on in your life. As you work on this exercise you will become aware of moments when you speak to yourself. When something isn't working out, you will probably use expletives to curse an object, yourself, or the world. When you want to make sure you remember what you have to do on a busy day, you may itemize tasks out loud. You may also talk to yourself when circumstances cause you to comment on your own behavior, criticizing or praising yourself, or when you want to nudge yourself along, cheer yourself on, or badger and bully yourself into doing what you have to do. I find that I always talk to myself if I enter a room and come to a dead stop because I can't remember what I was going to do there. I then give myself directions and reassure myself that if I return to where I started, I may remember what I was after in the first place. You may also play games in order to entertain yourself when you are bored. Choose circumstances to test these kinds of talking to yourself before you go to the next step.

Most monologues occur when a character is in crisis. He will talk to himself as he seeks control over his frustrations by trying to solve a problem. Before you begin to work on monologues, become familiar with the process of talking to yourself by creating circumstances that will provoke your need to speak out loud. You need a strong immediate preceding, present or future circumstance to trigger your need to talk out loud.

Make choices that have meaning for you: your neighbor may have just complained about the noise you make when you rehearse. You may have just been fired. You may just have heard that you are going to be flown out to the West Coast to test for a major film. You may have been invited to the Metropolitan Opera for New Year's Eve. You may be feeling depressed on the day of an important audition, and unable to find anything to wear that makes you feel confident. You may be preparing to see a friend or relative with whom you have had a painful argument. You may be having trouble with your computer, and have been kept on hold with the support system for twenty minutes. The possibilities are endless.

Planning

As you begin to plan your exercise, you will discover what makes you talk to yourself when you are alone. You will discover that, as Hagen wrote, "the thoughts you voice are only part of your thought process," because "while uttering one thing, your mind is racing with other nonverbal thoughts related to the circumstances."[8]

Rehearsal

Be sure to have complete surrounding circumstances. Don't build the exercise only on the words. Ask yourself what else you are doing under those particular circumstances.

Do not feel that you have to tell the whole story so that the audience understands what is happening.

Find the truth of talking to yourself. You do not need to speak in whole sentences. Hagen warned students not to plan or organize their words and thoughts, because "they have little *external* logic or sequence. They have the *inner* logic arising from their connection to the circumstances."[9]

Let the real outer objects and the visualized inner objects source your responses. If you find that you are repeating certain phrases every time you rehearse, avoid saying them unless they are genuinely provoked.

Practical Application

This technique should be applied to all soliloquies, in either a contemporary or a classical play.

EXERCISE 9: TALKING TO THE AUDIENCE

Purpose

Playwrights often direct actors to address the audience. This exercise helps you talk to the audience without having to step out of character or disrupt the created reality of the play. When you have a speech directed to the audience, the audience becomes your partner. You will learn what you need to do to believe that the audience belongs in the world of the play.

What You Do

You create circumstances where you tell the story of a play, novel or film, recount a dream, gossip about an acquaintance, vent about a personal experience, or reminisce about or analyze a past event in your own life. Choose someone you know who would be the right person for you to be talking to about the subject matter you select. You place that person in the area where the audience is sitting. In your mind you visualize the extended part of your own room where the person is sitting. Because you know the person to whom you are speaking, you also know the specifics of why you are telling this particular story at this particular time, and how you expect it to be received.

Rehearsal

Make sure that you give yourself complete surrounding circumstances, and that your physical life is unrelated to your verbal objective.

Decide if you are in the middle of your story or if you are just launching into it. If the latter is the case, what sparked the need for you to talk now?

Become more mindful of what you do when you talk to someone. Experiment with telling a friend the story of a movie you just saw. You will probably find yourself looking away in order to contact the inner objects that flow from the subject matter.

When you practice and present the exercise in class, do not keep looking at the person to whom you are speaking. Remember that you only look at the person you are speaking to intermittently, to see if they are getting what you are saying, or when you want to be more emphatic.

Don't expect a response from the other person.

Place the person you are talking to near a member of the audience, but in such a way that you don't have to worry about making eye contact with anyone sitting in the audience.

Be careful not to script or structure your thoughts.

Variations: After you feel comfortable talking to one person in the audience, try talking to three or four. Then experiment talking to a group of people whom you endow. When you talk to a group, you make contact with one person at a time. Place the people you will be talking to in the group in such a way that you do not actually make contact with a member of the audience.

Practical Application

The technique of talking to the audience will help you bring the reality of the world of the audience together with the reality of the world of the play.

EXERCISE 10: HISTORICAL IMAGINATION

The final exercise connects everything you have learned and adds research to your preparation.

Purpose

This is a great exercise, because as you delve into and learn about history, you connect yourself to all those who have ever lived. You learn to make living in an earlier era as real, vivid and specific for yourself as your own life.

What You Do

Unlike the other exercises, you choose a character from a play set in another time as the basis for your exercise. Plays set before you were born are the best choice.

Planning

Follow the six steps and set up an everyday circumstance, such as getting ready for bed, writing a letter, getting dressed or having breakfast. You can also choose a time when you are alone doing an activity that you find relaxing, such as reading, embroidering or painting. The circumstances for your exercise should not be related to the crisis in the play you have chosen. In order to do this exercise, you will need to know as much as you can about the period. You will discover that your character has human characteristics with which you can identify. Do as much as you can to feed your imagination about all aspects of people's lives in the period in which the play is set. Look for biographies, autobiographies, historical novels, and picture books of clothing, buildings, and art of the period. Watch movies set in the time of your play. Go to museums and actual historical locations in your own city. When you travel, as you visit different historic places, let yourself fantasize about living there in an earlier time.

When you do the exercise, bring the same sense of specific detail that you have discovered in your own life to the life of your character. Possibilities could include Nora wrapping Christmas presents for her family in Ibsen's *A Doll House*, or Astrov in Chekhov's *Uncle Vanya* working on his maps. Remember, the circumstances for your exercise should not be related to the crisis in the play.

Since you will not have the actual objects, furniture and clothing of the period, you will have to endow a great deal. Use your research. Thrift stores are a wonderful resource for inexpensive garments that can be assembled into clothing that approximates the style of the period you are researching.

Practical Application

This exercise should help you avoid making overly simplistic, judgmental conclusions about the lifestyle of characters in plays that are set in a different time. If your character is sophisticated and wealthy, and you don't think you, the actor, are, you might mistakenly try to affect behavior and attitudes that seem sophisticated. Wouldn't it be more fun to imagine that *you*, the character, are as used to everything connected to *your* lifestyle as you, the actor, are to your own lifestyle?

OVERALL GUIDELINES FOR APPROACHING THE EXERCISES

□ It is important to understand that Hagen's exercises, as readily accessible as they may seem, are deceptively sophisticated. Doing any exercise once is relatively meaningless. It is like a raindrop falling into the ocean. However, a committed approach to the exercises—returning to them again and again, combining them, and consistently applying them to scene work—will pay off.

☐ None of Hagen's exercises work without destination. They are all built upon the physical destination exercise. I cannot emphasize this enough.

☐ Work on each exercise until you and your teacher determine that you are ready to move on to the next.

☐ You have all the facts and experiences of your life at your disposal—use them to create the circumstances for your exercise. Do not invent scenarios that are totally foreign to you. Do not plan a short story with a beginning, middle and end. Don't be a playwright. You do not create a character when you do any of these exercises. The reason for this is that we want you to discover the hundreds of different selves you have inside of you, and what makes each one surface. You will see how circumstances change you and cause you to do everything you do.

☐ You will be selecting and working with real objects when you prepare these exercises. Pantomime is not part of this technique. No *air props*.

☐ Even though you are alone in each exercise, you do not have to be quiet. Depending upon the circumstances, you may have some moments when you sigh, grunt, groan, curse, hum, sing or mumble to yourself.

☐ One hour of actual rehearsal is needed to prepare a three-minute exercise for class. The three-minute time frame is not arbitrary. Actively selecting what happens in those three minutes will help you appreciate the lessons of each exercise. It is also a time frame short enough to prevent you from directing yourself.

☐ The exercise may seem so easy that you think you don't need to rehearse it before you come to class, and so you simply think about it. Not rehearsing the exercise will only postpone facing the occupational challenges of the actor. Rehearsal ultimately frees you, even though, along the way, you run the risk of becoming mechanical or playing remembered behavior (i.e., trying to repeat something that you remember happening in a prior rehearsal) rather than living spontaneously in the moment.

☐ It is important to rehearse at a time that is different from the actual time that you have chosen for your exercise. (Working during the actual time is research, not rehearsal.) Commit to your choices and be thorough.

☐ Get in the habit of rehearsing in the clothes that you will wear when you present your exercise in class.

☐ It will take time for you to become familiar with the equipment in your classroom, which should have an assortment of furniture, a portable door and door frames with which to create a living room, kitchen, bedroom or office space. Make any necessary changes in your actual routine so that you will be able to execute the exercise in class. For instance, if you are setting the table and usually get the plates out of a cupboard on the wall, you may need to have them already sitting on a counter because the studio does not have wall cupboards.

☐ It is crucial to plan ahead. Double-check the props and furniture that are in your classroom space, and make adjustments at home when you rehearse. This will enable you to follow through when you do your exercise in class. For instance, if you plan to use the sink, rehearse with and without running water, so that you will be able to follow through in class with a nonoperational faucet.

☐ Be sure to rehearse with every object you plan to use in the exercise. When a student brings objects to class with which he hasn't rehearsed, he learns on the spot how important rehearsal is. Not being prepared is an embarrassing experience. This seems so obvious, but I have watched many a student become thrown when an action takes longer or is more difficult to execute than he had anticipated. Remember that objects often have a life of their own, and that there are certain actions that cannot be made to go faster than they actually do.

☐ You may also discover, while you are in the middle of your exercise, that you need something on your set that you had not anticipated needing. Students often buy flowers from the local deli to use in their scene. When they go to remove the wrapping from the flowers, they discover that they need scissors, which they don't have. They can't undo the wrapping, so they finally rip it off, only to discover that they have no way to dispose of it because they forgot to bring a wastebasket. At that moment, we see the phenomenally *real* split second of the actor's realization and desperation. The absence of a needed object, no matter how small, can destroy the illusion of a simple exercise and ruin the actor's faith in his circumstances.

☐ Organize. List the objects you will bring from your home to class, and pack everything after your final rehearsal.

☐ Every so often, a student will try to concentrate on an activity which does not require as much concentration as he is giving it. This abnormal concentration produces inordinate tension onstage. Remember that you only focus on an object when you encounter an obstacle that demands your attention. Normally, your mind is filled with thoughts produced by your surrounding circumstances. Even activities like ironing and sewing require only minimal awareness, not intense concentration.

☐ Do not set or script your thought process. New thoughts may move in on you every time you rehearse or present your exercise in class. Let them.

☐ Be aware that some real objects may upstage you if you actually use them in an exercise. Students in the audience quickly see that certain realities can be disruptive. The noise from a real radio, blender, coffeemaker or hair dryer provides too much reality onstage. Whenever you turn on a radio that actually works in an exercise, everyone starts listening to the radio, and audience members have to fight to watch the exercise. Unwittingly, you have upstaged yourself. You may need the physical body of the object, but it doesn't have to actually work.

☐ Motivate your choices as specifically as possible. For instance, if you are asked why a radio is in the scene, your response shouldn't be that you always have it on. This is a good illustration of using a generalization about your life when making an acting choice. Instead, ask, "Why a radio at this moment?" If you really want the radio on, you will have to record the program that would be on during the time your exercise is taking place. You should use it only because it supports your action in the scene— it soothes you when you have heard bad news or are feeling homesick, psyches you up for a hot date, or supplies the weather forecast that helps you decide what to wear.

To the beginning actor, the approach I have put forth may seem overly complicated and, at the same time, simplistic, and it may lead some to question what all this has to do with acting. The answer is *everything*. Actors rehearse and prepare before they go before the public. When an actor works in class, he is also going before the public, not to entertain, but to test his choices and discover the work he still has to do. The ability to follow through on chosen actions, be they physical, verbal or psychological, is essential in creating life onstage.

Remember, perfecting your craft brings you closer to attaining the ultimate in your art—portraying what Uta Hagen described as "a human being onstage without artificial theatrics."[10]

Your experiences when working on these exercises will become valuable touchstones as you grow as an actor. They will humanize you. They will stimulate your imagination. They will lead you to create characters who are alive, unique and authentic. As you begin to combine the exercises, and as you begin to instinctively apply these lessons to every role, you will have the satisfaction and joy of finding your performances to be richer and more complete than you ever envisioned. More I cannot wish you.

ENDNOTES/SOURCES

1. Hagen, Uta, *A Challenge for the Actor*, New York: Scribner, 1991, pp. 55, 202, 124.
2. Ibid., p. 49.
3. Ibid., p. 50.
4. Hagen, Uta, with Haskel Frankel, *Respect for Acting*, New York: Wiley, 1973, p. 7.
5. Hagen, *A Challenge for the Actor*, p. 83.
6. Ibid., p. 134.
7. Ibid., p. 154.
8. Ibid., p. 198.
9. Ibid., p. 199.
10. Ibid., p. 123.

RECOMMENDED READING LIST

Gussow, Mel, "Uta Hagen, Tony-Winning Broadway Star and Teacher of Actors, Dies at 84," *New York Times*, January 14, 2004, p. A31.

Hagen, Uta, *A Challenge for the Actor*, New York: Scribner's, 1991.
Hagen's definitive revision of her earlier work, in which she describes in greater depth the techniques that serious artists must master when working on a role.

_____, *Sources, A Memoir*, Performing Arts Journal Publications, 1983.

Hagen, Uta, with Haskel Frankel, *Respect for Acting*, New York: Wiley, 1973.
Hagen's extremely popular first book on acting, written with Haskel Frankel, in which she set down her exercises and approach to text.

Spector, Susan, *Uta Hagen, The Early Years: 1919–1951*, dissertation, New York University, Bobst Library, 1982.
The story of Uta Hagen's development as an artist, culled from her personal journals, interviews and research.

_____, and Stephen Urkowitz, "Uta Hagen and Eva Le Gallienne," *Women in American Theatre*, Helen Krich Chinoy and Linda Walsh Jenkins, eds., New York: Theatre Communications Group, 2006.

Uta Hagen's Acting Class, Karen Ludwig, dir., New York: Hal Leonard, 2003.
A video series documenting Hagen's teaching, including critiquing and reworking scenes, and teaching the ten exercises.

Zucker, Carole, *In the Company of Actors: Reflections on the Craft of Acting*, New York: Routledge, 2001.
Interviews with sixteen celebrated actors.

UTA HAGEN was one of the most influential American acting teachers of the twentieth century. She began her professional life in theater in 1937, when Eva Le Gallienne cast Hagen as Ophelia in her production of *Hamlet*. In 1938, her Broadway career began when she was cast as Nina in *The Seagull*, with Alfred Lunt and Lynn Fontanne. In 1943 she played Desdemona in the historic Paul Robeson production of *Othello*, directed by Margaret Webster, and she played Blanche DuBois in the legendary second company of *A Streetcar Named Desire* in 1948. She won two Tony Awards: one in 1951, for her portrayal of Georgie in Clifford Odets's *The Country Girl* (for which she also received a Drama Critics Award and a Donaldson Award), and the other in 1962 for her creation of the role of Martha in Edward Albee's *Who's Afraid of Virginia Woolf?* (for which she also received a Drama Critics Award).

In 1947, Harold Clurman directed Hagen on Broadway in *The Whole World Over*, a Soviet comedy by Konstantine Simonov, adapted by Thelma Schnee. Hagen credited Clurman with guiding her to delve more deeply into the craft of acting. He encouraged her to strive for the humanity of Eleonora Duse and to eschew formalism in her work. It was in this same production that Hagen met her future husband, Herbert Berghof.

Hagen's mother was trained as an opera singer, and her father was a famed art historian and musicologist. Both were from Germany, and she was raised with a European sensibility. Herbert Berghof, the most important influence in her life, had immigrated to the United States in 1939 from his native Vienna, where he had studied at the Royal Academy of Art under Alexander Moissi and Max Reinhardt. He had been a leading actor in Max Reinhardt's company and had some one hundred roles under his belt when he came to the United States.

Berghof was one of the founding members of the Actors Studio. In 1941, he began teaching with Edwin Piscator at the Dramatic Workshop of the New School of Social Research, and later joined the faculty of the Neighborhood Playhouse. He began his own acting school, the HB Studio on Bank Street in Greenwich Village, in 1945, and brought Hagen to teach there in 1947.

Hagen was also a wonderful writer, and you can read about her life, influences and technique in her own fervent words in *Respect for Acting*, *A Challenge for the Actor* and *Sources, a Memoir*. Her life onstage was devoted to practicing her craft, and her life in the classroom was devoted to articulating the technique that encourages and enables the actor "to reveal a living soul" onstage (as she wrote in *A Challenge for the Actor*). The challenge she puts before every actor is the one by which she always lived.

After the death of Herbert Berghof in 1990, Hagen took over the leadership of the HB Studio and picked up her own challenge with an insatiable fervor. Her message is tough, honest, clear and uncompromising. She believed that consummate artistry requires talent, skill, a point of view about the world, a passionate need to communicate and an uncompromising avoidance of slick tricks and cliché in one's work. She knew that being an artist takes time, a lifelong dedication to hard work, a state of innocence, and great curiosity about the human condition.

At the age of 80, at the height of her power, she was still giving and sustaining performances that exemplified her writing and were a testimony to the fact that acting is a great art. She appeared in Nicholas Wright's *Mrs. Klein* in March 1995. It was first produced at the HB Playwright's Foundation and Theatre, moved Off-Broadway to great acclaim, and then toured extensively. Hagen then starred in the HB Playwrights Foundation and Theatre's mounting of *Collected Stories* by Donald Margulies in 1998. This production also moved Off-Broadway and once again received critical acclaim. It toured, and in 2000 it was remounted at the Stratford Festival in Ontario and played in Montreal, as well. William Carden, the former artistic director of the HB Playwrights Foundation and Theatre, directed both productions. Uta Hagen starred with David Hyde Pierce in Richard Alfieri's play, *Six Dance Lessons in Six Weeks*, in Los Angeles in 2001. This was her last performance onstage. Throughout 1998–1999 she taught a series of master classes, featured in the video series *Uta Hagen's Acting Class*, which documents her work as a teacher.

Hagen received many awards throughout her career, including a London Theatre Critics Award for *Who's Afraid of Virginia Woolf?* (1964); an OBIE Award for her performance in *Mrs. Klein* (1996); the New York Mayor's Liberty Medal (1986); the John Houseman Award and the Campostella Award for distinguished service (1987); induction into the Theater Hall of Fame (1981), the Wisconsin Theatre Hall of Fame (1983) and the American Academy of Arts and Sciences in Cambridge, Massachusetts (1999); the national Medal of Honor for the Arts, presented by the President of the United States (2003); and several honorary degrees and lifetime achievement awards.

Mastering of Hagen's technique takes time and patience, a great deal of experience, and a lot of trial and error. The work of artists using this technique is so fresh and alive that audiences never think about the actors and their acting. Hagen's legacy continues through the dedicated teaching and formidable acting of her gifted students and colleagues at the HB Studio and The HB Playwrights Foundation and Theatre.

CAROL ROSENFELD, an actress and director, has been on the faculty of the Herbert Berghof Studio in New York City since 1969. Since 1979, she has also almost single-handedly brought Hagen's work to Canada, where she has worked with some of the finest Canadian actors in intensive workshops in Toronto, Vancouver, Calgary, Halifax, Winnipeg and at the Shaw Festival at

Niagara-on-the-Lake. She also taught at the National Theatre School of Canada for ten years. From 1972–1977, as head of acting at Rutgers University, she developed the undergraduate acting program into a four-year course. She also taught the first MFA class to graduate from the Mason Gross School of the Arts. She was the acting coach for the acting company of the National Theatre of the Deaf for ten years. In 1987, she was invited by the Institut del Teatre in Barcelona to work with leading actors from the major theater companies in that city and, later, the Actors' Union of Denmark sponsored her workshop in Copenhagen. Productions she has directed include *Picnic* by William Inge, *The Road to Mecca* by Athol Fugard, *The Substance of Fire* by Jon Robin Baitz, *The Millionairess* by G. B. Shaw, *Collected Stories* by Donald Margulies and Edgar Lee Masters's *Spoon River Anthology*. She is currently writing *Moments, a Workbook for Acting and Living.*

ACTING WITH THE WISDOM OF OUR BODIES

A Physical Approach to Acting
Inspired by Jerzy Grotowski

Stephen Wangh

What we do with our bodies affects what we feel in our hearts. Polish director Jerzy Grotowski put it this way: "Memories are always physical reactions. It is our skin which has not forgotten, our eyes which have not forgotten."[1] Grotowski suggested that, by listening to the wisdom of our bodies, we can release the emotions, power and precision we need to act onstage.

□

Actors are asked to do the impossible: they are required to repeat memorized lines night after night as if they were speaking those words for the first time. They are expected to experience strong, honest, personal emotions while pretending to be someone else. And they must perform intimate actions *naturally*, while speaking loud enough for several hundred people to hear. Acting, more than any other art, is a paradoxical practice, a juggling act that requires the artist to do many contradictory things at the same time. And acting *technique* is any approach to these paradoxes that gives performers the courage to undertake such impossible tasks.

Jerzy Grotowski predicated his teaching upon the idea this courage is not something we need to *learn*; it is something each of us possessed when we were young, but have since forgotten. After all, when we were growing up, accomplishing the impossible was an everyday event. At age one, for instance, when we were learning to walk, we never worried that balancing the great weight of our bodies on two little legs was impossible. We never said to ourselves, "Oh no, I'm a terrible walker. I'll never be able to do this." No matter how many times we fell down, we got back up and tried again, for we had not yet learned to think of falling down as "failure." It was just a natural part of the process of learning.

The same was true of our imaginations: as children we had no trouble playing at being superheroes or princesses or animals or monsters. We undertook these impossible roles without shame or self-consciousness, and we could visualize "imaginary circumstances" whenever we wanted to. Robert Benedetti puts it this way: "A child can look at a floating twig and see a great ocean liner, and he doesn't have to deny the existence of the twig to do so. He simply transforms his interpretation of what he is seeing. Yet when student actors are asked to visualize a scene, they invariably close their eyes or stare blankly into space, as if the things they might really see around them hindered their ability to pretend. They have lost the child's ability to contact and accept reality and then *use* it to create an even more vivid illusion."[2]

Jerzy Grotowski believed that this wisdom of childhood, this youthful courage to imagine and to attempt the impossible, is never really lost; it is only buried within us, waiting to be freed. Because of this, he described acting training as a *via negativa*, a "way backwards" to things we once knew. Rather than a matter of learning to *do* things, it is an *un*doing of the tensions and habits we have acquired, a letting go of the fears and hesitations that undermine our courage and get in our way.

Of course, this *un*doing is not always easy. We have developed our tensions, habits and inhibitions for good reasons, and anyone who has not gained such inhibitions—anyone who continues to act out all his emotional impulses—can get into serious trouble. But to act onstage we need free access to all the wonderful and terrifying thoughts and impulses we have so carefully put away over the years. The question is how to gain that access.

Some acting methods suggest that the best way to get beyond our ingrained habits and tensions is to relax the body and turn inward, getting in touch with old memories. Others rely on the actor's ability to invent "imaginary circumstances." Grotowski agreed with both these aims, but he suggested that the most direct route back to the emotional freedom we once knew is to activate our bodies, and let them reveal to us the images and the memories they contain.

□

In the fall of 1967, I was a graduate student at NYU's School of the Arts. One day the director of the program announced that twenty of us would be taking part in an intensive four-week acting workshop with a young Polish theater director named Jerzy Grotowski. None of us had any idea who this Grotowski was. Some had heard rumors that he had recently taught a training workshop for Peter Brook's company in England, and that several of the actors in that workshop had dropped out because the work was too strenuous for them. But all we were told was to show up the next Monday morning, the men in shorts and the women in leotards, prepared to work hard.

The work that Grotowski presented to us, with the aid of his chief actor, Ryszard Cieslak, was physical—very physical. It included headstands and rolls and a set of physical isolations he called *les exercices plastiques*. At first, as we struggled with these forms, we found ourselves quite overwhelmed with the pure physical difficulty they presented. But Grotowski insisted that the difficulty of the exercises was not a problem; in fact, it was a good thing. "The real value [of the exercises]," he said, "lies in [your] *not* being able to do them."[3]

But what did he mean by this? Was he simply confronting us with our ineptitude, or was he trying to sound enigmatic? It didn't occur to us that he meant exactly what he was saying: that the value of this work lay in the *encounter* we had with the forms, not with their *accomplishment*, and that the frustration, fear and exhilaration we felt while struggling with these physical challenges were central to the work. Grotowski was encouraging us to notice that, while trying to accomplish the "impossible," we were having strong emotional reactions to the work itself. And he was suggesting that these reactions were not to be dismissed as "acting problems," but rather to be seen as inviting doorways into our emotional life.

Many actors fear that their difficulties with a role, their feelings about their fellow actors or their reactions to an acting exercise are "acting problems" that they need to overcome. Some acting teachers even tell their students to leave personal thoughts and feelings "outside the studio." But Grotowski suggested the opposite. "If during creation we hide the things that function in our personal lives," he wrote, "you may be sure that our creativity will fall."[4] The result of this attitude was that, in our work with Grotowski, everything we thought and felt, every impulse or image that we had, began to actually feed our work. While the *forms* he taught were physical, their *effect* was to connect our bodies with our emotions and our imaginations.

For me, this was a revelation. Before I studied with Jerzy Grotowski, I had often found acting to be a sort of out-of-body experience. I was often fearful, disconnected and self-conscious while performing, and I felt as if I didn't know quite what to do with my hands. But I always supposed that that was just the way it felt to be onstage—except once.

The spring before Grotowski came to NYU, while I was taking an acting class with Lloyd Richards, something strange had happened. I was working on a scene from Arthur Miller's *All My Sons*, and things were going as usual for me—I could play the scene, and I could react to my scene partner, but I experienced myself as not entirely *there* while performing. But then, the last time my partner and I presented our scene, everything seemed different. I had the feeling I was fully inside the reality of the play, fully *present* in the acting moment onstage.

Years later, when I read Stanislavsky's book *Creating a Role*, I understood that I had experienced what Stanislavsky called the feeling of "I am" on the stage. But that day in Lloyd Richards's class, I couldn't comprehend what had happened. The only thing that had been different that day was that my scene partner and I had begun our scene right after coming from Kristin Linklater's voice class, where we had spent an hour shaking out our bodies and warming up our voices. I suspected that my ease in the *All My Sons* scene must have had something to do with that warm-up, but I didn't understand how these events were connected.

The next fall, when I worked with Grotowski, my experience with the *All My Sons* scene became comprehensible. As I learned to pay attention to what was happening within my body, I found myself less and less distracted by what was going on in my mind. Grotowski's *plastique* exercises seemed to capture and transform the energy of my habitual self-consciousness into usable acting impulses. The more I worked in that way, the more I found myself experiencing the wonderful sensation Stanislavsky had called "I am."

In fact, as a young man, Jerzy Grotowski had gone to Moscow to study acting with students of Stanislavsky's. Years later, he said, "When I was a student in the school of dramatic arts . . . I founded the entire base of my theatrical knowledge on the principles of Stanislavsky. As an actor, I was possessed by Stanislavsky. I was a fanatic."[5]

But the work that so inspired Grotowski was not quite the same training that most Americans think of as the "Stanislavsky approach." Many Americans think of Stanislavsky's acting work as a largely mental process, a sensation- and memory-based technique by which actors search internally for emotional truth. Such internal, psychological exercises actually make up only a small part of Stanislavsky's work, though, for two reasons, they dominated American acting training throughout the twentieth century.

The first reason is that American acting training really began with the formation of the Group Theatre by Harold Clurman, Stella Adler and Lee Strasberg. These three had studied with Richard Boleslavsky and Maria Ouspenskaya, two actors who left Russia in 1923 after working with Stanislavsky early in his career. In those early years, Stanislavsky had been struggling to overcome his personal tendency toward being too external and mechanical in his acting, so at that time he had, indeed, concentrated on teaching inner, psychological exercises.

The second reason is that, although Stanislavsky's book *An Actor Prepares* was published in English in 1936, his second training book, *Building a Character*, was not translated until 1948, and the third, *Creating a Role*, not until 1961. And it is only in these later works that Stanislavsky described how his own understanding of acting technique had grown and changed over time. As he worked, Stanislavsky had come to realize that in his early years he had focused too narrowly on psychological exercises. As time went on, he came to insist more and more on the importance of physical action. Thus, in *Creating a Role* he wrote, "An actor on the stage need only sense the smallest modicum of organic physical truth in his action or general state and instantly his emotions will respond to his inner faith in the genuineness of what his body is doing. In our case it is incomparably easier to call forth real truth and faith in it in the region of our physical than of our spiritual nature."[6]

In fact, this insight—that the actor can use the body to awaken his emotional life—was not original to Stanislavsky. Early in the nineteenth century, the French acting coach François Delsarte had written, "Gesture is the direct agent of the heart . . . In a word, it is the spirit of which speech is merely the letter."[7] Delsarte had tried to create an acting system that depended not upon mental action, but upon physical gesture, but he had made the error of trying to prescribe a fixed vocabulary of movements for each human emotion, teaching his students particular gestures to convey particular emotions. This rigid format led many actors to external, mechanical acting—exactly the kind of empty, melodramatic gesticulation against which Konstantin Stanislavsky reacted half a century later.

Some great actors naturally understood how physical choices could lead them to emotional truth. Sanford Meisner tells this story about the nineteenth-century English actor William Charles Macready: "Before playing a certain scene in *The Merchant of Venice*, [Macready] used to try to shake the iron ladder backstage that was embedded in the brick. He'd try and try, and would get furious because he couldn't budge it. *Then* he went on and played the scene."[8]

Even the young Stanislavsky himself, while searching for inner, psychological techniques, had moments when he perceived how his body could inspire emotional truth. In *Creating a Role* he relates notes he had made early in his career on rehearsal techniques for the Russian play *Woe from Wit*: "There has been one instant when I really felt that I was there and believed in my own feelings. This was when I opened the door into the antechamber and pushed aside a large armchair; I really felt the physical effort entailed in this act . . . It was dissipated as soon as I walked away from the armchair."[9]

When he tried to make sense of this experience, Stanislavsky supposed that it was caused by the reality of the object, the armchair. "This experience teaches me the exceptional importance of the part played by an *object* in helping me to get into the state of 'I am.'" But I suspect that it was not the armchair that had made this moment so real for Stanislavsky, but rather the *effort* involved in pushing the chair, for it is the engagement of our muscles that often awakens emotional sources in us.

By the 1930s, Stanislavsky was convinced that he had gone too far in a purely psychological direction, and he declared that a physical approach to acting might be more dependable for an actor than a purely psychological one. In *Creating a Role* he concluded, "In every *physical action*, unless it is purely mechanical, there is concealed some *inner action*, some feelings."[10]

During the 1930s, the acting teachers Michael Chekhov and Sonia Moore tried to introduce physically-based versions of Stanislavsky's work to American acting students. By then, Lee Strasberg's "method" work had become *the* interpretation of Stanislavsky for many American actors, and it was only many years later that some of Strasberg's own students started to rediscover how the body could serve as a source for emotional truth. Warren Robertson, for instance, has related how he began to discover ways in which physical choices could be used to augment Strasberg's own exercises. "I often have an actor do an affective memory exercise on his feet instead of sitting in a chair. And at moments I'll have him try to integrate feelings into his body. I'll have him lift his hand and wave goodbye, and he will remember, without even trying, who he is waving good-bye to. The body is a means of finding a specific feeling."[11]

Even Strasberg's son, John, has said, "A lot of the people who are doing body work are aware of the fact that memory is in the muscle, even sense memory. Therefore, you can trigger it from the outside in as well as from the inside out."[12] So, by now, many actors and teachers who derive their inspiration from Stanislavsky have come to the same conclusion Grotowski reached: that the actor's body is a powerful resource in the search for emotional truth.

WHAT IS PHYSICAL ACTING?

It is impossible, in the course of this short chapter, to present a thorough overview of physical acting training, but in the next few pages, I will try to give you a quick glimpse of how this training proceeds. As you read, bear in mind that what most impressed Grotowski about Stanislavsky was not his *technique*, per se, but the fact that he dared to ask, over and over, "What must an actor do to be fully alive onstage?"—even when his own answers to that question kept changing. "Stanislavsky propounded the most important questions and he supplied his own answers," Grotowski wrote. "Throughout his numerous years of research his method evolved, but his disciples did not."[13]

What is important in any acting technique is not the answers it provides, but rather the space it offers for you to propound the most important questions for yourself. What particular challenges do *you* encounter in your acting? What kinds of exercises excite you and speak to your needs? What makes acting truly alive for you?

THE ACTOR'S WARM-UP

One of Stanislavsky's central questions was: How can an actor get ready to work? In *An Actor Prepares*, he posed the problem this way: "You know that a sculptor kneads his clay before he begins to use it, and a singer warms up his voice before his concert. We need to do something similar to tune our inner strings, to test the keys, the pedals and the stops."[14]

But how can an actor tune his *instrument* when that instrument is not just his body and voice, but his emotional life—his rage, tears and love? Physical acting training suggests that you take this question seriously and personally. What can you do to tune your inner strings? What kind of warm-up will prepare you to play the music of character and emotion upon your body and soul?

To answer this question, I encourage actors to become aware of what their bodies are telling them, of where their minds are leading them, and of the relationship between the two. I suggest that they explore questions like:

☐ How does your inner life change when you run around the room, curl up in a corner or stare out the window?

☐ Where does your mind take you when your eyes look out that window? What would happen if you let your whole body follow your eyes?

☐ What happens to you when you make or break eye contact with another actor? What happens to you if you smile or grimace when you do?

☐ What do you feel inside as you stretch or move your body?

I encourage actors to discover the answers to such questions actively, by experimentation. When you experiment, you often find that your body will clearly supply the answers to such questions. You may notice, as you search for answers, that your body seems to actually *contain* emotions, and that physical forms—even simple exercises like stretches or aerobics—connect you with the thoughts and feelings you need for your acting work. More importantly, you may find that the very task of asking such warm-up questions awakens within you the ability to discover the answers you seek.

In my book, *An Acrobat of the Heart*, I describe several exercises designed to help you explore the question, "What is an actor's warm-up?" But in the end, it is up to you to discover your own warm-up, for a warm-up is not simply a regimen or a fixed set of exercises. It is a gift you give your body, voice and mind to ready yourself for the acting work you are about to undertake. And each day your warm-up may be different, depending on what experiences you are coming from and what rehearsal or performance you are warming up for.

After these basic warm-up lessons, I introduce my students to some of Grotowski's full-body exercises.

CONNECTING THE WHOLE BODY

Many of those who saw Eleonora Duse onstage at the beginning of the twentieth century reported that she was a most amazing actress. Lee Strasberg described one performance this way: "Duse had a strange way of smiling. It seemed to come from the toes. It seemed to move through the body and arrive at the face and mouth and resembled the sun coming out of the clouds."[15]

This connectedness is something that every child possesses, but most of us seem to have lost, for we have spent years learning to sit in chairs, raise our hands before speaking, and mask our strongest emotions with false smiles. We have packed away our full-bodied emotions, and we have disconnected our faces and voices from the energies in our lower bodies. So it is not so surprising that our smiles no longer "come from the toes."

In order to rediscover those forgotten connections, we begin our training by freeing our spines from their normal task of keeping us vertical and our legs from their usual job of carrying us around. We do *undulations*, which carry energy from one end of the body to the other, and we practice kicks and somersaults, headstands and back-bends . . . not to train ourselves as acrobats, but to take ourselves out of the vertical and permit the expression of the joy, violence and sexuality that lie hidden in the lower half of our bodies.

When you undertake this work, you may delight in the pure energy of the physical exercises themselves—for rolling and leaping and standing on your hands are, in themselves, very exhilarating. But more important, you will discover that the joys, fears and struggles you encounter while undertaking these exercises can be converted into imagery and gestures that you can use in your acting. In fact, as you roll and bend and stand on your hands, you may notice that even your thoughts *about* the work, anxieties about the exercises, opinions about your body and anger at the acting class can be turned into sources of creative acting imagery.

After studying these full-body exercises, we move on to an exploration of what Grotowski called *les exercices plastiques*. These are physical isolations that allow you to explore the connections between particular physical gestures and personal imagery and emotion. At first they are practiced methodically, progressing through the body, part by part—the eyes, the face, the head, the neck, the shoulders, etc. But soon the *plastiques* begin to flow on their own, leading you from movement to movement and from image to image. Working with the *plastiques*, you start to notice how each physical choice you make can inspire a memory, a thought, or an emotional impulse, and you begin to perceive the unique information your body holds for you.

Of course, each actor finds slightly different physical connections in these exercises, and yet there are certain forms that seem to have similar effects for many people. Kicking hard with the legs, for instance, or striking backwards with the elbows can inspire anger; reaching upward with the arms may evoke feelings of yearning; opening across the chest can release tears; and running in place can produce pure fear.

In Grotowski's workshop, the *plastique* of running by shifting the weight left and right completely surprised me. As I began to run harder and harder, leaping left and right faster and faster, I found myself, at first, just short of breath, but when Grotowski encouraged us to glance backwards over our shoulders as we ran, something sent a shiver down my spine. It was not that I actually *saw* something chasing me; it was more like a suspicion, a possibility, a fear that something I could not quite see was there. And as I started to run harder, I sensed that whatever was back there was gaining on me. Each time I looked back, I wanted to run faster, and the faster I ran, the more frightened I felt. What had begun as a technical physical activity, running in place, was now provoking a real emotional reaction.

With this experience, I began to understand that, in the *plastique* work, what I did with my eyes was essential. If I looked forward while I ran, reaching my arms in front of me, I experienced entirely different images and emotions than if I looked backward over my shoulder. And that was true with each *plastique*: each one was really a combination of a physical movement and an eye gesture. The eye focus inspired me to imagine what it was that was provoking my body to move, and the effort of the body work convinced my heart that what I was imagining was real.

One way to think of the *plastique* exercises is as a series of *provocations*, keys you can use to unlock the doors of your emotional life. The wonderful thing about these keys is that you can pick them up or put them down at will, unlocking whichever emotional doors you need for a particular role, for, unlike your emotions or your memories themselves, these keys are controlled by the voluntary muscles of your body. As Stanislavsky wrote in *Creating a Role*, "With faith in your physical actions on the stage you will feel emotions, akin to the external life of your part, which possess a logical bond with your soul. The body is biddable; feelings are capricious."[16]

In our physical acting training, we spend many hours exploring the connections between our bodies, our images and our emotions. We examine how changing the amount of physical effort affects the work; we try working faster or slower; we try sticking with images for a long time or letting them constantly change. In these ways we learn how to make physical choices upon which we can depend in performances, night after night.

Connecting with our feelings is only one of many tasks acting requires. As I pointed out at the beginning of this chapter, the art of acting is filled with paradoxes, and one of the greatest is that, while we delve into our own inner feelings, we must simultaneously listen and respond to our scene partner's. Every acting training method must confront this problem in some way.

In Meisner technique, for instance, an actor begins with the *repetition exercise*, which teaches him to be entirely *in the moment*, listening and reacting to his scene partner. Once the actor is able to go with all the changes this listening provokes, he takes on the further problem of concentrating on an *activity*—at first a physical one and later a mental/emotional one—as he listens. American "method" actors approach this paradox from the opposite direction, learning first to get in touch with personal memories, sensations, and other inner experiences that activate strong emotions. Then they deal with the difficulty of simultaneously listening to their scene partners.

Our physical acting training approaches this paradox from another direction. The *plastique* exercises train us to perceive our *inner actions*, our memories, emotions and thoughts, not as something inside ourselves, but as *reactions* we are having to images on the outside. When we run in place, for instance, the images we may perceive behind us are, of course, simply thoughts inside our minds; but while we run, we experience them as if they were actually outside.

Since the *plastiques* allow us to *see* our inner world as if it were *out there*, when we listen to our scene partners, we find that our inner, emotional sources and our partner's words are both impinging upon us from the same place: they are both coming from *out there*. As a result, the paradoxical acting problem of following our *inner actions* while reacting to an *outer reality* ceases to be a paradox—the two activities are really one and the same. This experience forms the very core of physical acting work, the realization that all acting—even the *inner*, emotional part of it—is not an *action* but a *reaction* to something that is happening *to* us. The corollary of this perception is that our central task as actors is to stay open to receive, see and listen.

Of course, in our physical acting training, this *listening* is not something we do only with our ears—it is a full-body process. We train ourselves to be awake and vulnerable not only to the words our scene partner speaks to us, but to her movements, facial expressions and rhythms. To do so, we use some exercises similar to Meisner's *repetition exercises*, but we also learn to receive and react with our bodies as a whole.

Finally, before entering scene work, we add vocal training to the body work. We begin our vocal training by connecting our breath and sound with the bodily awareness and physical precision we have been studying. We explore how vowels and pitch are connected with resonators, gesture and movement, and we study the ticklish problem of exactly how much effort to use when producing sound. We discover how changes in pitch and placement can evoke images and emotions just as precisely and repeatedly as gesture and movement do. Then we add the consonants, tasting and feeling them, perceiving the power and precision they provide for the emotional life that the vowels have unleashed. Only then do we begin to work with words and text.

Coming to language in this way, you may find that the *meaning* of your lines derives not only from the thoughts the words convey, but also from the very sounds of those words. Each phrase you speak is more than just a group of words now; it is a vocal gesture, a way of attacking or touching or reaching out to others onstage. And every word and phrase you utter can spontaneously evoke within you the *action* and *subtext* it contains. (The importance of this approach becomes especially evident when you work with plays by poetic writers like Tennessee Williams or August Wilson, and especially when you undertake Shakespeare or Lorca.)

Finally, when we have integrated our voices, bodies and emotional instruments, we are ready to begin scene work. We begin not by sitting down to figure out the *beats* of the scene, but on our feet, letting the words of our texts drive our physical impulses, and allowing our whole beings to *embody* and interpret what we might otherwise do sitting at a table before getting up to act.

Approached in this way, scenes often start to stage themselves. The changes of distance between you and your scene partner, the movements and blocking and stage business, are not simply directorial inventions imposed on the scene; they are acting impulses that emerge organically out of the text itself. The actions, intentions and objectives you play are not problems you need to sit down and figure out; they exist within the impulses, shapes and sounds that your body and voice are inventing for you as you work.

For the physical actor, the *beats* and the *blocking* of a scene are not two separate things. Together they constitute what Grotowski called the *score* of a scene. "When one refers to the score of physical actions," Grotowski clarified, "this does not mean the gestures or external details—*blocking*. Physical action, rather, combines impulse and intention. What do you want to do to your partner? How do you wish to make him/her react? Action emanates always from some intention toward the Other, made manifest through the body."[17]

Thus, the physical approach to acting is not a rejection of Stanislavsky's work. It is an extension of his insights into the physical realm. Our listening and reacting exercises are similar to Meisner's *repetition exercise*, our image work is related to Strasberg's *sense memory* exercise, and the blocking which arises from our physical impulses is like a score of *actions* and *intentions*.

There are many approaches to acting, and there are many acting teachers in this world. But what is important about an acting *technique* is not the technique itself, but how it serves your particular needs as an artist. Similarly, what matters most in choosing a teacher is whether that person's particular teaching style frees *you* to feel powerful and creative in your art. In the end, no one can teach you how to act. The most a teacher can do is provide a safe space in which you can rediscover the sensitivity, power and truth that already reside within you. As Eleonora Duse once said, "He who claims to teach Art understands nothing whatsoever about it."[18]

ENDNOTES/SOURCES

1. Grotowski, Jerzy, *Towards a Poor Theatre*, Eugenio Barba, ed., London: Methuen, 1976, p. 185.

2. Benedetti, Robert, *The Actor at Work*, Englewood Cliffs, NJ: Prentice Hall, 1976.

3. Crawley, Tom, "The Stone in the Soup, Grotowski's First American Workshop," unpublished manuscript, 1978, pp. ii, 13.

4. Grotowski, p. 199.

5. Richards, Thomas, *At Work with Grotowski on Physical Actions*, London: Routledge, 1995, p. 6.

6. Stanislavsky, Konstantin [Stanislavski, Constantine], *Creating a Role*, Elizabeth Reynolds Hapgood, trans., New York: Theatre Arts Books, 1961, p. 150.

7. Delsarte, François, *Delsarte System of Oratory: Containing All the Literary Remains of François Delsarte Given in His Own Words*, Abby I. Alger, trans., New York: Edgar S. Werner, 1883, pp. 446–447.

8. Meisner, Sanford, and Dennis Longwell, *Sanford Meisner on Acting*, New York: Vintage, 1987, p. 80.

9. Stanislavsky, *Creating a Role*, p. 26.

10. Ibid., p. 228.

11. Mekler, Eva, *The New Generation of Acting Teachers*, New York: Penguin, 1987, p. 113.

12. Ibid., p. 106.

13. Grotowski, p. 184.

14. Stanislavsky, Konstantin [Stanislavski, Constantine], *An Actor Prepares*, Elizabeth Reynolds Hapgood, trans., London: Methuen, 1936, p. 250.

15. Strasberg, Lee, *A Dream of Passion: The Development of the Method*, Evangeline Morphos, ed., Boston: Little, Brown, 1987, p. 17.

16. Stanislavsky, *Creating a Role*, p. 154.

17. Wolford, Lisa, *Grotowski's Objective Drama Research*, Jackson: University Press of Mississippi, 1996, p. 63.

18. Pandolfi, Vito, ed., "Lettere di Eleonora Duse," *Antologia del Grande Attore*, Bari: Editori Laterza, 1954; translated by Vivien Leone in *Actors on Acting*, Toby Cole and Helen Krich Chinoy, eds., New York: Three Rivers Press, 1995, p. 467.

RECOMMENDED READING LIST

Benedetti, Robert, *The Actor at Work, Eighth Edition*, Boston: Allyn & Bacon, 2000.

Burzynski, Tadeusz, and Zbigniew Osiński, *Grotowski's Laboratory*, Warsaw: Interpress Publishers, 1979.

Delsarte, François, *Delsarte System of Oratory: Containing All the Literary Remains of François Delsarte Given in His Own Words*, Abby I. Alger, trans., New York: Edgar S. Werner, 1883.

Duse, Eleonora, "On Acting," *Actors on Acting*, Toby Cole and Helen Krich Chinoy, eds., New York: Three Rivers Press, 1995.
Vivien Leone translates excerpts from Eleonora Duse's letters, which were originally published as "Lettere di Eleonora Duse," edited by Vito Pandolfi, in *Antologia del Grande Attore*, Bari: Editori Laterza, 1954.

Grotowski, Jerzy, *Towards a Poor Theatre*, Eugenio Barba, ed., London: Methuen, 1976; New York: Routledge, 2002.
This book of essays and interviews with Jerzy Grotowski contains his most thorough discussions of the training work he developed with the Polish Laboratory Theatre in the 1960s. Some of it is difficult to follow, but it gives one a good sense of the man, his opinions and his style of teaching.

Kumiega, Jennifer, *The Theatre of Grotowski*, London: Methuen, 1987.
This book places Grotowski's physical training techniques in the context of the plays his company was creating.

Linklater, Kristin, *Freeing the Natural Voice*, New York: Drama Publishers, 1976.
This book outlines Linklater's approach to vocal training. An exercise-filled book, it makes one hungry for the presence of the teacher, but if you can't work with Kristin, this book will give you a taste of her wisdom and an appreciation for her specificity.

_____, *Freeing Shakespeare's Voice: The Actor's Guide to Talking the Text*, New York: Theatre Communications Group, 1992.
This book explains Linklater's approach to vocal training for Shakespeare. Its exercises on vowels and consonants are particularly useful.

Meisner, Sanford, and Dennis Longwell, *Sanford Meisner on Acting*, New York: Vintage, 1987.

Mekler, Eva, *The New Generation of Acting Teachers*, New York: Penguin, 1987.

Moore, Sonia, *Stanislavski Revealed: The Actor's Guide to Spontaneity on Stage*, New York: Applause, 2000.
Sonia Moore studied with Stanislavsky during his last years of teaching in Russia. This book reveals how very body-centered Stanislavsky's work became in his later years.

Richards, Thomas, *At Work with Grotowski on Physical Actions*, London: Routledge, 1995.

Thomas Richards worked with Jerzy Grotowski at Pontedera, Italy, in the 1990s. In this book, Richards explains the deep psychophysical direction Grotowski took with his work.

Schechner, Richard, and Lisa Wolford, eds., *The Grotowski Sourcebook*, London: Routledge, 1997.
This book offers readings about Grotowski's entire career with contextualizing comments by the editors.

Stanislavsky, Konstantin [Stanislavski, Constantine], *An Actor Prepares*, Elizabeth Reynolds Hapgood, trans., New York: Theatre Arts Books, 1989.

_____, *Building a Character*, Elisabeth Reynolds Hapgood, trans., New York: Theatre Arts Books, 1994.
_____, *Creating a Role*. Elizabeth Reynolds Hapgood, trans., New York: Theatre Arts Books, 1989.
These two books allow actors who have read only *An Actor Prepares* to see how Stanislavsky became more and more interested in physical action in his later years.

Strasberg, Lee, *A Dream of Passion: The Development of the Method*, Evangeline Morphos, ed., New York: Plume, 1988.

Wangh, Stephen, *An Acrobat of the Heart: A Physical Approach to Acting Inspired by the Work of Jerzy Grotowski*, New York: Vintage, 2000.
This book explains in detail how the physical approach to acting progresses from training exercises to scene and character work. The last section of the book includes chapters on the psychological, political and spiritual aspects of acting training, and the final chapter is entitled, "How to Choose an Acting Teacher."

Wolford, Lisa, *Grotowski's Objective Drama Research*, Jackson: University Press of Mississippi, 1996.

Zarrilli, Phillip B., ed., *Acting (Re)Considered: A Theoretical and Practical Guide*, London: Routledge, 2002.
Zarrilli's book exposes the reader to many non-Western approaches to acting. It enables actors trained in traditional American techniques to think in new ways about the relationship between the body and the emotions.

JERZY GROTOWSKI was born in Rzeszow, Poland, in 1933. From 1951 to 1955, he studied acting at the State Higher Theatre School in Kraków. In 1955–1956, he studied directing at the Lunacharsky State Institute of Theatre Arts (GITIS) in Moscow, and in 1958 he studied with Yuri Aleksandrovich

Zawadsky, who had been a student of Stanislavsky and Vakhtangov. He also studied mime (with Marcel Marceau) and Indian and Chinese theater forms. In 1959, Grotowski and Ludwik Flaszen took over the Theatre of Thirteen Rows in the small Polish town of Opole. In 1965, they moved their group to Wrocław (known as "Breslau" in German), and in 1966 they renamed it the Institute for the Study of Acting Methods (and later, the Polish Laboratory Theatre). That year, Grotowski also began leading workshops outside of Poland, and in 1967 he came to the United States for the first time to conduct a workshop at New York University's Tisch School of the Arts.

The Polish Laboratory Theatre's productions of *Acropolis*, *The Constant Prince* and *Apocalypsis cum Figuris* made Grotowski's work world-famous in 1968 and 1969. But in 1970, he declared, "We live in a *post-theater* age. What is coming is not a new wave of theater, but something that will take the place occupied by it." (Burzynski, Tadeusz, and Zbigniew Osiński, *Grotowski's Laboratory*, Warsaw: Interpress Publishers, 1979, p. 101) At this point he began to create "holidays," paratheatrical rural retreats in which he invited nonactors to experience the "active culture" of the artist. In the late 1970s, he abandoned these participatory experiments to initiate "the Theater of Sources." For this experiential research, Grotowski invited shamans and teachers of ritual from all over the world to lead his students in a quest for "those elements of the ancient rituals of various world cultures which have a precise and therefore objective impact on participants." (Wolford, Lisa, *Grotowski's Objective Drama Research*, Jackson: University Press of Mississippi, 1996, p. 9) This work, which he called "objective drama," led Grotowski finally toward what Peter Brook has called "art as vehicle," a method of self-investigation for actors. He continued this work at the Centro per la Sperimentazione e la Ricerca Teatrale in Pontedera, Italy, until his death in 1999.

STEPHEN WANGH was born in 1943 and grew up in New York City. He graduated from Brandeis University in 1964, and after working as assistant to Joe Papp at the New York Shakespeare Festival, he attended the Yale School of Drama and New York University's School of the Arts. In 1967, while studying directing at NYU, he took part in a four-week workshop with Jerzy Grotowski.

When he graduated from NYU in 1968, Wangh founded the New York Free Theater, a political street-theater company. In 1973 he and Linda Putnam created Reality Theater in Boston, and in 1976 he became assistant professor of dramatic arts at Emerson College. Wangh began teaching at New York University in 1980, while at the same time founding the Actor's Space training program and Present Stage in Northampton, Massachusetts. He teaches and directs in Europe, Asia and America. He is arts professor in NYU's Tisch School of the Arts and visiting faculty at Naropa University in Boulder, Colorado.

His book, *An Acrobat of the Heart: A Physical Approach to Acting Inspired by the Work of Jerzy Grotowski*, was published by Vintage Books in

2000. His plays include *Class!*, *Calamity!* and *Goin' Downtown*. He was dramaturg for Moisés Kaufman's *Gross Indecency: The Three Trials of Oscar Wilde*, and associate writer for *The Laramie Project*. Visit his website, http://homepages.nyu.edu/~sw1, for more information.

THE SIX VIEWPOINTS

Mary Overlie

Influenced as a child by the painters of a small community of artists working in Montana, I developed a project to find the materials and principles involved in making theater. This project finally lured me to New York City and into an art community that I call the deconstructionists: artists working with mechanics rather than expression. I assembled the Six Viewpoints while working within this community. As performance was deconstructed in the real-time experiences of making dances, the raw materials were exposed, and from this the theory and its practices slowly came into focus. I had started to piece this work together in 1977, and in 1978 began to enter this work as a part of the theater training for the Experimental Theater Wing, a studio of the undergraduate theater department of New York University. This process kept developing, and was finally finished in 2002 as a complete theory. When I looked back I realized with a shock that it had taken twenty-seven years.

The Six Viewpoints began with dancers' questions about choreography, and has evolved into an investigation into theater in the era when so much crossover happened in the arts. The Six Viewpoints work can be seen and written about from the perspective of acting, directing, choreographing or dancing, and in Viewpoints work the term "theater" refers to both dance and drama. The following chapter is written from the perspective of acting training.

All art functions through the arrangement of information into specific logic systems. Logic is the means through which art delivers its messages and effects and becomes significant to us. Logic is one of the keys that links art to life. The Six Viewpoints presents a new structural approach to theater through a new arrangement of logic. The concepts framed in the Six Viewpoints are linked to an era of rethinking art—the process of training to be an artist, the definition of what it is to be an artist and the messages art endeavors to deliver to its audiences. The basis of this work is founded on very simple principles, yet these principles are easily misunderstood because of their radical shift in logic. Discovering the principles that this logic reveals and forming a verbal expression of these new concepts have been arduous and thrilling work.

This chapter is a small portion of a great deal of writing that I have done over the last seventeen years. With the exception of this chapter, this work has never been published. My need to present the entire logic has made me very reluctant to publish anything less thorough. I am pleased to contribute to this book, the first work in print on the Six Viewpoints.

THE SIX VIEWPOINTS PERSPECTIVE

The Six Viewpoints presents, through practical experiential practices, a different understanding of communication and approach to dialogue. It releases the existing materials of theater, formerly organized into various rigid hierarchical orders, into a fluid state for reexamination. It defines and makes practicable a new perspective on art that came into being in the late 1950s and continued to develop throughout the '60s and '70s.

At that time, the processes of minimalism and deconstruction caused a change in basic perspectives on art. Simply working with materials and concepts by accepting them on their own merit became a major source for art. This shift redrew the lines defining art around an entirely different set of concerns. The new work focused on bringing the audience beyond a definitive message, reaching instead toward a more fluid dialogue with possibilities and interaction. It was distasteful to make statements such as, "This is how I think of the world," which seemed overly concerned with the familiar and intent on distilling what had already been learned, thus removing the art, the artist and the audience from the adventure and challenge of pure experience. This new movement was more interested in taking things apart to access more information. Contemplation and redefinition and the accidental, incidental and everyday became primary sources of art. This repositioning of the source of art from imagination and visions to observation and interaction de-prioritized hierarchical ownership of art, and resulted in the massive shift away from the artist's being defined as a creator/originator. Absorbed in a dialogue with materials, the new artist could be more accurately defined as an observer/participant. Artists developed an entirely different set of skills, which focused on their ability to read space with their bodies, dissect time from various perspectives, and listen and see without the prejudice of the creator.

During this era in New York, a large number of artists from many disciplines were approaching the shift from creator/originator to observer/participant, each from an entirely different angle. Their commonality was in the process of taking things apart to expose more information, an approach that circumvented the requirement to create a definitive statement or, in many cases, a final product. These new artists worked under the supposition that structure could be discerned rather than imposed. This creative process, and the art it produced, centered on witnessing and interacting, and, in turn, redefined the role or activity of the audience. The audience, no longer presented with a finite vision from the artist, instead joined the artist as observers/participants. The redefinition of the role of the artist and the relationship of artist to audience created an environment of heightened equality or extreme democracy.

This release of hierarchy may indicate sheer chaos to the hierarchically subdued mind. Far from being chaotic or passive, this new interpretation of creativity and art was based on the sound principle that the act of seeing or witnessing generates its own structures. These structures produce their own progress without a preconceived and definitive statement created by a singular person/artist. This may sound like a relaxed and undemanding approach for the artist, but this new type of work is enormously strenuous. It demands concentration beyond the self, and a constant vigilance that you keep your own knowledge under strict control, so that you can be receptive to what the materials or events are actually trying to communicate, beyond what you think you already know. You might say that this new practice of art is a practice of not knowing, as opposed to knowing. To the hierarchically trained mind, this concept might seem mystical rather than practical, and definitely not something that could actually work in the world of creation. But, in all actuality, this is the system that all human beings enter when they encounter the unknown.

Viewpoints is an elaborate articulation of this artistic and philosophical process, composed of the isolation of the practical materials of theater and their languages, conceptual frames and established physical and mental practices.

Viewpoints is designed to help artists develop their own aesthetic perceptions by isolating six basic theatrical materials, so that each can be explored while the artists focus on developing their perceptual and interactive abilities. Because this work is done directly by the artist, not coached by a director, teacher or other higher authority, it promotes the development of a personal source of information, an intricate personal vocabulary pertaining to each material, and personal integrity. This work cannot be taught in a right/wrong, good/bad format. Guidance is only given to insure clarity of focus and separation of each of the six languages. One of the seminal points of Viewpoints is that it is not art, but simply a preparation system for making art.

To underline this point, the initial stages of these training practices are not presented in the context of theatrical events or scene work. The artist is asked simply to stand in a bare room and discover the languages of space, shape, time, emotion, movement and story. The goal of this work is to arrive at a dialogue with the six materials, to actually begin to communicate with them on your own. At the beginning of this work, and throughout its study, the artist and the materials must be given equal value. Because of the importance of nonhierarchical position, choice is of no importance in much of this work. In fact, it must be aggressively avoided. Space is as important as the artist, and makes as many moves on the artist as the artist makes on it. Choices come much later in this study, and when they enter, the artist is in an entirely different relationship to the process of choice-making and creativity.

Viewpoints practices are not theater games. If they are taken as such, perceptual development is short-circuited by the context of enthusiasm, competition and conviction. Viewpoints work is much more like the practice of kung fu or Japanese ink-brush drawing. Work is done in strictly deconstructed parts and reassembled much later. It is always dependent on what transpires in the moment. For instance, in the Stanislavsky system, the product—that is, the play— is necessary for the actor to understand and participate in the training. In contrast, the Six Viewpoints unhooks the actor from the issues of acting a character in a play, placing him in the theater with the deconstructed languages that surround him. This process defines a theater through deconstruction that is based on dialogue with the languages rather than traditional definitions of creativity. I sometimes refer to the Six Viewpoints as a process of "inventing the wheel backwards," because it has taken the highly organized and established idea of theater—what it is and what it is for—and inverted it, bringing the actor back to the raw materials.

To understand the Six Viewpoints, it is helpful to see it in the context of the artistic community that surrounds its development. In any study of the Six Viewpoints, it is helpful to be familiar with the work of these artists:

- Dance—Trisha Brown, Lucinda Childs, Merce Cunningham, Barbara Dilley, Simone Forti, David Gordon, Meredith Monk, Yvonne Rainer.
- Sculpture—Gene Highstein, Richard Nonas, Richard Serra, Keith Sonnier.
- Music—John Cage, Ornette Coleman, Philip Glass.
- Theater—JoAnne Akalaitis, Lee Breuer, Willem Dafoe, Richard Foreman, Elizabeth LeCompte, Ruth Maleczech, Judith Malina and Julian Beck, Sam Shepard, Ron Vawter, Robert Wilson.

These artists have worked extensively to train themselves to witness and simply work with what they perceive. Each is a highly accomplished deconstructionist who evokes powerful art from the simplest means and allows the materials to speak directly to the audience.

This idea of deconstructing is fundamental to the Six Viewpoints, and leads directly to finding new perceptions of reality to bring to an audience. Theater companies such as Mabou Mines, The Wooster Group, the Ontological-Hysteric Theater and The Living Theatre have experimented with the nature of narrative logic, actor-driven theater, language as sound, scripts as pictures, and timing as the score for action. By incorporating these and many other active sources, the definition of acting technique became much broader and, in many ways, more detailed. These groups deconstructed theater, then reconstructed it from the material they found. In the work of Robert Wilson (Byrd Hoffman Foundation), space and time became narrative lines; in the work of Lee Breuer (Mabou Mines), the story became an entity that could travel backward and forward simultaneously to create a message that added up to *a situation*; Elizabeth LeCompte (The Wooster Group) makes theater that is deeply musical, connecting the actors to the logic of the story through incredibly detailed timing; in the work of Richard Foreman (Ontological-Hysteric Theater), the actors become properties along with the set. The words become a snowstorm, rather than trying to keep things straight so they can be added up to mean one thing, pushing the audience toward the realization that meaning is a selfish and overwhelming force that does not necessarily do anyone any good. In all this work, the deconstruction process has brought an investigation into the nature and function of communication.

Ultimately, this work is the physical embodiment of a new philosophical step, called postmodernism. This new approach to art turns the entire western concept of thought on its ear by changing the definition and goal of intellectual and artistic pursuit. Rather than focusing on judgment and the establishment of certainty, postmodernism emphasizes inclusiveness and equality of information. This is in direct contrast to modernism, which works on reaching definitive descriptions of problems and endeavors to search for more perfect solutions. It is a mind-bending task to transition from a modernist perspective, stressing the need make a definitive statement in the pursuit of solutions, to the postmodern perspective, with its focus on dialogue and belief in the arrival rather than creation of solutions.

The Six Viewpoints helps define this radically different entrance into theater through both a theoretical and a practical process, employing minimalism and deconstruction. Using these two tools results in a part-by-part analysis of theater that encompasses a much more extensive definition of action than is drawn on by traditional theatrical approaches.

THE SIX VIEWPOINTS LANGUAGES

Viewpoints understands theater to consist of space, shape (design), time, emotion, movement and story (logic).

Separating theater into these six languages replaces the former hierarchy, centering on story and emotion, with a regard for each of the six languages as equal. This placement of equal attention establishes what is referred to as "the Horizontal" in Viewpoints work.

SOLID-STATE THEATER

Theater and acting training based on using all six languages simultaneously.

THEATER DECONSTRUCTED INTO SIX SEPARATE LANGUAGES

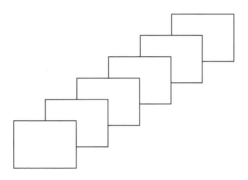

Traditional theater has these languages arranged in a hierarchical order:

Story

Emotion

Timing

Shape/Design

Movement

Space/Blocking

Note that these languages are connected, interdependent and supportive of the story in this relationship. When one language is moved, the rest must move in the same direction in order to remain a cohesive structure.

Viewpoints has deconstructed this order to fully investigate each of the six languages:

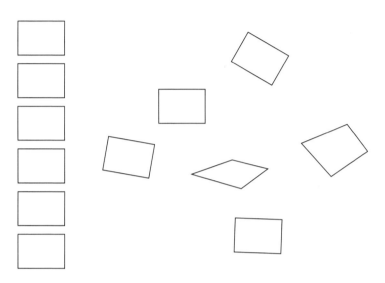

This deconstruction releases the verticality of hierarchy, since the six are no longer dependent on each other to support the main focus, leading to a profound new philosophical perspective that I refer to as the Horizontal.

Working from the Horizontal, the actor is free to construct performance through a choice of materials. An actor may choose to construct a performance through a focus on spatial interaction or physical movement. Once the Horizontal is established in practice, the actor is able to find new entrances into action, stepping from the language of one material into another and discovering a multitude of possibilities. This work inevitably leads to what I call the Matrix. This Matrix is constructed of a subtle intersection of the six languages, and the actor enters it by being able to change whichever language he or she is speaking mid-action or from moment to moment. It is a little like skiing down a field of moguls: shifting from a space language to a shape language to a time language within the process of picking up a cup or saying, "I love you," is like the body shifting its concentration at top speed while encountering the moguls. The actor can, through the Six Viewpoints, develop a dialogue onstage that weaves space into time and then switches to emotion before traveling on to the next moment. Through this process, the actor is anchored in a highly mobile environment and maintains an extreme mobility of perspective on communication and possibility. The Matrix practice is designed specifically for the actor to enter into an experiential dialogue based on contemplation and immersion. In this interaction, actors redefine language, becoming highly fluid conduits with other performers, the audience and the director.

This training process is deceptively simple in light of the complex behavior that results. As the performer enters the physical practices, the entire philosophical structure of the Six Viewpoints comes easily and naturally. This is because the artist is placed in the position of being his own guide. Most of the education in Viewpoints actor training comes from the actors' direct contact with the six languages through the practices. For example, when the actor is allowed to stand in space as a pure language, space quickly becomes tangible and full of information that it transmits directly to the performer. In the Six Viewpoints practices, there is no need for the teacher to point out the qualities embodied in each of these languages. In fact, since the education that space has to impart to the performer is nonverbal, the instructor cannot begin to do justice to it. Through this type of training, the actors become readers, mentally, emotionally and physically, and begin to develop their own skill with the six languages. Through this process, they are anchored onstage in an expanded personal communication process. This develops what I call the "Original Anarchist"—one who knows through experience what the right action is, and who can listen with great humility and clarity to others without losing himself.

The development of the Original Anarchist frees the actors from acting by allowing them to enter into a dialogue with what pre-exists in a production or a specific role. Actors are both humbled and strengthened by the experience of a much longer interaction with the languages of their trade. Acting with the six materials constructs an acting base in which personal emotions are but one aspect of an actor's technique.

Actors come to understand that space has its own emotion, that their emotions can be caused by the space, that design can communicate as powerfully as words, and that logic is a delicate and highly flexible tool of communication between audience and performer.

They can enter a scene through the language of design, using a shape in their body to create the role and communicate with the other actors. In taking this route, they find that the language of shape is carrying on its own dialogue with the other shapes, and all they have to do is read this dialogue and participate in it. In this situation, the actors are not really creating; they are skillfully following along as the medium of shape carries them forward into action. Through this work, actors find that the issue of motivation, so important to live performance, can come purely from one or more of the languages. Once this awareness becomes rooted in the acting practice, actors find that they have many more options and entrances into action via the Matrix of the six separated languages. The Viewpoints approach to acting considers each of these languages as a performer, and the actors simply interact with them. The actors' ability to shift focus among each of these six languages brings the necessary awareness to act in the Matrix.

With the removal of hierarchy, the Six Viewpoints philosophy and training works to establish a truth that is contingent on real materials. This work proposes the idea that the actor is not obliged to convince the audience, but can join them in an investigation. The Six Viewpoints defines the actor as an investigator, responsible for becoming a highly tuned instrument of investigation and communication. This act of witnessing becomes the key to Viewpoints acting training.

Viewpoints training progresses through a system of studies. The practices are applied to these steps in various ways, providing entrances into the materials. To give an idea of how the Six Viewpoints works, I have made a brief description of a few Viewpoints practices.

SHAPE OF THE STUDY

- Locating the Horizontal: Learning how to clearly deconstruct and differentiate between space, shape, time, emotion, movement and story.
- Entering the Horizontal: Learning how to enter into each of these perceptual languages in order to gain direct experiential knowledge.
- Working Without Knowing: Learning how to recognize and interact with structure in the moment.
- Shaping Choices: Learning how to use multiple focuses.

- ☐ Formulating Logic: Learning how to construct from the horizontal.
- ☐ Realism vs. Abstraction: Learning how to work critically.

LOCATING THE HORIZONTAL

It is necessary to learn how to deconstruct theater to achieve the Horizontal. In this step, the six materials or languages can be freed from the solid-state structure of theater. Viewpoints presents a study of theater that distinguishes between the material and personal motivation, symbolism, process or product. To achieve the Horizontal in a practical sense, you must be able to differentiate between the languages of the six materials. This can be done by going into a studio and choosing to focus on one of the materials. Once you understand that it is possible to focus on one material at a time, you can say to yourself and others, "Now look at space, now at time, now at shapes, now at movement, now at story, now at emotion." It is necessary to give each of these materials time to come into focus. I tell actors that it takes about thirty-six hours with each focus to begin to fully perceive the languages. This advice hints at the benefits and necessity of repeated practice in this work.

Deconstructing Space

Students deconstruct and explore space in the Six Viewpoints simply by walking into a room and observing (a basic Viewpoints practice). Through this physical activity, the artist as observer/participant begins to discover the spatial angles that connect one corner to the other, the door to the window, etc. The patterns, dimensions and architectural details become an expanding creative palette. Now I am looking at the space; I am not looking at objects, movement, time, my presence in this room, or the reason that I am in the room.

The primary practice for this work is called "Walk and Stop." Actors simply alternate walking and stopping in a studio or stage. This extremely minimal set of instructions helps actors avoid the temptation to elaborate on performance possibilities, such as adding body shapes, adding timing, or working with any of the languages in a way that might confuse their discovery of basic spatial principals. Walking and Stopping carries you into space to meditate on your perceptions, distance, and the rituals of space. In this work, the actors make observations such as, "I am three feet, ten inches from X," "I can see X from where I stand," "I look like this in relationship to X," "The length of the room is X," "I can execute this floor pattern in this space," "I feel strong here and weak there." There are thousands of bits of spatial information actors can discover once they begin to recognize space as a separate language.

Architectural detail alone, separate from distance and other languages of space, is a powerful and influential spatial language in acting. When actors are able to work with an awareness of the architecture, they can use it as a magnifying glass to enlarge their own presence. Actor Richard Burton made great use of architecture, including his position on the set, to bring the audience into the world he occupied. Studying his entrances, you see that he uses the space with great articulation, focusing the architecture to frame his action rather than standing apart from his environment. In Viewpoints study, this branch of space, architectural space, has been given special practices because of the richness of the information and the usefulness it has for the actor as a performance awareness tool.

The longer you work with spatial awareness, the more you will discover in your own performance.

Deconstructing Shape

Shape or design can be deconstructed into a separate language by simply observing the body as it creates design. Through this process, familiarity is developed with symmetry and asymmetry, curved and straight lines, balanced and unbalanced form. This study brings actors to an awareness of their plastic communication. Shape is the primary tool for such theatrical aesthetics as commedia dell'arte, Kabuki, Inuit and Balinese theater.

Actors who have an awareness of what they look like have a more powerful presence onstage. Viewpoints separates the shape language from formal studies such as ballet, Grotowski *plastiques*, and other traditional forms in order to give actors contact with this language as a raw material. As actors develop awareness in this language, it is much easier for them to acquire other formal, shape-based performance languages. By isolating this material as an experiential perception beyond form, the actor acquires shape awareness rather than a set vocabulary.

The basic practice for isolating shape is called "Shape 1–1." This should be practiced both solo and with a partner. To practice, the actor moves his or her body into a position, then stops, tries to see the form, moves again, stops, sees, etc. In duet form, the actors move one at a time, each taking time to absorb the other and the collective, then change to a new shape. As this practice progresses, the actor can speed up the process until his moves from one shape to another are continuous, and the witnesses of his mind and senses are so acute that they may keep up with the rapidity of the passing formal languages of shape.

Familiarity with shape and investigation of its language requires stillness and observation. It is somewhat mysterious that, in this work, the slower you proceed, the quicker the language of shape will begin to speak. Perhaps the answer to this strange principle is that shape occupies its own sense of time, and by surrendering to it we see it with greater and greater clarity.

When you isolate shape as a separate focus, you find that constant activity is not required onstage. Instead, like a vase in the window, the actor's visual presence interacts in the scene with a highly active language of its own. As actors begin to realize the techniques of using this theatrical material, staying present when there is no action or line to play, they find incredible pleasure and strength in knowing that they are acting through the sheer design of their bodies.

Another interesting attribute of this training is that the practices that lead to isolating its languages must start long before any dialogue about good or interesting shapes can be considered. Interest in shape without judgment allows the actor's perceptions to penetrate to the finest levels of focus. This special focus also brings the discovery that the individual actor does not need to be in creative command, but simply in conversation. This is a profound ensemble-building component of Viewpoints training. As the actor's ability to perceive and interact with design develops, the languages of shape begin to generate more uses and articulation than the individual artist could possibly provide from his own creativity. In addition to the primary practices used to isolate a focus on shape, there are approximately seven basic shape practices involved in the study of the Six Viewpoints, and many more practices that have been invented by directors using Viewpoints.

Deconstructing Time

The languages of time possess, in my mind, the most dramatic and emotional impact of the materials in theater. They encompass automatic and calculated rhythm, duration, tempo, speed and impulse.

Their effect on performers and audience is unexpectedly and deceptively profound for a material that is presented as an abstract and arbitrary language in our current civilization.

To locate time, it is imperative to study it outside of formal systems, since we have reified and codified time to such an extent that it is all but impossible for us to contact it as a pure material. Our modern habitat discourages and inhibits us from reading time on our own. We rarely make or take our own time and do not develop the ability to read the time of others, surrendering our own sense of this material to the powerful and often maniacal social clock that ticks in every corner of our lives. The idea that "time is money" is firmly fixed in most people's minds. In the theater, however, time is a material that reaches beyond our sense of practicality and touches the nerves of our very existence. This is true for the actor, the director and the audience. The Six Viewpoints lays a foundation for time awareness before going into other practices that involve the study of boundless time and impulse.

Time is an exacting language that cannot be experienced without total surrender. This may sound intimidating to all but the most physically accomplished, but the simplicity of the Six Viewpoints is isolation of materials. The beautiful physical work that comes from this surrender is a by-product of the ability to focus exclusively on the material itself. Once the surrender has been accomplished by sheer focused detail, time has the mysterious and thrilling ability to arrange physical fulfillment of its needs with total precision. When the actor is working in time as a pure material, separate from space or logic, it guides the body to go where it demands. When time is deconstructed from the whole and relocated in the Horizontal, it is found to have its own kinesthetic vocabulary.

The first practice for deconstructing and locating time employs a new focus on the practice of Walk and Stop. As with the first Walk and Stop, this new approach also requires that the actor use no movements other than walking and stopping. Staying with the simple, unarticulated body insures that the concentration can remain on time, just as it had previously insured that the focus would stay on space. The actor simply focuses on length of time standing, length of time walking and speed of walking, either solo or in a group. The collected experiences begin to form a focus that reveals time in one of its most basic languages, that of duration.

It is extremely important to explore the language of time as duration, although from the outset this requires nerve, patience and devotion. There is a wonderful benefit for the actor who passes through this work. Actors trained to entertain the audience by using excitement and high emotion become locked into a limited understanding of the use of time, and begin to believe that the audience demands a certain kind of timing in order to be satisfied with their performance. Since, in Viewpoints work, there is no idea of entertainment, the focus of this primary practice exposes time as a solid and ever-present material, moving the actor past preconceived fears of audience judgment. This turns timing into a territory where time exists independently and communicates on its own terms.

To enrich this base, Viewpoints training has many practices to approach other languages of time for which we have not yet established any labels—crunch time, wrinkled time, shattered time, cloud time. Moving in an unknown time frame, the actor becomes familiar with a more subtle world. He discovers that it is possible to be in a time language that is far removed from our common and limited vocabulary. Time is also studied through practices in repetition, through which the actor finds the appreciation of variation and the subtlety of communication; patterning, through which the actor finds compositional control; and impulse, through which the actor finds the language of responding and acting at the very edge of time—perhaps you could say where time begins.

All these practices build a simple awareness and articulation of timing. Reading time in this manner builds confidence and accuracy and connects actor to actor, audience to actor, and director to both. Ensemble skills are automatically developed, since in practicing the perceiving of time, actors work in a powerful universal language that binds people, animals, mountains and planets together.

The skill of responding without hesitation develops automatically as the actor locates and is located within the principles of the material. As actors practice isolating time, they begin to develop an absolute willingness to respond. These practices in time remove the painful problem of second-guessing. When this language is not manipulated, but rather discerned, it creates a sublime, supportive, subliminal connectedness.

Deconstructing Emotion

What is the basic language of emotion? Viewpoints finds emotion in what it calls "the dog-sniff-dog world"—presence and the reading of presence by ourselves and others. Emotion cannot be discerned as a separate material until it is separated from its traditional partner, story. Again, this is a difficult task for the actor. Reification has these two stuck together as inextricably as layers in plywood.

The basic practice to locate this material as a pure and independent part of theater requires actors to sit and let themselves be observed at length, with no focus or activity to distract them. It involves observing and being observed without blocking the normal thought patterns, the feelings that float in and out in daily life. The Six Viewpoints initially studies emotion through presence practices to develop the actors' ability to observe and embrace their inner life, and to expand their willingness and ability to share that inner world with others. Finally, these practices develop actors' ability to invite the audience into the very subtle world of being.

The basis of the language of emotion in Viewpoints work is our ability to interact in the present from a natural flow of being. In order to establish the presence of the actors, hours of self-observation and performances, built on ordinary behavior in daily life, are required. This focus demonstrates to actors that they are interesting to watch and capable of being watched without a role to carry them. Truly interesting actors are fully present with themselves and able to deliver that presence to the audience with confidence, detail and generosity. The practice of presence gives actors a double focus of maintaining their own, fully lived life while developing the life of the character. This adds dimension to their acting and makes it possible for them to communicate directly with the audience over and beyond the life of their character.

The basic Viewpoints practice for emotion is called Presence Work. Actors sit on chairs, allowing their thoughts, breathing, movements, feelings and even physical sensations of biofeedback to remain active in their awareness. As they sit, the actors begin to open themselves to the experience of being watched. They work on looking directly into the eyes of their audience, and then reverse the conditions, looking away so that they are seen without being able to see. Focusing on the emotional transitions caused by each of these gazes allows the actor to work on blocking information, transitions of thought and feeling.

In this approach to emotion, the artist is only a reader. The more detailed the actors become in their perception of what is transpiring, the clearer the material of emotion becomes. This practice of presence clears a path for actors to encounter what we call emotions, both in themselves and in the audience. If you can let the space speak, for instance, you will find yourself performing with it. This principle applies to each of these languages. When actors accomplish the horizontal location of their presence, they enter the "dog-sniff-dog world." Humans function, as do other animals, through the rapid and subtle sensing of presence. This is the Viewpoints equivalent of traditional interpretations of acting as located in emotion. The difference is that, in Viewpoints work, emotion is only one material among six equal materials, neither more nor less important than the others. In this subtle emotional work, many emotions are allowed to be onstage at one time. Emotions shift free of the dictates of the story, perhaps focusing on the effects of the space or the thought of going home to a lonely dog after the performance. It is actually more life-like to realize that, in response to a given situation, a person may feel sad, happy, fearful and expansive at the same time.

The practice of focusing the senses through Presence Work also helps the actor realize that the audience can read far more than is normally assumed. As the actors sit in front of their audience with nothing in the world to do but be there, they begin to realize that they can direct the audience's concentration by placing their own awareness. In loosening the definition of emotion, the practices allow the actor to see that, just as time has many languages that have no labels, there are many emotions that have no names and no common recorded verbal history, but do, nonetheless, exist. In fact, everything has a presence and communicates emotion. A chair communicates an emotional presence, and if we look at it in a deconstructed, horizontal manner, it can be just as important as, or more important than, an actor's own emotions.

Another important practice, Scripted Movement, is used to reveal emotion from an entirely different perspective and language. Scripted Movement explores emotion by placing the focus entirely outside the realm of the actor. This practice is as strenuous as Presence Work is dimensional. The effort that the actor must initially apply, and the zeal and discipline he or she must then maintain, eventually reveal a fascinating new acting technique and source of emotion. I call this type of emotional language *ex-acting*, meaning that emotions are generated and fulfilled strictly in an exterior structure, much like the exoskeletal structure of some insects. This practice is entered by setting a detailed blocking that includes small gestures, spatial blocking, timing and visual focus. The actor must create this structure and commit it to memory before the second part of the practice can be added. Next, a scene is selected by an outside party. Having accomplished this, the performers memorize their lines and begin to work the scene to study how the blocking and other parts of the physical script can be justified into the context of the written script. The actors begin to see a whole language of detailed emotional content that is based on the juxtaposition between the set physical script and the text script. They consider the possibility that the emotional content of the words may be revealed to a much greater extent if they do not follow the meaning of the words with their bodies. Eventually, the actor can begin to separate the actions from the words and float in a world of several focuses at one time, forging an emotional dialogue that comes from his exterior struggle with the disparate elements thrown into the scene. No longer carrying the burden of thinking the characters are more important than they are, or committed to keeping the emotional material steadily aligned with the plot, the actors can isolate emotion as a material separate from story, thereby developing into acute observer/participants in the emotional life of the theater.

In deconstructing theater to focus exclusively on emotion, the actor must separate emotion from story as a primary issue and then place emotion in an equal relationship to the other five materials. Then the actor begins to see that sitting still, staring at a spot on a rug, tensing and relaxing his body, and taking a long time before speaking can reach a powerful and unnamable emotional communication that can electrically charge the senses of the audience.

Deconstructing Movement

Movement is easier to identify than any of the other materials. Perhaps this is because it is our most immediate and tangible medium. In Viewpoints training, movement is the main tool used to prepare the body for the highly specialized demands created by the postmodern definition of art, and of the artist as the observer/participant. It is through movement that the actor learns skeletal alignment, which leads to clarity in reading at what degree the body is facing the wall or the proscenium. It is through movement that the body meets the challenges of time, experiments with shape and explores a deep source of emotion (as Grotowski discovered). At the heart of this material lies the seed of the Original Anarchist—our reality anchored for us by our physical participation in existence and the common bonds of pain, health, touch, hunger.

To approach movement through the deconstructive quest of the Six Viewpoints, the actor must remove this material from all its disciplines and applications and find a pure definition that allows access to the basic material. To be deconstructed as a separate voice, movement must be carefully isolated from the languages of time, space and shape. Most people cannot conceive of movement existing without seeing it moving through space and taking a certain form in the body—but, in fact, the properties of movement have nothing to do with form or space. Excluding these other materials, while tightening the focus on movement, not only challenges the actor's discipline of deconstruction, but also introduces him to a wonderful new world of expression that has nothing to do with dance, sports or pedestrian movement. This language is the closest thing I can think of to pure sensuality. When separated from solid-state theater, dance or sports, movement is comprised of many properties—gravity, fulcrum, balance, pendulum action, kinetic response and sensation, just to name a few. Through Viewpoints practices, the body becomes knowledgeable of and integrated with internal and external forces of movement. The basic Viewpoints practice for creating pure movement focus is similar to the basic space practice of simply standing in the room. Movement practice guides the actor to discover movement by moving from pure sensation in the body. Through this simple practice, the actor will develop knowledge of movement's basic properties without any of the additional sculpturing of movement found in dance or other physical training. It may seem that employing this principle would result in a room full of actors writhing around in uncontrolled mayhem, but actually, the language of movement is naturally ordered and graceful.

In explanation and defense of this rather libertarian practice and point of view, it should be pointed out that the great athlete, the efficient farmer and the talented golfer are all people who have had a natural and self-led introduction to the nature of movement as a basis for their eventual development. Furthermore, it is common for our society to believe that the body must be tamed and organized by exterior forms. Viewpoints practice directly opposes this idea of movement in human development.

We count on the body's movement to get us through the day mostly unguided. We have been taught to use this language to accomplish things, and are shy about thinking of it as a language on its own. I have found that most actors are grateful for the opportunity to work with Viewpoints movement practices, as opposed to their traditional dance classes. Movement comes to the actors' recognition much faster through sensation than through formal systems requiring movement memory. The type of physical training that supports Viewpoints work has specific attributes. At the end of this explanation of the Six Viewpoints, I have made a description of the types of training that support this work and why.

Over the years, I have found that actors enter the theater in many ways: through their bodies, through specific concepts of space, through emotional exchange, through communicating with the form and appearance of their bodies, and through time. In approaching deconstruction of solid-state theater, an actor will have a natural affinity for one of these materials, and because of that attachment he will tend to place the other, less familiar, five languages as secondary or supporting characters to his favorite language. Actors may also have difficulty differentiating among the materials because they explore them all through their favorite medium, unconsciously unable to remove it from the practices. In seeking to locate movement, physically oriented actors are often deeply challenged to locate space. They have such an acute internal focus on sensation that space disappears for them.

Deconstructing Story

Viewpoints exercises isolate story as a discrete material by looking at narrative as flexible logic. Long ago, in developing the Six Viewpoints technique, I decided to call this element "story," instead of the more universal label, "logic," to challenge both abstractionists and traditional storytellers, and to push them past presumed aesthetic boundaries. Viewed from the Six Viewpoints perspective, story, at its basic level, is nothing more than an arrangement of information. If we put the saltshaker behind or in front of the pepper, we are selecting this arrangement from thousands if not millions of options, each with its own meaning.

Story and logic, easily engender conditions of prejudice because of their proximity to hierarchical thinking. Story and logic are processes of ordering and prioritizing information. We normally require this hierarchical action to comply with traditional hierarchical standards: a story must touch on a truth, and its logic must be irrefutable. Unfortunately, these goals have nothing to do with the fundamental issues of the material of logic, so it is necessary for an artist to reach beyond this natural hierarchical block in order to find this material and its languages.

In deconstructing theater and locating the material of story, it is extremely important for actors to seek experiential understanding of the nature of pure logic. Many actors think abstraction tells no story when, in reality, it is a perfectly thought-out structure containing a beginning, middle and end. Many actors, along with other artists who embrace the idea of the abstract in art, believe that this type of work has nothing to do with a story that exists in some pure world of objects, paint, words or sound. For an actor approaching the material of story as a pure voice, both ideas are wrong.

There are a multitude of Viewpoints practices that aid the actor in identifying the material of story. A primary example of a story practice is the Running Story. In this practice, the story or logic should be held with the lightest grasp, so that at the slightest tremble the story can jump boundaries, colliding with other stories and changing into something totally different. An actor might start out as an insect, creeping along the floor, and then arch his or her back to form a bridge that begins making connections between door and wall, window and floor. From there, the actor might turn into the water beneath the bridge, roll over on the floor, end up in a teacup at the Mad Hatter's tea party and begin writing the story as Lewis Carroll. In a group practice, the stories of other actors must be transferred into the individual's story by means of justification. It is not necessary or even desirable to know the story or logic of the other actors. For each actor, the story that is unfolding is centered only on his own reality.

This practice conditions the actor to the nature of story, in which information and developments can change at any moment for thousands of reasons. Acquiring an understanding of this aspect of story benefits the actor, who must deal with many characters' motivations and story lines while creating his own logical sequence of events.

A more advanced story practice places the actors into a story that is being created from three unrelated texts at one time by instant justification. This justification, much like the development of emotional motivation from the tensions between text and blocking in the Scripted Movement practice, allows the actor to explore story as an observer/participant. In both these practices, the actor must work with great concentration and flexibility to keep up with what is happening, rather than making something happen. As a result, the actor begins to learn from story. The difference is massively significant when you think of the artist shifting between creator and observer. It also has great social implications when this process is applied to our interpretations of truth and information.

Deconstructing the material of story from the other materials of theater provides endless possibilities for experimenting with meaning. A more advanced story practice is to play with possible logic structures: a performance could start in the middle and proceed simultaneously toward the beginning and end. This seemingly abstract idea is, in actuality, more like most real-life stories. Another option in playing with logic would be to begin with information that seems to progress in a logical structure, but suddenly starts to fragment or shatter into a multiplicity of opinions and directions of information. There can be many simultaneous logics functioning in any given set of experiences.

Story is a powerful and necessary tool, and it can also be an enormous trap. We order information into stories as a survival tool. In real life, if we were unable to relate the logic of a situation we would not survive very long. The way we tell a story will often determine the outcome. We are constantly adjusting the telling of stories in different ways to create different effects.

Actors working with a Viewpoints-based understanding of story must focus on communicating with the audience. This is critical because the more deeply actors understand the function of logic for the audience, the more information they are able to offer the audience. People are natural sleuths—it is a necessity of life. We must try to find out what something means and where it fits into the structure that we know. Accepting this condition, the actor can play very complicated logics with confidence, because he or she knows that the audience will be working to find out what is being said.

In the initial isolation of story, basic Viewpoints practices ask the actors to investigate common objects such as refrigerators, mailboxes and wastebaskets. The actor begins to discover that everything has a story, and that we know these stories as intimately as we know the human dramas we have learned as children. It is common knowledge that refrigerators have personality and histories, but it is not articulated knowledge. This practice sets the idea of story apart from the human dilemma and focuses on the issue of collected data. When the actor allows the story to speak for itself, the audience automatically jumps on for the ride.

ENTERING THE HORIZONTAL

In the Horizontal, actors, having developed the ability to separate the materials, now step into the structure of the work, improvising with combining the materials to build a fluid observer/participant flow of action. Entering the Horizontal is the equivalent of getting the feel for the weight of a hammer, knowing the right consistency for mixing cement, or experiencing what it takes to draw a line on paper. Once the languages have been found, the actors must then become proficient at working in them. Entering the Horizontal, entering the Viewpoints, means working *in* space, time, shape, movement, story and emotion on an improvisational level. The Viewpoints are not yet encountered on an abstract or creative level. The work remains anchored in a physical reality. This step in the progression of the practice slowly begins to form the foundation for creative choices that will be anchored in horizontal practice, identifying temporary hierarchical structures through observation and participation.

WORKING WITHOUT KNOWING

Working Without Knowing means that the outcome is not predicted, yet a product emerges. This is accomplished through improvisation focused toward acknowledging what has been created. The actors work to become skilled observers using memory recall and repetition, while acting as full participants, refusing to predict or guide the end result. With this step, the actors have arrived at the heart of Viewpoints study. They recognize the event as it appears, gradually developing the ability to hold several simultaneous focuses while continuing to be aware of what is transpiring.

The actors learn to identify structural possibilities, products and events while remaining in a horizontal, nonhierarchical equality with the materials. Holding several focuses at one time, the actors develop the ability to sustain duality. This is the beginning of the establishment of the Matrix. At this stage of the study, the actors automatically develop the ability to listen, respond, hold focus, shift focus, coordinate body and mind, remove boundaries and find fluidity of thought.

The most important skill developed at this level of work is the ability to *change lenses* while engaged in action. Changing lenses involves moving awareness from one language to another while maintaining a single action. For example, an actor may be in a dialogue that is based on space—e.g., sitting near a wall—and then change that perception into the language of emotion. The new lens of emotion will take the action in a different direction without the actors consciously making a change. The actors, employing a strict focus on the new lens of emotion, develop the ability to follow its messages in a subtle shift of direction, eventually entering the Matrix in multi-layered, complex shifts from one material to another.

The use of the practice of Walk and Stop, combined with shape language in a Viewpoints practice called Japanese Garden, gradually begins to build into this complexity by allowing actors to observe, without losing their ability to work or predetermining what they want to happen. This practice puts an ensemble into a room with five instructions—walk, stop, stand, sit or lie down. The bodies become living temples in a determined spatial arrangement that offers a whole visual entity for contemplation, yet no one actor has created the picture they are meditating on. This is a slow and quiet practice that allows the actors time to absorb form, recall events, and enter into a dialogue with space and the simple shapes of standing, sitting and lying down. To create this step of development, Working Without Knowing, the actors must be in a dialogue with the languages or materials of theater without being responsible for creating them. Protected at this level from having to know, the actors develop strength and security through discovering the possibilities that come from interaction with the materials.

If this level of the work is given the time that it requires, it closes the door on a debilitating kind of judgment and opens it to creative innovation. Working Without Knowing uses the Viewpoints to let the actor take a swim in performance before it is defined into the structure of a play. This swim should produce a big personal soup of additional resources in terms of images, options and forms.

If you are prepared for the unknown, you are standing in a place that assures that you can make art from mistakes, misunder-standings and all other real-life events that surround you. You can make art that carries life, rather than predictability.

SHAPING CHOICES

This is mind-expanding work. With careful practice, performers can grow from being competent actors to rocket scientists. Actors who are able to work in all six languages, making independent choices that come together in one character, are thrilling to watch.

In this step, performers start to make choices in the diversity of a nonhierarchical world. Actors begin to actually use, rather than interact with, the materials located by Viewpoints. At the beginning of this work the actors should focus on limiting themselves to the choice of two languages at one time. Maintaining two thought processes takes a great deal of practice, and actors must be allowed to move slowly. If this work feels comfortable at first, actors are most likely working in a vertical dialogue. A vertical dialogue has only one focus and is much easier to handle. A vertical use of space means that the actor allows the space to be dictated by the story. For example, in a scene involving a conflict with another character, an actor working vertically would characteristically face his opponent and move forward. A horizontal approach to the relationship of story and space gives the actor the options of sitting perfectly still, looking off into the distance, or advancing slowly in a direction away from the scene partner.

FORMULATING LOGIC/STORIES

The Six Viewpoints work defines story as information placed in a particular logical order. It is important to understand that in this approach to theater, working with story always comes after prolonged research of the other five materials or languages. Through practicing action and developing the lenses for interaction, the artist comes to appreciate how the various elements relate to each other and form logic. As the skill to perceive logic develops, the issue of finding one's own meaning and content begins to confront the artist. This is the big conceptual step in Viewpoints work. Making a story or creating logic is arduous work, because there are so many lines that have to be folded into a logical structure in order to form communication. Large decisions must be made about the shape and point of the communication. The big questions of what are you trying to say and how are you going to say it finally come to sit in the studio with the director and the performer. Whatever logic coordinates are chosen must be developed along consequent lines. If the logic is structurally weak, the play or performance will be weak and ineffective. If you decide that you are directing chaos, then you must be vigilant that it is real chaos, not indicated chaos. If you want to direct indicated chaos then you must be sure that it is indicated chaos. If you are directing a set, traditional structure, then the material, choices and performance must hold true to that structure.

Once they have explored the nature of structure, artists must make individual choices about what they want to communicate and find the discipline to hold true to that structure. The stronger the disciplines, the more effective the communication. One way Viewpoints work deals with this issue is through the conceptual frame of the Piano, which imagines that the audience is an instrument that can be played by the actors and director. This analogy is meant to suggest to the actors that members of the audience also see and interact with space, shape, time, movement, story and emotion. When this is accomplished, the artists are free to bring any message they wish to the audience, using any materials they wish, confident that the audience is capable of reading anything that is presented to it with discipline. The Six Viewpoints states that the audience is as sensitive as the artists who play it. The actors' work is to establish the sensitivity of the Piano. Viewpoints sees audience members as masters of investigation who love the twists and turns of a good piece of new logic, played in any and all of the materials of the theater, just as the actor loves to communicate with these same materials.

Much of this work should already be established as the practice of Presence Work is explored. In Presence Work, the actor comes to understand that he can communicate to the audience everything that is transpiring simply by being present. With this underlying knowledge, the artists should begin to understand that if they are working in space, the audience will be able to see this and read its meaning.

REALISM VS. ABSTRACTION

Debates over the issues of abstract and realistic art inevitably come up in any Viewpoints study. Emerging from this horizontal procedure into theater, actors are faced with the question, "What is real, and what is not?" The deconstruction of theater makes this an interesting and important question. Suddenly it is time to look at the castle that was left behind, and the territory into which we have moved. What is the definition of performance, and how does the artist place himself in the dialogue of this debate?

To truly embrace the teachings of this work, it is necessary to understand that the distinction between abstraction and realism is an aesthetic choice. In the end, all art draws from abstract form, from elemental materials. All theater is built from time, movement, emotion, logic, space and shape. Rodgers and Hammerstein's *South Pacific* is made of the same materials as Robert Wilson's *A Letter for Queen Victoria*. In applying this work of the horizontal, it is up to the artists to make the choice between the styles commonly called "realism" and "abstraction." In making this choice, artists define where they stand in the historical dialogue of their art form, and can enter that dialogue with a responsible voice. Finally, this choice of abstract vs. realism takes the study of these materials into the serious and challenging question of self-expression, and the substance of artists' personal aesthetics and beliefs in relationship to the world.

PHILOSOPHICAL FRAME OF THE VIEWPOINTS

In order to fully understand the context of the Six Viewpoints and its historical background, it is important to understand its relationship to postmodernism and compare this philosophy to modern and classical beliefs.

Postmodernism is actually easy to understand when seen through the theory of Viewpoints. Over the years, I have developed the illustration below to express postmodernism in relationship to the two philosophies that preceded and led to it. If you compare this drawing to the last of the Six Viewpoints drawings at the beginning of this chapter, you will see the similarity in structure. This similarity was discovered over many years of work and caused a great expansion in my understanding of this work on a philosophical level.

CLASSICISM

MODERNISM

POSTMODERNISM

Classicism and modernism investigated reality in a vertical order. Both philosophies employed the assumption that absolute universal laws could be established, and believed that all information could be naturally ordered into a common set of rules that supported this organization. Toward the end of the modernist period, the investigation became so detailed, through deconstruction and application of minimalism, that it caused a deep separation of information. This separation of essential or basic materials resulted in a loss of hierarchy. As a result, the vertical or hierarchical order of information changed to a horizontal position in which all information was regarded as having equal importance. Difference became the new focus; consensus was established through identifying patterns of agreement. Mobility of information increased in this new horizontal world as the learned and held hierarchical patterns were removed, creating a much more complex understanding of reality. In this repositioning, our attention is placed on our ability to read and interact, rather than to establish one reality that others must be persuaded to join and support. The scientific effect of this new perspective can be found in the development of the chaos and string theories.

The difference between classical, modern and postmodern statements is that the first two try to establish a truth that is permanent and the third tries to examine information to see what truth arises. Postmodernism accepts that any truth will change in time as more information is known or as the circumstances vary. The first two processes offer a security of absolute knowledge; they are anchored in their emphasis on structures. What anchors postmodernism is direct experience and contemplation. Postmodernism offers a dialogue in which many truths can be entertained at one time.

At this point in time, postmodernism seems to us to be extremely complex. I believe that much of the complexity we perceive is due to the still prevalent training in hierarchical structure. Many modernists see postmodernism as a dangerous, wishy-washy infection. While I do not believe that this is true, I do think that the failings of all three philosophical positions can be argued. The hierarchical beliefs that caused the exemptions of large amounts of information, demanding polarization and resulting in exclusion, have affected our lives in negative ways. On the other hand, the current confusion—caused by misunderstanding this new postmodern philosophy that is so sensitively dependent on dialogue—is dangerous indeed. Rather than choosing one side or another, I prefer to see the situation as an ongoing effort to evolve a new thinking on how to improve society, art and thought. In this dialogue, the Six Viewpoints focuses on training the artist to understand and function as a responsible, self-reliant individual.

It is important to note that one of this work's postmodern qualities is inclusion rather than exclusion of the achievements of the past. The Six Viewpoints does not place the artist, actor, director, dancer or choreographer in an either-or situation. This training is not at war with Grotowski, Stanislavsky-based or classical training. This is because it functions in a postmodern "both-and" structure, rather than a classical or modern "either-or" condition.

When you remove information from a hierarchical form, the only thing left is practical dialogue. It is, therefore, impossible to understand postmodernism, and the small part of it called the Six Viewpoints, divorced from physical experience. The practice of the Six Viewpoints necessitates a highly detailed physical training for the artist, since, in this work, the body is the instrument of observation and participation.

Although this seems to indicate an overwhelming new demand on the actor, it is actually much easier to enter into and acquire than traditional dance training.

THE SIX VIEWPOINTS PHYSICAL TRAINING

On this pivotal issue, Viewpoints theory uses a fusion of different physical techniques—Contact Improvisation, created by Steve Paxton; Allan Wayne technique; the body-mind centering training of Bonnie Cohen; and the floor barre work of Jean Hamilton. Other training techniques that rely on the breakdown of the moving body can also be included in Viewpoints studies, but the techniques that I have listed have a traditional interface with this theory. In order to give the reader a clearer picture of what this type of training encompasses, I offer a brief description of these systems and their influence on the actor's development in this work.

CONTACT IMPROVISATION

The study of Contact Improvisation brings the actor into 360-degree spatial conditioning and builds collaborative ensemble skills through the interdependent conditions of the study. This work gives actors firsthand experience with the principles found in new physics and chaos theory. Contact delivers the basic joy of physical existence, the pleasure of the animal nature of our reflexive mind/body relationship. Its study removes the constraints society places on the body, teaching a highly developed sense of play based on attention to the details of the physical forces that are exerted on us in daily life. This work imparts knowledge of gravity, fulcrums, weight distribution, weight transference, momentum and balance.

JEAN HAMILTON'S FLOOR BARRE

The technique of Jean Hamilton trains the actor to articulate in both diastole (initiating from the periphery) and proximal (initiating from the joint) paths of movement. This study, in turn, increases articulation and strength of the spine, foot and knee through fine muscle development. Floor barre work gives the actor a sense of great stability and control over his body. Actors discover that their bodies can transform in shape and range of motion as a physical reality. Through this experience of transformation, the actor learns that nothing is finite. The Hamilton work extends the conception of what control really means in an ever-expanding universe. This work is done individually and without example, so that the student is placed in a dialogue with his personal will and ability to think and accomplish change. It also helps students develop the ability to concentrate on small details.

BONNIE BAINBRIDGE COHEN'S BODY-MIND CENTERING

The Bonnie Cohen work is an elaborate study of the body systems that cover developmental movement patterning, which stimulates brain development; the fluid systems, which influence and connect us to the fact that we are largely made of water; the bone systems; and the muscle systems. Through this highly aerobic study of the movement patterns stemming from each of these systems, the actor establishes a physical connection to the bodily elements that that connect us to the planet and to the evolution of our human form.

ALLAN WAYNE WORK

Wayne work focuses on joint support and strengthening the fine muscle systems of the body, and produces very fine motor control and a fluid movement structure. A multidimensional approach to the moving body connects this work to the improvisational base of Viewpoints practices.

□

All these techniques have been applied for many years to Viewpoints training, and are essential to the actor in this study. Each of these techniques gives the actor a tool with which to stand in the six languages with reception and balance. Study of these techniques increases the actors' natural movement vocabulary and knowledge of their bodies in connection to the brain function, ensemble work and performance. These techniques bring the actor into contact with the origins of conceptual dance in the late sixties, a specific physical bond that forges a technical and theoretical connection to the work of such companies as Mabou Mines, The Wooster Group, and Robert Wilson's Byrd Hoffman Foundation, as well as the underlying principles found in the work of sculptors Richard Serra, Dan Flavin, Robert Morris and Richard Nonas. Of course, having grown out of a dance perspective, this work is substantiated in the choreography of Trisha Brown, Lucinda Childs, Steve Paxton, Wendell Beavers and Paul Langland, to name just a few. It is through these techniques that theater and dance have been crossed to create an expansion of expression in theater.

VIEWPOINTS IN CONTEXT AS AN EXPRESSION OF AMERICAN ART

While Viewpoints is a product of the experimentation of the 1960s and '70s, these concepts and the art they produced did not actually give rise to my original idea. That credit is reserved for the landscape of Montana and the modern artists I grew up with in that vast state. Many readers will no doubt recognize the names of painters Robert and Gennie DeWeese from Robert M. Pirsig's widely read American classic, *Zen and the Art of Motorcycle Maintenance*. I met them in 1953 and enlisted them as my art parents, a role that Gennie continues to occupy to this day. It was through their tutelage in Montana that I first began to understand the benefits of breaking art down into a technical dialogue. I learned to recognize how articulating differences and using concepts and technical vocabularies opened the eye to see and freed the mind to create options. It was under this influence that I began to study theater, dance and choreography. Most of my studies occurred during artists' weeklong visits to the DeWeese home, where they partied, critiqued and created art together. There was always an energetic dialogue, based on the history of painting and dealing with articulating technical terminology. As a child, observing their example, I reasoned that if I could find words for the materials and process of theater, it would elevate the form to a better standing in the arts and help it grow formally.

This early history is evidence of a deep relationship between Viewpoints and visual art. This connection has continued to run through every phase of this work, ultimately unfolding a vision of the inside-out or backward nature of this work.

A STILL WIDER CONTEXTUAL FRAME

Finally, the landscape of Montana itself contributed to the development of Viewpoints work. The vastness of this land was ultimately the petri dish in which my first thoughts about Viewpoints were formed, and to fully understand the nature of this work, one must consider the physical influence of the landscape. The minimalism and high altitudes of the Montana landscape, and the sparse population, engender a sense of clarity and vision and allow time to think about distant things. Distance itself encourages a sense of taking time and of timelessness. One feels in contact with the world, as though it is possible to reinvent everything that has already been discovered from the bare elements that started it all. The minimalism of this landscape is strangely empowering. At the same time, the endless space inspires awe. In this place, there is no need to separate from the environment in order to find yourself. You find yourself through your surroundings, or you don't find yourself at all.

RECOMMENDED READING LIST

Burbules, Nicholas, "Reasonable Doubt: Toward a Postmodern Defense of Reason as an Educational Aim," *Critical Conversations in Philosophy of Realism*, Wendy Kohli, ed., New York: Routledge, 1995.
This paper and any of Burbules's works are greatly informative writings on postmodernism. In all his writings, what stands out the most for me is the honest and difficult struggle Burbules wages with articulation of postmodern thought and structure.

Cleaver, Eldridge, *Soul on Ice*, New York: Delta, 1999.
This book, originally published in 1968, is a tightly focused sociological record of the social climate that surrounded the first step of the Six Viewpoints theory. Cleaver gives a perfect view into the powerful beliefs brought about by the sudden descent into nonhierarchical structure.

Gleick, James, *Chaos: Making a New Science*, New York: Penguin, 1988.
Zulav, Gary, *The Dancing Wu Li Masters: An Overview of the New Physics*, New York: Bantam, 1984.
These two books are beautiful examples of the type of structural thought found in the Six Viewpoints. Both theories offer entirely different approaches to what is referred to as the Horizontal in the Six Viewpoints. The similarity is due to the fact that all three theories deal with a new way of looking at phenomena and the change of perspective resulting from this investigation. I feel that both these books look at what Viewpoints expresses, but in the world of science, and, in doing so, corroborate the method, thinking and findings of my theory in fascinating and often deeply moving new terms.

Havel, Vaslav, *Disturbing the Peace: A Conversation with Karel Huizdala*, New York: Vintage, 1991.
This book is an example of what can happen when the Horizontal is applied to politics. It has often been my hope that the Six Viewpoints work would contribute to finding the path toward a new political system called for by Czech Republic president and artist Vaslav Havel in this book. Perhaps the Six Viewpoints, by pointing out how a human being can interact in a nonhierarchical environment, can lay some foundation for a new social structure and a new way of dealing with conflict.

Natoli, Joseph P., and Linda Hutcheon, eds., *A Postmodern Reader*, Albany: State University of New York Press, 1993.
This book contains many examples of postmodern philosophy and provides very good mental practices for the student of Viewpoints. The contrast of the physical exploration of postmodernism, found in Viewpoints, with the metaphysical exploration of pure philosophy provides an interesting exercise in connecting the dots. This book is an informative example of the complexity

of postmodern philosophy, as opposed to the simplicity of the Six Viewpoints approach to postmodernism.

Raban, Jonathan, *Passage to Juneau: A Sea and Its Meanings*, New York: Vintage Departures, 2000.
This book is a beautiful example of a profound respect for nature. I have included it on this reading list because concentrating on nature is at the core of the Six Viewpoints work, ultimately forging the qualities of the Original Anarchist. In the many passages describing the quality of the waters surrounding the San Juan Islands, the reader can embrace the quality of what actors experience as they feel space and form or work in unusual time. Raban's poetical descriptions touch what is available in the materials of theater when they are explored on the Horizontal.

Since 1976, MARY OVERLIE has devoted herself to conceiving and developing the Six Viewpoints Theory.

She was born and raised in Bozeman, Montana, and, at seventeen, hopped a freight train to Berkeley, California, where she studied and performed with the Jane Lapiner Dance Company, the San Francisco Mime Troupe and the Margaret Jenkins Studio. At the Jenkins Studio she was first introduced to Cunningham technique. Her love of Cunningham's work led her to meet and perform with Grand Union member Barbara Dilley at the Whitney Museum. Overlie moved to New York City in 1970, and for the next seven years she danced with an improvisational dance company, the Natural History of the American Dancer.

Overlie became a renowned dancer and choreographer in New York. Her choreographic debut was in 1977 with "Painter's Dream," which performed to sold-out audiences at The Kitchen and was described by *New York Times* dance critic Jennifer Dunning as "a dance work as delicately inevitable as the whorled interior of a seashell." Overlie performed at Judson Church, Danspace at St. Mark's Church, the Museum of Modern Art, and numerous other galleries and performance spaces. She founded and maintained the Mary Overlie Dance Company from 1978 to 1986, whose members included Paul Langland, Nina Martin and Wendell Beavers. To date, she has choreographed over one hundred dance pieces, many of which have toured internationally.

She first set down her Viewpoints principles in 1976. Then, in 1978, Overlie was the first faculty member hired by Ron Argelander of the drama department at NYU's Tisch School of the Arts to establish the Experimental Theatre Wing. Her Six Viewpoints training has been adopted as a basis for ETW's core curriculum. In addition, Overlie served as artistic director of the ETW Paris branch from 1985 to 1987, and as artistic director of ETW in New York from 1989 to 1991. In January of 1998, Overlie was honored with a national conference at NYU on the subject of her Viewpoints Theory. Today she continues to develop her Viewpoints Theory as a master teacher at Tisch.

Overlie has written and directed the plays *Skies over America*, with a score by Ornette Coleman, and *What Happened to the Future*. She directed Marleen Sterowitz's *For the First Forty Years I Was Looking for My God*, and has collaborated with noted theater directors Lawrence Sacharow, Lee Breuer, JoAnne Akalaitis, Brian Jucha and Anne Bogart. Seven of the plays on which she has collaborated have won OBIE awards.

In addition to her own work as a performer, teacher and choreographer, Overlie has founded multiple performance organizations and designed curricula for arts institutes internationally. She is a cofounder of Danspace at St. Mark's Church and Movement Research, two New York–based organizations, still in existence, that were formed in the late 1970s to investigate new dance forms. She is also a cofounder of the Pro Series Workshops of the Internationale Tanzwochen Wien in Vienna, for which she served as artistic coordinator from 1991 to 1997. She has been a guest faculty member for the European Dance Development Center and the Classical Dance Academy for the Hogh School for Art in Arnhem, Holland.

Along with other grants, Overlie has been awarded an NEA choreographic fellowship grant. She has also received two New York Dance and Performance Awards (or Bessies), the first in 1984 for the creation of the Studies Project at Movement Research, and the second in 1998 for lifetime achievement. Overlie feels that her work and success result from remaining true to her free spirit. She has fished for salmon in the Puget Sound for income; operated her own bread-making business in San Francisco; created a loft construction business in New York; managed "Food Restaurant," an artist-run restaurant in SoHo; thought about becoming a ski bum instead of dancing; and climbed in the Sierra Mountains. Overlie recommends all of these activities as studies in the Six Viewpoints Theory. After twenty-seven years of studio research, Overlie completed her Six Viewpoints Theory in April 2002. She is currently wrestling with translating her experiences, theories and practices from studio to paper.

PRACTICAL AESTHETICS: AN OVERVIEW

Robert Bella

THE HISTORY OF PRACTICAL AESTHETICS

All an actor needs is will, bravery, and common sense.

—DAVID MAMET

"Near the close of the last millennium, MoMamet came down from the mountaintop, bringing with him the Three Commandments . . ." Or something like that.

Actually the birth of Practical Aesthetics was far less messianic. As a young man, David Mamet studied acting with Sanford Meisner at The Neighborhood Playhouse in New York City. Mamet wasn't asked back for the program's second year.

As a result, Mamet set out to teach himself those things that he could not get from formalized actor training. Eventually, he wound up teaching his theories as a professor at Vermont's Goddard College. There he encountered the Green Mountains, the late sixties drug culture and William H. Macy. The two young men moved to Chicago and formed the Saint Nicholas Theater Company, where they fine-tuned the methodology with which they had been experimenting in Vermont.

In 1983, Mamet and Macy founded the Atlantic Theater Company (ATC). At the time, ATC was primarily focused on the actor training program it offered through New York University's undergraduate drama department. They called their new school the Practical Aesthetics Workshop (PAW).

For two years, Mamet and Macy trained a core group of NYU students. The outgrowth of one classroom assignment was *A Practical Handbook for the Actor*, which has since become required reading at drama schools around the world. Eventually, that core group became the foundation of ATC's acting ensemble. Atlantic, which began producing plays in 1985, has become a highly respected Off-Broadway theater company. Through the Atlantic Acting School, Mamet's teachings continue to be passed on to future generations of theater artists.

THE INSPIRATION FOR PRACTICAL AESTHETICS

Practical: capable of being put to use.
Aesthetics: a particular theory of beauty or art.

> Most acting training is based on shame and guilt. If you have studied acting, you have been asked to do exercises you didn't understand, and when you did them, as your teacher adjudged, badly, you submitted guiltily to the criticism. You have also been asked to do exercises you *did* understand, but whose application to the craft of acting escaped you, and you were ashamed to ask that their usefulness be explained.
>
> —DAVID MAMET

Anyone can learn to act, and to act well. Some people are born with a gift for acting, and they may progress in learning how to act at a faster rate than others. But having *talent* doesn't mean they have *craft*.

Mamet had many issues with actor training in America that he hoped to address through Practical Aesthetics. He felt that acting classes, more often than not, left students frustrated and confused, either through flaws in the technique or, sometimes, because of the teachers themselves.

David said that acting is *a craft*, a learnable skill that can be defined in extremely simple and specific terms—much like playing the piano or building a house. Like any craft, acting has guidelines that are consistent and repeatable. If you apply yourself to those defined terms, you will then become an actor. You do not need to be blessed with talent, nor do you need to learn to be a better or different person. You simply need to be specific and diligent.

Mamet also perceived the tendency of modern American actors to focus on themselves, consciously and unconsciously, rather than on telling the story of the play. Mamet studied the role of drama in society and concluded that an actor's primary responsibility is not to himself, his emotions or his character, but rather to the audience. Mamet suggested that certain basic human truths could not be avoided when studying acting, and that the study of acting was as much the study of semantics and human behavior as it was anything else. He felt it was just as important for actors to read books about psychology, philosophy and dramatic structure as it was for them to read the Stanislavsky cycle. Stanislavsky, was simply trying to solve the same problems confronting any actor: how to make acting look believable, realistic, truthful, unrehearsed.

There are a million different answers, but the question is the same: How do I bring this theatrical event to life for the audience? In your quest for solutions, remember this—there is no *one technique.* Or, really, there is *only* one technique: *yours.*

THE PROCESS OF PRACTICAL AESTHETICS

> Keep your principles simple and few, so that you can rely
> on them at a moment's notice.
>
> —STOIC PHILOSOPHY

Practical Aesthetics can be broken down into three main categories:

1. Philosophy: the guiding principles behind the technique
2. Script Analysis: breaking a script down into usable language
3. Performance Technique: how one implements the analysis.

It would be impractical to attempt to fully examine each of these areas in this format. However, a brief explanation should shed a little light on the foundations and specifics of the technique.

I. PHILOSOPHY

Practical Aesthetics' guiding principles were culled from an impressive list of literary sources, very few of which would normally be considered *acting books.* To truly appreciate the knowledge contained in these works, you would do best to explore them yourself (see the recommended reading list at the end of this chapter). Some of the books are quite ancient in style and theory. Nevertheless, their intrinsic truths are so profound that they still ring out today.

Aristotle's Poetics

One of the technique's underlying goals is to shift the actor's focus back to the theatrical event as a whole, so it makes perfect sense to begin at the beginning, so to speak. Mamet reasoned that if an actor can understand the *principles* of dramatic writing, he can progress fairly simply to the *interpretation* of dramatic writing.

In *The Poetics*, Aristotle codified and encapsulated many of the fundamental conventions of Western drama. He did it so efficiently that today, over two thousand years later, *The Poetics* is still required reading in most dramatic writing programs. Acting schools should also require it. *The Poetics* contains the most important information any actor can ever learn. Some of Aristotle's points are no longer applicable, but the *essence* is still so penetrating that *The Poetics* is an indispensable guide for all theater artists.

Aristotle looked at the plays and theatrical events going on around him and noticed some basic similarities and essential truths. He recognized *a pattern* in drama, a pattern that mirrored life. He then expanded upon his observations, and the rest, as they say, is history. Aristotle noted that:

- The essence of drama is conflict.
- All stories have a beginning, middle and end.
- Every play has at least one main character or protagonist.
- The plot is driven forward by the needs of the protagonists.
- As the protagonists pursue their needs and desires, they encounter the antagonist(s).
- The antagonists provide escalating conflict with the protagonists.
- The result of this escalation of conflict is that The Protagonists have an epiphany, leading to a catharsis, and so, at the end of the story, the protagonists are different than they were in the beginning.
- Every character in a story is one of three things: a protagonist, an antagonist or a combination of both.
- Characters are defined by their actions.

This last point is especially important. For example, one could argue that Lester Burnham, Kevin Spacey's character, is the protagonist of the film *American Beauty*. His overall need, or *through-line*, might be to reclaim the joy in his life. Some of the forces of antagonism that he encounters are his boss, his wife and his daughter. Through the various conflicts the antagonists provide, Lester learns that he hates his job, his marriage has lost its passion, and he misses the carefree times of his youth. His ultimate catharsis is the realization that reclaiming his youth (by having sex with Mena Suvari's character) is not the real solution to his problem. He discovers that his love for his family is the true joy in his life, and what he needs to do is investigate those relationships more deeply and fully.

Thus, at the end, Lester is a far different person from who he was in the beginning. And how do we know this? By the things Lester does—his *actions*. As the film progresses, he quits his job, he starts smoking marijuana and he flirts with his daughter's best friend. Lester has a need; he encounters escalating conflicts as presented by the antagonists; he has an epiphany; and then he dies. Not purely Aristotelian, but the principles do help to break down the script rather easily.

The Illusion of Character

Always tell the truth. It's the easiest thing to remember.

—DAVID MAMET

One of the most controversial challenges Mamet made to acting theory has to do with the creation of character. As an actor, director and writer, he had encountered scores upon scores of American actors who were obsessed with the attempt to "become the character." To Mamet, this endeavor seemed, at best, misguided and, at worst, a tremendous waste of valuable time. Plain logic tells us that we are never *truthfully* anyone but ourselves.

If we *really* convinced ourselves that we were the characters, how could we ever account for all the necessary intrusions of reality? Actors in a play understand that they have to project, cheat out and hold for laughs. In films we do multiple takes, stand in front of green screens and long for the day when we will have great big paychecks and trailers awaiting us.

The character would never have to address these facts of life, but actors must. We might be able to deceive ourselves *briefly*, but it certainly does seem the proverbial "long way 'round the barn." Why as actors would we set out to do anything that, by its very nature, leads us to be untruthful to ourselves or to the world around us?

Mamet said character is an illusion created in the imagination of the audience. You don't have to believe the play is real, nor do you have to become your character in order to create a believable illusion. To Mamet, the very attempt to do these difficult, nonessential things is what leads most actors to the tremendous sense of failure and frustration they experience.

Aristotle tells us that characters are defined as the sum of their actions—in other words, "People are what people do." We do not call firefighters "America's heroes" because they wear a uniform, nor because of their inner emotional life, upbringing or cultural heritage. We identify them as heroes because they risk their lives in the line of duty; because they *run in* as others are *running out* . . . because of their *actions*.

Mamet reasoned that actors would do better to identify a character's actions and then perform them than to try to believe they are who they're not. Why try to accept the unacceptable when you can truthfully perform a simple task? Why make an *interesting* choice when you can make a *thematic* one?

Actors always ask, "How can I create this character believably?" "What is my character's motivation?" "How should I deliver this line?" These are all valid questions, but perhaps the answers would be found more readily if some other questions preceded them. For example:

- Whose story is this?
- What is the main character's underlying need?
- What are the conflicts he or she encounters?
- How do these encounters alter the main character?
- Where does my role fit into that bigger picture?

Once you identify the protagonist's journey, it is usually quite simple to figure out your character's purpose within the story's overall structure. Hence, the *dramatic function* of your role will help you determine most of the individual choices you need to make.

If you understand *The Poetics*, you can analyze any moment, scene or character in any script. This is not to say that every story follows the Aristotelian model perfectly, but if you comprehend the foundations of drama—if you learn the classical rules, so to speak—it is easy to see where and how a writer is varying them.

Epictetus' Enchiridion

First say to yourself what you would be, and then do
what you have to do.

—EPICTETUS

Epictetus was a Greek slave who lived in Rome and was born about
the middle of the first century A.D. He was eventually emancipated,
and quickly became one of the leading teachers and philosophers of
Stoicism. Stoics held that an enlightened person would strive to
determine what in life was within his control, and what was not. Or,
put another way: "God, grant me the serenity to accept the things
I cannot change, the courage to change the things I can, and the wisdom to know the difference."

The author of this prayer wasn't a Stoic philosopher, but he
certainly seemed to understand the core of Epictetus' teachings. This
prayer has become a mainstay of countless self-help groups, and it
graces the walls of grandmothers' kitchens across America. Acting
schools should frame it and hang it on their walls as well. Many
actors would have far more satisfying careers if they merely abided
by this one simple homily.

"Why won't that agent sign me?" "I can't believe I didn't get that
part." "I really hope the critic from [fill in your favorite newspaper] likes
my performance." These are just a few of the many things actors fret
about that are *completely out of their control*. Why fight the unfightable?
Instead of worrying about what others think of your abilities, focus on
improving them and leave the rest to itself. Instead of going into audi-
tions to *get the part*, try instead to do a good job, and the odds that you'll
succeed will improve dramatically and instantaneously.

Mamet suggested that every actor would be very well served by
a little bit of stoicism. Be brave enough to accept those things over
which you have little or no control. Apply your will to change those
things you can control. Develop the common sense required to distinguish one from the other.

The Pursuit of Emotion

The very act of striving to create an emotional state in
oneself takes one out of the play. It is the ultimate self-
consciousness, and though it may be self-consciousness
in the service of an ideal, it is no less boring for that.

—DAVID MAMET

Have you ever been in love with someone you shouldn't be in love with—because they are unavailable (physically or emotionally) or because they aren't truly good for you, or *to* you? Well, you're an actor: Feel happy. Stop calling on the phone just to get the answering machine. *Feel* as though that awful void where your heart used to be isn't actually a pit full of pain, regret and fear.

If you have been in this situation, you'll know this is easier said than done. The subconscious does not accept direct suggestion. "Become the character." "See the fourth wall." "Get in touch with the character's feelings." "Feel sad." Feel *anything*. You cannot control your emotions—at least, not consistently, and not for any real length of time. If you could, you wouldn't be human. If humans could control their emotions there would be no wars, no tears and no therapists.

Mamet took this fundamental truth one step further. He said that attempting to control emotions was not only an inconsistent way of working; it was actually detrimental to the process of storytelling. The very attempt forces actors to concentrate on their feelings instead of their actions. They become wrapped up in their attempt to fool Mother Nature—"Am I feeling what I'm supposed to be feeling? Why are there so many distractions preventing me from gaining control of my emotions? If only we could get rid of that pesky crew/camera/audience, I would be able to concentrate more fully on my correct emotional state." The more you try to seize the abstract, the more you disengage from the story. As a result, the very fiber of the dramatic event becomes damaged. So, if you can't consistently control your emotions, what should you focus on? If you can't truly become the character, then what steps should you take?

Although the subconscious may not accept direct suggestion, it can be encouraged to come out and play. How? Think about something else. For example: You're in bed. It's late at night. You're exhausted. "Go to sleep, go to sleep, go to sleep . . ." is your mantra, and it never works. What does? Reading a book, turning on the television, counting sheep—concentrating on almost anything other than the obvious destination you want to force your subconscious toward.

Worry less about those things that are difficult to control. Focus instead on what you can control. *Acting* is not *feeling* or *believing*. *To act* is *to do*.

2. SCRIPT ANALYSIS

Many techniques espouse the importance of *doing*, or of *physical action*. But what constitutes an action? And exactly how do you determine the action of a scene? Mamet felt that the time spent breaking down the script was quite probably the most important investment an actor could make. You might look at script analysis as the "make the difficult easy" part of Stanislavsky's equation.

Mamet broke the process down into three simple steps (described in much greater detail in *A Practical Handbook for the Actor*). Over the years, the Atlantic has added one additional intermediary step (the second in this list), but the fundamental concept remains the same:

- ☐ What is my character literally doing?
- ☐ What does my character want?
- ☐ What is the essential action of what my character is doing?
- ☐ What does that action mean to me? It's *as if* . . .

What Is My Character Literally Doing?

The purpose of this step of analysis is to give you a place to begin. Most actors want to leap to interpretation—"How should I say this line?" Rather than immediately submerging yourself in how you will do the scene, first establish what the scene is, on its least complicated, most obvious level. (An early scene from *American Beauty* is included at the end of this chapter as an aid to understanding the various steps of analysis.) Here are some guidelines to bear in mind for this first step:

- ☐ Be as simple and literal as possible. Try not to determine what the character is feeling or thinking. Try not to be too interpretive.
- ☐ Phrase this step in the third person. When talking about the scene, say, "The character is . . ." rather than, "I am . . ." Stay objective for a little while as you study the character. Later you can become subjective.
- ☐ When all else fails, remember the "popcorn test." The popcorn test goes like this: Your friend leaves the room to get some popcorn; he comes back after the scene has started and asks you what is going on. Looking at the scene from *American Beauty*, you might say, "Lester is talking to his boss about how the company spends its money."

You now have a simple sentence that covers what your character is literally doing in the entire scene. From here you can go anywhere. By not being too interpretive, you've given yourself a solid place from which to start. Keeping it in the third person reminds you to study all your options before becoming immersed in the scene.

What Does My Character Want?

Atlantic added this question to serve as a bridge between Mamet's first and second steps. It can be an extremely useful tool to help you find your action. Determining what your character wants is the first of your interpretive choices. While the first step of script analysis, the *literal*, should be neutral (i.e., non-interpretive), the *want* should not be. Some other things to consider:

- Phrase the want in the third person. Again, it's extremely helpful to keep some distance between yourself and the character in the early steps of analysis. When you talk about your character in the first person, you often rob yourself of options and perspective. Think of it this way—what *you* want while talking to your boss about your job may not be what *Lester* wants.

- Ask yourself, "What can my character get from the other character *in this scene?*" This question will help keep you focused on the specific scene you are acting, and prevent you from getting lost in your character's through-line. Try to identify what your character wants the other character to *do*, rather than *feel*. Remember, the first is more within your actual control, and therefore easier to accomplish.

Let's revisit *American Beauty*. If Lester's through-line has to do with the search for joy in his life, one might reason that recognition and self-worth would be significant issues for him. His journey might start, then, in those situations that are most familiar—his job, his family, his friends. But rather than phrasing the want in terms of Lester's through-line (i.e., Lester wants recognition), we could state it in a way that is more physically attainable in this scene. You might say: Lester wants his boss to recognize Lester's value to the company.

What Is the Essential Action of What My Character Is Doing?

Mamet created a list of additional suggestions to help actors find the answer to this next step, while weeding out those actions that are difficult or impossible to play. An action must:

- Be physically capable of being done—something you can actually accomplish physically.
- Be fun to do. Whatever action you choose, it must be something that excites your sense of play. A good action gets your motor going.
- Be specific. The more specific your action is, the easier it is to perform.
- Have its test in the other person. You should be able to determine whether you are succeeding at your action by checking in with your scene partner, not yourself.
- Have a cap. The cap is the thing your partner will do that lets you know you have succeeded at your action. It is your end goal.
- Not be an errand. Any action that can be completed with one line of dialogue is an errand. Errands are not good actions because they won't motivate you through an entire scene.
- Not presuppose a physical or emotional state (i.e., sadness, excitement, etc.) An action should be do-able regardless of how you or your scene partner feel.
- Not be emotionally manipulative. An action should help you focus on affecting your partner's physical behavior, not his emotions.
- Be in line with the playwright's intentions. Every scene is open to interpretation, and for any one scene there can be numerous actions that might work. The trick is finding the one that motivates you, while staying true to the writer's vision.

Take a look at *American Beauty* for a moment. This is the analysis so far:

- What is my character literally doing?

  Lester is talking to his boss about how the company spends its money.

233

◻ What does my character want?

Lester wants his boss to recognize Lester's value to the company.

Now you must ask another question:

◻ What is the essential action of what my character is doing?

One possible answer might be: *To make him see the truth.*

The goal of identifying an essential action is to distill the various elements of a scene down to their *essential nature*. Imagine you are watching a play in a foreign language. The dialogue is a mystery to you, yet the heart of each scene is absolutely clear if you can follow what the actor is *doing*.

A couple of additional suggestions when it comes to actions:

◻ Phrase the action in the *first person*. This helps you to become subjective rather than objective. In answering the first two questions, it was important to keep some perspective, so those steps are phrased objectively—"My character is literally doing this," "My character wants that." But the action is the task *you* will be performing; it is the goal *you* pursue in the scene. So, when stating your action, say to yourself, "I'm going to make him see the truth."

◻ Ask yourself, "What is the obstacle for my scene partner's character? What is preventing my partner's character from giving my character what he or she wants? Based on that knowledge, what action can I play to get them past that obstacle?" The answer to that question will often be a good action for the scene.

In *American Beauty*, Lester wants his boss to recognize his value to the company. The obstacle for the boss is that he thinks Lester is expendable. In order to get him past that obstacle, your essential action in the scene could be *to make him see the truth.*

Now that you've distilled the scene down to its essence, the last step of analysis is:

What Does that Action Mean to Me? It's As If . . .

The purpose of the *as-if* is to allow you to understand in your body what it means to pursue the action. If the intention of script analysis is to help you break a character down into physical action, then the *as-if* is where you learn what that analysis means to you on a personal level.

To make him see the truth is one possible action that might be the essence of Lester Burnham's behavior in the above-mentioned scene from *American Beauty*. However, there are any number of potential truths that you could make someone see. Which kind of truth are you revealing in this scene? How important is it that you succeed at making your scene partner see this truth? (What is *at stake* for your character?) What is the essential nature of the relationship between Lester and his boss? (Does Lester perceive his boss as his inferior, his mentor, his enemy?) How does that essential relationship affect Lester's behavior and, hence, *your* actions? Through the creation of an imaginary story, an *as-if*, you will be able to answer many of these ancillary questions.

Here are a few guidelines that will help you choose a good *as-if*:

☐ Phrase the *as-if* in the first person. The *as-if* is a purely subjective step of analysis. You are no longer talking about the character, but rather trying to find a way to understand the character's behavior and actions in your own life.

☐ Create an *as-if* that captures the essence of the scene, rather than one that replicates the details of the scene. Often, actors find it easy to repeat the story of the script in their *as-if* (i.e., the scene is about someone breaking up with his significant other; the *as-if* is about you breaking up with your significant other). It's not that this method won't work—it will. It is simply not a good habit if the goal is to have a solid technique. You will often find that repeating the story of the script in your *as-if* will not unlock the multitude of options you might discover. (i.e., the way in which *the actor* breaks up with a significant other may not be the way in which *the character* breaks up with a significant other.) More importantly, this guideline will help keep your imagination strong and supple. If you rely on simply restating the script, what happens when you are cast in a role where there is no corollary experience in your life? (i.e., the scene is about getting fired, my *as-if* is about getting fired; the scene is about infidelity, my *as-if* is about infidelity; the scene is about *homicide*, my *as-if* is about . . . ?) Choose an *as-if* that clarifies the heart of the scene, rather than one that simply repeats the script.

☐ Make sure the *as-if* is a story your imagination can accept. The script is already a fantasy that may be hard for you to understand or accept. With the *as-if*, you are attempting to find a situation you *can* understand—one that engages your sense of play; one that makes it easier to act the scene. You will then apply that knowledge of what it means to pursue the action back to the text.

☐ The *as-if* should be an imaginary story—one that could happen, but hasn't already happened. In the *as-if*, you should engage your imagination, not your memory. The former will lead you to understand the scene's infinite range of possibilities; the latter will lead you to a very finite idea of how to play the scene. The imagination will send your creativity outward through an act of exploration; the memory will send your creativity inward, to an act of reproduction.

☐ Create an *as-if* that is in line with the playwright's intentions. Simply put, you don't want an *as-if* that leads you to physical behaviors and habits that will be contrary to the writer's vision.

☐ A good *as-if* will answer the question: "What happens if I don't succeed at getting my action?" If the answer to this question is, "Well, it doesn't really matter that much," then your *as-if* is not very good. Remember, your investment in your *as-if is* the character's investment in the scene. If your investment is not very important, then the audience will perceive the character's stakes in the scene as being equally trivial.

☐ A good *as-if* will answer the question: "Why now?" In other words, what specific event just occurred that made you speak up? What was the straw that broke the camel's back?

☐ Often, the best *as-if*'s are the things you think about while walking down the street—scenarios that are so potent that, while your conscious mind is taking a break, the subconscious decides to work out an issue, idea or fantasy.

For example, the action in the *American Beauty* scene is: *To make him see the truth.* A possible *as-if* for that scene and action might be:

It's *as-if* the President of the United States announces that in order to protect the environment, he is authorizing the wholesale cutting down of trees. "Fewer trees means fewer forest fires," he proclaims. You're at a town hall meeting that he is attending, and you speak up *to make him see the truth.* You say, "Perhaps the forest fires are occurring due to a lack of rainfall, which is possibly being created by the greenhouse effect, which might be a result of the lack of trees in the world."

This *as-if* doesn't restate the scene, but it does shed light on the essential nature of the relationships, the overall scene, the underlying dilemma, and what is at stake for your character. It will communicate to your body what it feels like to play the scene and action in your own life and, thereby make it easier for you to act the script. It is a story that should make you want to act, one that gets your motor going and launches you into the scene.

One important thing to bear in mind: the *as-if* is an early rehearsal device. You should not be thinking about the *as-if* while playing the scene in performance. The *as-if* is simply an exercise that lets your body understand the action. Create the muscle memory, create the habit, and then let the specific story go. The point of the *as-if* is not to *substitute* your own emotional life for the character's, but rather to utilize an imaginary situation to shed light on how to play the scene.

Script Analysis Wrap-up

The search for the *perfect* analysis will keep you *off* the stage and in the classroom.

—DAVID MAMET

There is no such thing as the perfect *as-if*, action or analysis. Your analysis is your *preparation*, not your *performance*. It's your homework. You might not ever discuss it with anyone involved with the production. You are simply looking for the phrases that get you ready to act. Once you've accomplished that goal, your analysis is done.

Move on. Because, at the end of the day, acting isn't an intellectual process, it's a physical process.

This is not to say that Script Analysis is unimportant. Quite the contrary, it's extremely important. The study of acting is the study of semantics. The words you choose in your analysis will have a particular effect on the way you perform the scene, so make sure that you choose those phrases very specifically—not only in regards to the script, but also in terms of your own personal semantics. In your analysis, it's essential that you incorporate the language you use when speaking to yourself in private.

Remember, Script Analysis is a system designed to help you identify the underlying conflicts in the scene, distill those conflicts into a few phrases that are easy to remember and simple to implement, and make your performance more precise and repeatable.

So, once you have these phrases, what do you do with them? How do you implement them? If Script Analysis teaches you to *think before you act*, then Performance Technique is where you learn to *act before you think*. Ideally, every performer has an equal balance of these two skills—one analytical, the other visceral.

3. PERFORMANCE TECHNIQUE

The Use of Language

Speak the speech, I pray you, as I pronounced it to you,
trippingly on the tongue . . .

—WILLIAM SHAKESPEARE
HAMLET (ACT III, SCENE II)

What is the meaning of the words "I love you"? Experience tells us they can have any number of possible meanings: "I adore you," "I want to have sex with you," "You're the funniest person I've ever met," "I'll talk to you later," "You make my life complete." The meaning of the phrase "I love you" is communicated by the *context* in which the words are spoken and the *intention* with which they are said. If this is a universal truth in life, then why is it not so in acting?

Actors, directors and teachers are always trying to figure out "how to say the line." We all assume there is some *correct* or *ideal* way a line should be delivered. In our search for the correct line reading, we forget that words can have infinite meaning, depending upon the situation. Real life is an endless improvisation, a negotiation based on what we want and how we perceive we can best obtain that objective.

A director, writer or teacher may have a preference as to how a line should be delivered. They may explain that preference in such a way as to make their choice seem like the *only* choice. But the reality is that life is more complex than that. There is no *one way* to any destination. The very concept belies human experience. There is no one way to say the line; there are a multitude of possible interpretations. So, which one do you choose? Mamet felt we'd all be well served by following Hamlet's advice to the players:

> Let your own discretion be your tutor. Suit the action to the word, the word to the action, with this special observance: that you o'erstep not the modesty of nature. For anything so overdone is from the purpose of playing, whose end, both at the first and now, was and is to hold, as 'twere, the mirror up to nature.

The writer has provided the words—*the context*. Script Analysis defines the action—*the intention*. How should you say the line? Perhaps, instead, you should ask, "How does my scene partner need to hear the line? What would be the best way to achieve my action in this moment?" Determine that, and then say the line in order to further that goal. Hold up the mirror by staying true to the natural improvisation in life.

Again, we must remember our job in its larger context. It is not to please the director, our teacher or ourselves. Our job is to affect the audience. What does the audience hope to experience? They want to be transported into the world of the script. They want to believe it is real. Hence the expression "willing suspension of disbelief." The audience willingly chooses to forget it is a play or movie; they suspend their disbelief and accept that the story is actually happening right in front of them for the very first time.

Unfortunately, it is more difficult for the performers to suspend their disbelief. Ideally, the actors have rehearsed and performed the lines many times before. They know exactly how the scene will progress. As a result, most performers wind up doing the line readings that the director prefers or that they think will get the desired response from the audience. But rote line readings are a far cry from life being revealed in a unique and fresh way.

In an attempt to solve this problem, many actors do an *impersonation* of saying the lines for the very first time. They put their attention on *re-creating* these "fresh" line readings, rather than *creating* a performance anew in each moment. They attempt to deny the truth: they have read the script; the rehearsal process actually took place; and they almost certainly know how the scene will end.

Mamet suggested that the best way to give the audience what they are looking for is to actually commit to life's improvisational nature. Instead of doing a line reading, determine your intention. Worry less about what seemed to work before, and ask yourself, "What might work now?" An improvisational approach to saying the lines solves the inherent dilemma. The actor does not actually know from moment to moment what approach will work best with his or her scene partner. By discovering the best way to say the lines in the moment, the performer will truly be creating his performance for the very first time, every time.

The Truth of the Moment

To deny nothing, invent nothing—accept everything, and get *on* with it.

—DAVID MAMET

An improvisational style of acting requires performers to have an acute awareness of what is going on around them. The *truth of the moment* is everything that is transpiring while an actor performs any given beat. The phrase encompasses your scene partner's state of being, your state of being, your understanding of the script, the director's notes, the audience's responses and far more. The truth of the moment is simply that—your knowledge of everything that is true about *this moment*. As Mamet is fond of saying, "It's all in, people."

Mamet wanted to eliminate the self-consciousness that derived from an actor's believing there were certain thoughts or impulses that were *in character* and others that were not. From the perspective of the audience, *you* are the character. They make no distinction. It is a function of the suspension of disbelief. Hence, whatever you are thinking or feeling by necessity must be what the character is thinking or feeling. There is no difference.

The audience will continue to suspend its disbelief until such time as the performers give them reason not to. Anything you do that makes the story seem less than real will cause the audience to disengage—for example, if you forget a line, fall off the stage, or pretend to be experiencing something that is not truthfully transpiring in the moment.

In the desire to do justice to the theatrical event, actors often try to create some kind of a result—whether it be emotional, intellectual or physical. But if that result is not motivated and justified by the interaction that is transpiring in front of the audiences' eyes, the illusion is shattered. For example, as an actor, how often have you tried to appear angry when, in fact, you were not? Do you actually think the audience can't tell the difference? This is what is commonly called "indicating": the actor attempts to *indicate* to the audience the reaction that either the script or the director seems to demand.

Mamet suggested that every reaction required by the script or the director could be broken down into physical acts that were absolutely within the performer's control, night after night, take after take. Instead of trying to *feel anger*, perhaps you might focus your attention on *putting someone in his place*. Rather than doing the line reading that worked last night, you could ask yourself, "What will it take to put my scene partner in their place in this moment?"

A complete understanding of the truth of the moment does not require the actor to fabricate results that are not really happening—*invent nothing*. Nor is the actor obligated to renounce reality—*deny nothing*. The actor is allowed to embrace all that is available to him in order to achieve his action—*accept everything*. As a result, you are ultimately freed to do as Mamet suggested—*get on with it*.

The Repetition Exercise

How does an actor think? He doesn't think—he does.

—SANFORD MEISNER

One of the greatest problems an actor faces is overcoming self-consciousness. The very nature of the profession compounds the challenge. We perform beneath bright lights in front of a crowd of onlookers; we have to remember our lines, our cues, our blocking; our careers rise or fall on the basis of a good or bad review.

What's the simplest way to overcome self-consciousness? Put your attention on something other than your fear or your desire to please. Give yourself a more important focus—your scene partner, your action.

Sanford Meisner created what he called the "word repetition game." It is an exercise designed to train actors to truly listen to each other, and then to respond impulsively. Mamet adopted and adapted Meisner's game to create what Practical Aesthetics calls the Repetition Exercise.

To learn and understand repetition, it is best to watch it being practiced. There are numerous suggestions and qualifiers that a teacher can make to clarify an actor's grasp of the various principles. However, the basics are quite simple. Practical Aesthetics implements the exercise in three stages:

> Stage 1: Straight Repetition
> Stage 2: Repetition with Actions
> Stage 3: Active Repetition

Stage 1: Straight Repetition

Each stage builds a deeper understanding of the following basic instructions, introduced in Stage 1:

> 1. Say something true about the other person.
> 2. Repeat until something makes you change.

In this stage, the exercise begins with Actor 1 identifying a simple truth about Actor 2. It can be as obvious as, "You have a blue shirt." Actor 2 then repeats the phrase back to Actor 1, after inverting the pronoun to apply it to himself: "I have a blue shirt." A typical Straight Repetition exchange might go as follows:

> ACTOR 1: You have a blue shirt.
> ACTOR 2: I have a blue shirt.
> ACTOR 1: You have a blue shirt.
> ACTOR 2: I have a blue shirt.

The actors continue repeating until something *makes* one of them change. One of them might notice a different article of clothing, or perhaps a smile might creep onto someone's face. As soon as an impulse occurs to make one of the actors change, the repetition phrases alter accordingly:

> ACTOR 1: You have a blue shirt.
> ACTOR 2: I have a blue shirt.
> ACTOR 1: You have a blue shirt.

ACTOR 2: You have black sneakers.
ACTOR 1: I have black sneakers.
ACTOR 2: You have black sneakers.
ACTOR 1: You are smiling.
ACTOR 2: I am smiling.
ACTOR 1: You are smiling.
ACTOR 2: I am smiling.

And so on. There are no right or wrong observations, and no predetermined time limits for any phrase. The actors do not strive to take turns changing, create dialogue, make it *interesting*, keep score or *win*. They simply make truthful observations about each other.

Eventually this first stage of repetition can move beyond the obvious surface truths to encompass deeper recognitions of behavior. Perhaps the smile was an attempt to flirt, or maybe it was a reflection of boredom or discomfort. If one of the actors recognizes this to be true from his point of view, then he can change the repetition phrase:

ACTOR 1: You are smiling.
ACTOR 2: I am smiling.
ACTOR 1: You think this is silly.
ACTOR 2: I think this is silly.
ACTOR 1: You think this is silly.
ACTOR 2: You're annoyed by that.

Stage 2: Repetition with Actions

In this stage, your action and *as-if* give you a perspective from which to *interpret* your partner's behavior. If you are Actor 1 and your action is to put someone in their place, you might perceive Actor 2's smiling in a very different way, especially if Actor 2's action is to teach you a lesson. Your analysis becomes the point of view from which you approach the exercise. You choose your words and use the tone of your voice to help you achieve your action:

ACTOR 1 *(Testing)*: You're smiling?
ACTOR 2 *(Confirming)*: I'm smiling.
ACTOR 1 *(Warning)*: You think you're in charge?
ACTOR 2 *(Challenging)*: I think I'm in charge.
ACTOR 1 *(Mocking)*: You think you're in charge.
ACTOR 2 *(Threatening)*: I think I'm in charge.

Stage 3: Active Repetition

Straight Repetition should be fairly neutral in the actor's approach to the spoken phrases. Repetition with Actions adds the layer of a very specific point of view by which to address the phrases. Active Repetition allows the performers to choose phrases that more *actively* approach the objective they are striving toward:

> ACTOR 1 *(Testing)*: You're smiling?
> ACTOR 2 *(Confirming)*: I'm smiling.
> ACTOR 1 *(Warning)*: Wipe that grin off your face.
> ACTOR 2 *(Challenging)*: Don't tell me what to do.
> ACTOR 1 *(Mocking)*: Don't tell you what to do?
> ACTOR 2 *(Threatening)*: Don't tell me what to do.
> ACTOR 1 *(Cautioning)*: Back off.
> ACTOR 2 *(Rebuking)*: Back off?

In this hypothetical scenario, Actor 1 saw the smile. The action (to put someone in his place) gave that actor a point of view about the smile. The performer then impulsively chose an active phrase in an attempt to achieve the objective. Abiding by the original principles, both actors would continue repeating the phrase until some new impulse caused one of them to change.

Performance Technique Wrap-up

We prepare in order to improvise.

—DAVID MAMET

The ultimate goal of Performance Technique is to give you a set of physical habits that complement your Script Analysis skills. The latter helps you to determine the actable phrases; the former shows you how to implement them. You have an action—your point of view. You have your lines and your scene partner. The rest is a structured improvisation. You negotiate from beat to beat in order to achieve your objective while constantly factoring in the truth of the moment.

The Repetition Exercise provides you with a way to practice your improvisational skills. Straight Repetition helps you to overcome self-consciousness by placing your attention on your partner. It teaches you to identify and verbalize the truth of the moment spontaneously. Repetition with Actions and Active Repetition take the basic habits one step further. You are now identifying and reacting to the truth of your partner's behavior with a very specific point of view. You then verbalize your point of view in words that *actively* help you attain your objective. The exercise provides you with a way to rehearse the scene impulsively on its most essential level—there's only you, your impulses and your partner.

Anything that occurs to you in the moment is potential fuel to further your goal. Whether you find your imagination being inspired by the text or not, you are freed of the obligation of assuming there is some *correct* inner state of being. The questions, "What is my subtext?" and "What should I be thinking or feeling?" then become quite simple to answer. You say the lines in the way your impulses tell you will be most effective in this moment. Your emotional life, your subtext, your inner thoughts will evolve from the pursuit of your action.

The writer has created *conflict*. The actor should attempt to create *order*. If you're pursuing a goal that is important to you, and your scene partners are pursuing their own important goals, then there will be *friction*. That friction will engender in you a truthful, spontaneous inner life. In effect, your scene partner's refusal to allow you to create order will let you know exactly how to act each moment, and it will give the audience the benefit of watching the story unfold right in front of its eyes, for the very first time, every time.

What happens if the director wants you to *set* your performance? No problem. The same principles apply. The only addition would be what some people refer to as *tactics* or *tools*. Tactics are specific do-able phrases that you can add on to your action—line by line, if necessary. In other words, if the director wants you to "be frightened" on a certain line, then on that particular line you might add the tactic *to beg* while pursuing your action. This still allows you to be improvisational from moment to moment, albeit in a narrower framework: How you beg on a certain line today will be slightly different than how you would do it tomorrow, because the truth of the moment will be different.

PRACTICAL AESTHETICS AND HABIT

What you rehearse is what you perform.

—DAVID MAMET

By creating Practical Aesthetics, Mamet hoped to demystify the craft of acting. He wanted to devise a technique that anyone could use, provided they approached the work with enough diligence, courage and common sense—a system that addressed the inherent complexity of the art form, but also one that actors could implement on a consistent basis.

The basic principles behind Practical Aesthetics are simple and few. They can be grasped very quickly by just about anyone. This is not to say that this chapter has covered all those concepts—there are Advanced Analysis and Performance Technique skills that were not investigated here, not to mention the other tools essential to developing as an actor, skills such as voice and speech work, physical alignment and flexibility. But even those abilities are relatively easy to *understand*. What does it take to *master* them? How does the old joke go? "How do you get to Carnegie Hall? . . . Practice, practice, practice."

The goal is to create a set of habits that will serve you in a moment's notice—skills that become second nature; habits so ingrained that their very use becomes an art form in itself. In *Zen in the Art of Archery*, Eugen Herrigel wrote, "One has to transcend technique so that the art becomes an 'artless art' growing out of the Unconscious." Or, as Stanislavsky put it, "Make the difficult easy, the easy habitual, and the habitual beautiful."

Whatever technique you devise, make sure to always honor your integrity, humanity and individuality. Remember, Stanislavsky also said, "The person you are is a thousand times more interesting than the best actor you could ever hope to be." And as you embark on the journey ahead, keep this thought, from William James's essay "Habit," in mind:

> Let no youth have any anxiety about the upshot of his education, whatever the line of it may be. If he keeps faithfully busy each hour of the working day, he may safely leave the final result to itself. He can with perfect certainty count on waking up some fine morning to find himself one of the competent ones of his generation, in whatever pursuit he may have singled out. Silently, between all the details of his business, the *power of judging* in all that class of matter will have built itself up within him as a possession that will never pass away. Young people should know this truth in advance. The ignorance of it has probably engendered more discouragement and faint-heartedness in youths embarking on arduous careers than all other causes put together.

ADDENDUM

A SCENE FROM *AMERICAN BEAUTY*
By Alan Ball

Interior Brad's office. Brad is seated behind his desk in his big corner office.

BRAD: I'm sure you can understand our need to cut corners around here.

(Lester sits across from him, looking small and isolated.)

LESTER: Oh, sure. Times are tight, and you gotta free up cash. Gotta spend money to make money. Right?

BRAD: Exactly. So . . .

(Brad stands, ready to usher Lester out.)

LESTER *(Blurts)*: Like the time when Mr. Flournoy used the company MasterCard to pay for that hooker, and then she used the card numbers and stayed at the St. Regis for, what was it, like, three months?

BRAD *(Startled)*: That's unsubstantiated gossip.

LESTER: That's fifty thousand dollars. That's somebody's salary. That's somebody who's gonna get fired because Craig has to pay women to fuck him!

BRAD: Jesus. Calm down. Nobody's getting fired yet. That's why we're having everyone write out a job description, mapping out in detail how they contribute. That way, management can assess who's valuable and—

LESTER: Who's expendable.

BRAD: It's just business.

LESTER *(Angry)*: I've been writing for this magazine for fourteen years, Brad. You've been here how long, a whole month?

BRAD *(Frank)*: I'm one of the good guys, Les. I'm trying to level with you. This is your one chance to save your job.

(Lester stares at him, powerless.)

ENDNOTES/SOURCES

Epigraphs/Excerpts:
(Page 223, 227, 239, 244, 245) Attributed to David Mamet by the author.
(Page 224) Mamet, David, from his Introduction to *A Practical Handbook for the Actor*, Melissa Bruder et al., New York: Vintage, 1986.
(Page 229) Epictetus, *Enchiridion*, George Long, trans., Amherst, NY: Prometheus Books, 1991.
(Page 229, 237, 240) Mamet, David, *True and False: Heresy and Common Sense for the Actor*, New York: Vintage, 1999.
(Page 241) Meisner, Sanford, and Dennis Longwell, *Sanford Meisner on Acting*, New York: Vintage, 1987.
(Page 247) Ball, Alan, *American Beauty: The Shooting Script*, New York: Newmarket Press, 1999, copyright Paramount Pictures.

RECOMMENDED READING LIST

Aristotle's Poetics, S. H. Butcher, trans., New York: Hill and Wang, 1961.
In *The Poetics*, Aristotle codifies and encapsulates many of the fundamental conventions of Western drama. Aristotle details a pattern in drama that mirrors life. He breaks down that pattern into a few simple principles that, more than two thousand years later, still hold true in modern drama. Actors can greatly improve their ability to understand scripts if they have a solid grasp of dramatic structure.

Bettelheim, Bruno, *The Uses of Enchantment: The Meaning and Importance of Fairy Tales*, New York: Vintage, 1989.
Bettelheim shows how fairy tales can teach children important life lessons. The lessons are presented in ways that allow children to externalize their own life questions and problems. The parallel to an audience's experience in theater is extremely revealing. Ultimately, Bettelheim helps to shed light on the identification process that occurs between the audience and the storyteller.

Bruder, Melissa, Lee Michael Cohn, Madeline Olnek, Nathaniel Pollack, Robert Previto and Scott Zigler, *A Practical Handbook for the Actor*, New York: Vintage, 1986.
A Practical Handbook for the Actor is currently the only detailed examination of Mamet's original teachings about Practical Aesthetics. It contains a summation of the various steps of Script Analysis as well as an overview of all the underlying philosophies behind the technique.

Campbell, Joseph, *The Hero with a Thousand Faces*, Princeton: Bolligen Series, 1972.

Campbell examines the world's complex and interwoven mythologies, folklore and religions from a unique perspective, providing an understanding of the underlying patterns in human nature. This classic study traces the story of the hero's journey and transformation through virtually all the mythologies of the world, revealing the one archetypical hero common to them all. Campbell investigates the storyteller's and the listener's underlying need to participate in the hero's journey.

Epictetus, *Enchiridion*, George Long, trans., Amherst, NY: Prometheus Books, 1991.
The *Enchiridion* is a summary of the teachings of the Stoic philosopher Epictetus. The handbook outlines the principles that the Stoics felt were essential to provide people with more tranquil and productive lives. Actors can benefit greatly from these theories both on the stage and throughout their careers.

Johnson, Michael G., and Tracey B. Henley, eds., *Reflections on "The Principles of Psychology,"* Volume One, Hillsdale, NJ: L. Erlbaum Associates, 1990.
In his essay "Habit" (reprinted in this collection), William James suggested that the ultimate goal of a good habit was "to make our nervous system our ally instead of our enemy . . . We must make automatic and habitual, as early as possible, as many useful actions as we can, and guard against the growing into ways that are likely to be disadvantageous to us, as we should guard against the plague."

Mamet, David, *On Directing Film*, New York: Penguin, 1991.
Mamet draws on sources from Aristotle to Hitchcock to Hemingway in order to explain what makes a good story work, and how those principles can be applied to writing and directing a script. The book is a great asset for anyone interested in creative writing and is a highly insightful look into Mamet's theories of drama.

_____, *Three Uses of the Knife: On the Nature and Purpose of Drama*, New York: Vintage, 2000.
Mamet's three lectures, originally delivered at Columbia University, are ostensibly about issues of dramatic structure, but as the essays unfold, Mamet continually explores the relationship between dramatic structure and the lives we live. He delves into the questions, "What makes good drama?" and "Why does drama matter in the modern age?"

_____, *True and False: Heresy and Common Sense for the Actor*, New York: Vintage, 1999.
This book's brief essays contain sound advice on how actors might apply themselves to a career in the performing arts. He investigates issues includ-

ing the proper consideration due the audition process, the selection of parts that one accepts and the creation of character. The essays challenge actors to question their understanding of their craft and their profession, and ultimately provide detailed clarification of Mamet's theories of drama and acting.

————, *Writing in Restaurants*, New York: Penguin, 1987.

This book collects twenty-eight essays on a variety of topics ranging from radio drama to middle-class fashion trends to the Academy Awards to the use of amplification in theaters. Highly entertaining and compelling, the essays provide an early glimpse into many of the underlying themes Mamet has investigated in his later essays and novels.

DAVID MAMET was born in Chicago in 1947. He studied at Goddard College in Vermont and at the Neighborhood Playhouse School of the Theatre in New York. He has taught at Goddard College, the Yale School of Drama, Harvard and New York University, and he lectures at the Atlantic Theater Company, of which he is a founding member. He was the first artistic director of Chicago's Saint Nicholas Theater Company and was a resident playwright at The Goodman Theatre in Chicago. In addition to numerous novels and essays, Mamet has written and directed the films *House of Games*, *Things Change*, *Homicide*, *Oleanna*, *The Spanish Prisoner*, *The Winslow Boy*, *State and Main*, *Heist* and *Spartan*. In 1984, he was awarded the Pulitzer Prize for his play *Glengarry Glen Ross*. Other acclaimed plays and screenplays include *Speed-the-Plow*, *American Buffalo*, *Sexual Perversity in Chicago*, *Hannibal*, *The Untouchables* and *Wag the Dog* and *The Verdict*, for which he received Academy Award nominations. Mamet currently lives in Los Angeles with his wife, actress-singer-songwriter Rebecca Pidgeon, and their three children.

ROBERT BELLA was born in Brooklyn, New York. He has a BFA from New York University's undergraduate drama department, where he has been an adjunct faculty member since 1987. Robert is a founding member of the Atlantic Theater Company. He has worked on over 100 plays as an actor, director, writer and producer. He has also served as Atlantic's producing director and associate artistic director, and as executive director of the Atlantic Acting School. As a master teacher for Atlantic, he has been instrumental in the ongoing development of Practical Aesthetics. Robert produced and directed the feature film *Colin Fitz*, which had its world premiere at the 1997 Sundance Film Festival. Acting credits include *This Revolution*, *Spartan*, *Magnolia*, *Colin Fitz*, *Money for Nothing*, *Homicide* and *Things Change*. Writing credits include a screenplay, *The Passion Dream Book* (based on a novel by Whitney Otto), and a stage adaptation of the film *Stand and Deliver* (available from the Dramatic Publishing Company).

INTERDISCIPLINARY TRAINING

Directing for Actors

Fritz Ertl

I teach directing to students who, initially at least, consider themselves actors. This is part of an interdisciplinary course of study that all incoming Playwrights Horizons Theater School (PHTS) students are required to take. In this program, the entire first-year curriculum is fixed, and just as the actors are required to take Directing and Design, so too must the incoming directors and designers study Acting, Movement, and Voice and Speech—and everyone must take Stage Management. The great benefit of such a program is that it mirrors the interdisciplinary nature of theater itself, where actors, designers and directors work collectively, not separately. The interdisciplinary approach to theater training, then, aims to produce fully rounded theater collaborators who, because they understand how the whole works, can better understand their own tasks. Obviously, every class in the interdisciplinary curriculum plays its role in this higher mission. The purpose here is not to describe the program as a whole, but to outline the role first-semester First Year Directing plays in developing young theater artists, both as all-around collaborators and as actors.

THEATER AS STORYTELLING

Historically, First Year Directing at PHTS has always begun with the one element that affects all the others—story. Every play tells a story, and, by extension, every collaborator involved in a theatrical production is a storyteller. While the playwright is usually the initial storyteller in a project, every collaborator who comes onboard after a script is written is, in effect, bringing her particular storytelling skills to the collaboration, and everyone needs to be working in concert to tell a *singular story*. It is crucial, then, that every theater artist develop the ability to tell story effectively, and toward this end I begin First Year Directing by outlining six Aristotelian components of a dramatic story: *plot, action, character, space, musicality* and *spectacle*. Over the course of the first semester, students will be asked to stage a dramatic story of their own invention for each of the six components, slowly building an arsenal of storytelling tools. The stories are nonverbal, are required to be five to ten minutes in length, and can be wholly original or based on myths, fairy tales or news events. While some students are petrified of the imperative to tell stories, after a few tries—and as their arsenals expand—most begin to really enjoy themselves. Even the most frightened students, who begin the semester protesting that they are, after all, *only* actors, so why should they have to learn how to tell a story—even such students come to understand that their craft as an actor is in the service of a story, and that they must learn to orchestrate their craft in relation to that story. In short, the playwright may write the story, but it is the actors who communicate that story to an audience; and the best actors are, among other things, marvelous storytellers.

PLOT

Nothing is more basic to a story than plot, yet constructing an effective plot can be maddeningly difficult. In explaining plot, I begin by differentiating between plot and story. Plot, as defined since Aristotle, is a sequence of events; story, on the other hand, is the significance (i.e., the meaning, point of view, themes) of that plot. To help clarify this distinction, when discussing scenes in the early weeks, I always begin with the same two questions: "What happens?" (i.e., "What is the plot?") and, "What is this the story of?" (i.e., "What is the meaning or point of view?") It is important that these two questions be answered in different terms. The plot of Sophocles' *Oedipus Rex*, for example, is clear and unchangeable, involving a series of events, beginning with Oedipus determined to root out the cause of the plague that is ravaging Thebes, and ending with him putting his own eyes out for being the very cause he was looking for. The story, on the other hand, can be interpreted in a number of ways. Is it the story of a man's hubris leading to his own downfall, or is it the story of a brutal world in which the gods play with men's ambitions simply to make them miserable? Both interpretations, and many others, are viable; each tells a different story, even though the plot stays the same. Deciding *which* story one wants to tell, and why, is an important decision for every storyteller, as a plot without a point of view is simply a sequence of events, not an informed, complete story. Accordingly, from day one in First Year Directing, students are trained to link plot with point of view—the product of the two being a story.

Once the difference between plot and story is established, we turn our attention to the details of what constitutes a plot. For this I turn again to Aristotle, who simply states that a successful plot must be "complete," by which he means that it must have a *beginning*, a *middle* and an *end*. Building on this Aristotelian base, it can be said that the beginning of a plot is an introduction to a *situation* in which the audience is given important background information regarding the characters and their setting, all of which will become significant later in the plot. After the situation has been established, something occurs to unsettle or complicate the situation; this *complication* constitutes a play's middle, and usually longest section, and builds through a series of rising events to the play's climax. After the climax comes the play's ending, or *resolution*, when the story examines how the situation to which we were introduced has been changed by the experiences of the complication. This tripartite structure describes a journey—the dramatic journey—without which no story can be complete. At this point, I assign each student the task of staging a short story of her own creation, with only one requirement: that its plot contain a beginning, a middle and an end; that is, that it describe a dramatic journey; that is, that it be complete.

Not surprisingly, most of the early attempts are woefully incomplete. In fact, many students resist the imperative for wholeness with every ounce of their being, preferring to tell stories in which nothing happens, where there is no complication, where the story ends exactly as it began, then insisting that that this is how they see the world. These stories (or non-stories) afford the opportunity to introduce another Aristotelian imperative: the need for a plot to have *magnitude*. For Aristotle, magnitude meant tragic import, and necessitated a hero falling from great heights to the lower depths: the so-called reversal of fortune. While our own modern sensibility doesn't always require such an enormous change, something still needs to have changed by play's end for the plot to be complete. A simple rule for drama might be stated thus: no change = no journey = no drama. Invariably, several savvy students will challenge this rule, citing plays whose plots seem to defy the imperative for change, the most common being *Waiting for Godot*. In this well-known absurdist play, we are introduced to Estragon and Vladimir, two tramps passing time in a meaningless world. The plot is complicated with the introduction of Pozzo and Lucky, who bring news that Godot is coming. This leads the tramps, and us in the audience, to expect a change in the characters' meaningless circumstances once Godot appears. Godot, alas, does not appear, and in the play's resolution—once it is clear that he is not coming—the tramps have no recourse but to resume passing time as they were at the beginning. Can a plot that ends as it began be complete? The answer in this case is yes, the key to its completeness being the possibility of change and the desire for change on the part of the characters during the play's complication. Before ending exactly where they began, the protagonists journey through many options and possibilities for change. In fact, much of the play involves them imagining their world changed. Returning to the actions of the top of the play works as a resolution only once these imaginings prove ineffective at bringing about the desired change (the climax being when Estragon and Vladimir realize Godot is not coming), thus completing a journey that has been fraught with urgency. In fact, so urgent is the characters' desire for change that we experience the ultimate lack of change as nothing short of a reversal of fortune—a truly modern tragedy replete with modern magnitude. Upon close inspection, every drama, regardless of its aesthetic orientation, chronicles a journey of change.

Beckett's plays are helpful examples when teaching story to young artists because they illustrate the idea that a play doesn't have to be *well made* to be complete. As mentioned above, it is the smartest students who fear completeness the most, primarily because they understand how *patently* complete mediocre stories are, particularly in mainstream Hollywood films and prime-time television shows. In such stories, every component is painfully clear. Watching the beginning, one is acutely aware that everything being introduced will become important later on; then something occurs to upset the situation, and it is clear the plot has entered the complication and the climax (still 20 minutes away) can already be guessed at with confidence; and finally, after the climax, the story resolves in a manner that most clearly communicates the story's simplistic message or moral. In such stories, the tripartite structure (situation, complication, resolution) becomes formulaic, and while completeness is accomplished, it is done in a reductive manner. It is not surprising, then, that the best students, having viewed hundreds of such stories already in their young lives, equate completeness with simplicity. But such an equation is really a syllogism: completeness is a requirement of a story; mainstream stories are simplistic; ergo, complete stories are simplistic. Like all syllogisms, once this is spelled out in black and white, the lapse in logic becomes clear. In the case of storytelling, the answer is simple: if you wish to avoid simplistic stories, don't reject completeness; rather, embrace complexity! A story needs to be complete in its own terms, and a simplistic story will resolve simplistically, while a complex story will resolve in a complex manner. Which brings us back to Beckett, whose plays are at once complex and complete, the complexity being felt in the profundity of their tragic resolution.

Accepting completeness as a necessary component of art in general, and stories in particular, is a foundational lesson for all students at PHTS—for the actors as much as for the directors. Once one accepts the imperative of wholeness, one can turn one's attentions to the two storytelling tools that pertain most to the actor's craft: character and action.

CHARACTER AND ACTION

Character is the combination of physical and psychological attributes that identify an individual. Adjectives are quite useful when describing a character, as a character is physically either short or tall, masculine or feminine, erect and stately or stooped and lowly. Psychologically, the character is ambitious or timid, demanding or easygoing, obsessive-compulsive or sloppy—the list of character adjectives is obviously endless. But characters don't exist in a vacuum; that is, they don't exist merely to exhibit their character traits. Each of the characters has a life history filled with experiences that have informed these traits, and each character, as a product of his or her life experience, *wants something* all the time. Which brings us to action.

For Aristotle, action was the main, driving force behind the plot, impelling the story forward. While this definition is still apt, since Stanislavsky, action has taken on a more specific meaning, focusing on the desires and objectives of the play's characters. Action, in short, is what characters *do* in pursuit of what they *want* (the objective). It is important that character, action, and objective be integrated, and to that end I begin the discussion of each scene for this assignment with a series of questions: "Who are these characters, what do they want, and what do they do to get it?" Note the progression from a question about character traits, to one about objectives, to one about actions. In the case of Oedipus, he's a headstrong, stubborn leader of men (who is he?); he wants to rid Thebes of the horrible plague that is ravaging it (what does he want?); and he spares no end to discover the source of the plague, interrogating everyone and considering every possibility (what does he do to get it?). Finally, in order for plot, character, and action to be fully dramatic, the plot must be driven by the actions of characters *interacting*. This is absolutely crucial, as dramatic complication is usually the result of characters' conflicting objectives. What would happen in *Macbeth*, for example, if an exceedingly ambitious wife didn't drive Macbeth to his murders? He well might ignore the witches' prophecy and continue serving his king as a dutiful thane, and there would be no drama. Hence, character and action are the primary agents of the plot itself, and without them functioning in unison it is impossible to have a complete story.

Most students understand the idea of action in theory, but almost all struggle to master it in practice. In many cases, the director and her actors understand the action of a scene, yet their understanding is not communicated to the audience—usually because the action is internalized; that is, not properly physicalized. These cases illustrate well another major lesson of First Year Directing: psychological action (i.e., intentions or motivations) can only be understood through physical actions (i.e., what people *visibly* do onstage). If it is important in the introduction to establish that a character desperately wants to be seen as mature and deserving of her new peer group, we need to see her trying various tactics to convince her peers of her worth, switching from one tactic to another when she feels the first tactic is not working. If the actress feels various tactical impulses internally (maybe I should be friendly, maybe I should show off, maybe I should act cool, etc.) but only physicalizes one tactic, say acting cool and aloof, we—the audience—might very well conclude that the character is simply aloof, and we will not understand what the scene is about. We will be off the story because the full variety of the main character's action was not properly physicalized.

Learning to physicalize action is a profoundly important lesson for the theater artist to learn, and one that is resisted by first-year students for several understandable reasons. First, just as the best students resist completeness because they equate it with simplistic, formulaic plotting, they also resist physicalizing action because they equate it with the greatest sin of twentieth-century performance: *indicating*. This fear is well founded, as poorly physicalized action will indeed manifest as indicating; but again, there is a lapse in logic undergirding this fear, as properly physicalized action will not be interpreted as indicating. In fact, as my colleagues teaching acting assure me, learning how to physicalize action without indicating is the single most difficult lesson for an actor and, therefore, it must constitute a large part of every actor's training. Treating the issue in directing class is useful because the focus is not specifically on individual performances, yet everyone in the class can see when action is internalized, when it is physicalized effectively, and when it is indicated. Thus, even if they don't learn a specific technique for physicalizing actions in directing class, actors are converted to the idea that doing so is necessary.

There is a second misconception that must be overcome before the idea of physicalized action can be fully learned by students, and that concerns the role of emotion in a dramatic story. One of the great appeals of the theater and cinema is that they dramatize human emotions. One could even say that theater and cinema chronicle the emotional truth of each successive generation. For example: Oedipus putting his eyes out, Stanley Kowalski calling out, "Stella!" over and over again, and Prior quaking with fear in his bed at the sight of Tony Kushner's angel are three dramatic moments from theater history that define three distinct eras. Because emotion is so visible and important in the theater, it is not surprising that young theater artists want to focus their craft on the manufacturing of emotions. In response to this impulse, one of the primary objectives of First Year Directing at PHTS is to teach students that their task as dramatic storytellers is not so much to manufacture emotion as it is to contextualize it. Let us return to our example from above, in which a character desperately wants to be accepted as mature and deserving of attention. If the actor doesn't clarify the character's action, and the character suddenly bursts into tears at the end, we will have no understanding of her tears and, while the actress playing the role might be quite moved by her character's frustration, we in the audience will be left unmoved, perhaps even annoyed by an emotional outburst we don't understand. If, on the other hand, we see her struggle to get respect and attention, only to fail in her attempt, then her tears will move us as much as they do the performer. It is the primary job of actors and directors, working collaboratively, to fully embody the action of the play; only then will emotions be effective. There is perhaps no quicker way for an actor to learn this than in a Directing class.

PERSONAL POINT OF VIEW

There are few things I enjoy teaching more than the imperative for every artist to bring a personal point of view to her work. Toward this end, the first semester curriculum requires students to stage dramatic stories of their own creation rather than work on preexisting text. Having to tell their own stories immediately raises a question in each student's mind: "What kind of stories do I want to tell?" And in answering that question—or at least struggling to answer it—students discover their own point of view. I begin by suggesting that they work personally, but am careful to distinguish between personal and autobiographical. A literal transcription of something that happened to one might indeed lead to a personal story, but so might an utter fiction. What is most important is that the students are telling stories they feel passionate about; stories that somehow convey their love or anger or questions about the world they live in; in short, stories that capture their personal point of view. Unlike the imperatives to create complete stories and to physicalize action, students rarely resist, conceptually, the imperative to work personally—most likely because there is a long history of equating art with self-expression. Nevertheless, really connecting to one's personal core is difficult for many students. Most often they are simply cautious about revealing their point of view, for fear it will be discounted as unsophisticated or untrue. On a very important level, the entire first-year curriculum at PHTS is about overcoming these fears that block students from discovering and claiming their own voices, and my insistence that they work personally is echoed loudly in every other First Year class. "What makes you happy? What makes you angry? What don't you understand about the world you live in?" These are the questions

I ask over and over again to help students find their themes. Once they have connected with their own interests, I encourage them to explore various ways to develop these interests into stories. The idea of a premise (the magic if) is a great place to start. Let us say, for example, that a student has been greatly influenced by his mother's grave illness, from which she fortunately recovered. "What *if* she hadn't recovered?" I might ask the student. "Can you create a story built upon this premise?" Other students are more drawn to events in the news, or scholarly discourses, or fairy tales as springboards for stories they are passionate about, and each of these options is discussed as a legitimate possibility. Slowly, over the course of the first semester, virtually every student finds his or her voice, making each a better storyteller and, by extension, a better actor, designer and director.

SPACE

The first three tools—plot, character and action—all deal with dramatic structure. I sometimes refer to them, with only a little irony, as the holy trinity of story. Understanding how to analyze a plot and translating that plot into the physical actions of interacting characters—this is the primary task of *all* theater artists. As such, these three tools will be reviewed and reexamined in virtually every acting and directing class that students take at PHTS over their entire four-year career. The next three tools, *space, musicality* and *spectacle*, all deal with the materials of the theater itself. They are the tools that allow one to render a story with pictures and sound, creating visual and aural landscapes that house the story even as they tell the story. If the three tools that comprise the holy trinity of story require students to develop their skills as writers, *space, musicality* and *spectacle* require them to develop their skills as visual artists and musicians. The change of focus is a welcome relief for all involved.

All theater begins with an empty space. It is the job of the director and his collaborators to shape and color this void to meet the needs of their story. Many questions need to be answered before a fully rendered space can be realized: to begin, in what kind of world does the play take place? Is it a detailed, natural world, filled with real furniture and real knickknacks and real doors—like a Victorian comedy, for example? Or is it a more abstract world, mostly bare, with few if any natural details—like a Beckett play? Also, do the details of the world change over the course of the story? Drama loves change, so it is not surprising that dramatic settings are usually transformational. Sometimes they transform by changing the location: operas and musicals, for example, are noted for scenery that flies in and out, changing locales from act to act. A similar effect can be had in a simpler fashion with a more minimalist treatment of space. Imagine a bare stage with only one chair, stage center. That chair can transform simply by having the performers treat it differently from scene to scene, so that in scene one the chair is a car seat; that same chair becomes a throne in scene two; and then, for the concluding scene three, our plain chair becomes an electric chair. These are two very different approaches to effecting theatrical transformations, the first being more literal, the second being more purely imaginative. Perhaps the most theatrically satisfying changes are those in which the locale itself doesn't change, but the audience's perception of that locale does. For example, we are in a dark void with no doors; stage center is a large cube on which the play's only character sits. The lone character wants to get out of the void but can find no egress. Suddenly the box slides to the side, revealing an exit through the floor. In this moment the audience, like the protagonist, sees the space anew. It is no longer a self-contained void without a way out, but part of a larger world, and the way to access that world is to go underneath the one to which we have been introduced. Such transformations, which can be called *revelations of space*, are truly satisfying, as they are characteristic of a highly theatrical play-world.

Once the nature of the play-world has been addressed, the storytelling collaborators must next consider the placement and role of the audience in the space. Nineteenth-century naturalism promoted the idea of the imaginary fourth wall, which clearly separated the audience from the action, allowing them to observe the action as if looking through a hole in the wall. Spatially, the audience is distinctly separate from the play's action in such treatments, allowing for a cool, scientific assessment of the action. But most theater, both before and since the nineteenth century, has been interested in a more interactive relationship between performance and audience. In addition to common strategies used to break the so-called fourth wall—characters addressing the audience, for example—more radical treatments of space are also to be seen in our current theater. Some of these treatments require the audience to move from station to station to watch different parts of the play (what the English call promenade staging), others place the audience onstage with the action (often called environmental staging), still others keep the audience seated separately from the action, but give the audience a role in the drama, for example, as witnesses in a court or as members of a congregation. Whether such choices are legitimate or gratuitous depends on whether the unusual treatment of space, and the audience's place in it, actually furthers the story. For example, a story about how men and women perceive each other might work very well with the audience segregated by gender and looking at each other across the action in the middle. An effective story by a recent student involved a murder case in which the members of the audience were both the suspects and the victims and were all hideously murdered at a séance, seated around the table holding hands! Very clever staging, to be sure, but also in keeping with the desired effect of every mystery story, which is to scare the daylights out of the viewers as they attempt to solve the mystery. It is important to explore conceptually the relationship of audience to performance when examining space; if one doesn't, students will most often revert to the fourth wall as the default option, an aesthetic norm very much fed by the popularity of cinema that, as a mediated rather than live event, inherently separates audience from performers. The great joy of theater, however, is that it is live, and that what is happening onstage is happening in real time. As such, young theater artists need to explore every means possible to interact with their audience, always expanding their theatrical imaginations rather than limiting them.

Finally, once the more conceptual issues have been dealt with and a space created, it is time to put the story *into* the space. Rather than just staging, or *blocking*, I encourage young directors to think in terms of a series of moving pictures—not unlike the effect of looking at a reel of film, one frame at a time. Each frame, of course, must be composed in an artful manner, yet also tell a story. One key to accomplishing this is in the spatial relationships that exist between the people on stage, and the story inherent in these spatial relationships. Two characters standing at opposite ends of the stage tell a different story than the same two characters standing face to face; yet another story is told with them back to back, or when one of them is standing while the other is on one knee. But these are all static pictures, without a context. Since the crux of drama is in change, let us examine how changing pictures can reflect the journey of the story. Consider the simple story of two brothers, one a king, the other an outcast and beggar. By play's end the two have switched roles. Is it possible to tell this story spatially? The obvious way of doing so is to have the first king occupy a vertically superior position to his lowly brother during the introduction, and to have them switch positions during the resolution. The middle—that is, the complication—would tell the story of how this change comes about. Obviously, learning to shape action *in space* is one of the most important skills a director needs to develop.

A careful consideration of space has a profound effect on developing theater artists, especially insofar as space requires the students to use their theatrical imaginations. As stated above, all theater begins with an empty space; how that space is filled and shaped is limited only by the theatrical imaginations of the theater artists involved in a production. So, while time must of course be spent on technical issues, such as how to balance a composition and why diagonals are important, equal time is spent encouraging students to fully challenge their theatrical imaginations and create a theater that looks and works like none ever seen before. In the same way that most students revert to the fourth wall until challenged, so do most students accept a whole series of related theatrical idioms as some kind of norm. The whole issue of entrances serves as a good example. In the space where I teach Directing at PHTS, there is one door, which students sometimes use for exits and entrances; there are also several flats that can be arranged to create the effect of wings, a configuration which is also used regularly to help with entrances and exits. Both these approaches work well when there are a limited number of locales in a story, but the students get into trouble when their stories range across a variety of locales—for example, crossing from one apartment to another, then into a bathroom, then out onto the street. Invariably, the students solve the problem of delineating the various spaces by having the actors involved mime opening or closing a door as they enter each new space. To my mind, nothing signals a paucity of theatrical imagination more than these mimed doors, and I cajole and harangue students to consider different ways to solve the problem. Perhaps there's some kind of treatment on the floor—a circle, for example—and each time a character exits the circle and reenters, she is in a new place. Perhaps there is a flat upstage center, and each time a character exits she crosses upstage of that flat, emerging in a new locale once on the other side. Or, maybe a live, onstage percussionist signals the opening of each door with a sharp beat on his snare drum. Or, perhaps a light cue signals the change. The possibilities are indeed endless, and to accept one solution as *normal*—particularly one as literal as the mimed opening of the doors—is detrimental to imaginative theater.

Once students are sold on the idea that no theatrical idiom or convention is normal, they can each begin to develop their own theatrical styles. In effect, they are developing their formal points of view, which is as important as developing a point of view in relation to content. In fact, the two are inseparable, as form gives shape to content and—as ever—form is most exciting in the theater when it truly embodies the content. This lesson is as important for the actor to learn as for the director, and it is always interesting to note that the best actors in the class are highly imaginative and open to a variety of theatrical idioms. If great actors are great storytellers, the best also excel as sculptors of space, understanding how to move through space and what effect their moving image in space has on an audience, understanding also when to give and when to take focus and— perhaps most importantly—knowing how to share space with an audience. In an earlier age, these skills all fell under the rubric of stage deportment, but even today the actor must deport herself onstage in an effective manner in order to succeed in communicating the story. Again, it may be the director who introduces specific idioms to a production, but it is the actor who must embody them in the space, and training actors to be willing collaborators in the treatment of space is an important agenda of the PHTS curriculum.

MUSICALITY

If space requires students to consider the visual picture, controlling everything that is seen in a theatrical production, musicality requires students to master everything that is heard—what I call the aural track. Because we live in a culture that is so obsessively visual, we sometimes forget how important and ubiquitous is sound. To begin, sound comes from various sources in the theater. As characters move through space they invariably generate sound: the sounds of walking, interacting with scenery and props, breathing, and—the most prevalent source—talking. In addition, there may be music in a scene, either as an organic component (i.e., the characters are listening to music onstage) or as a cinematic underscoring that helps capture the mood or place of a scene. There may also be recorded special effects, usually used to enhance the visual track, as when a recorded sound cue of a door closing is used in lieu of a real door. But regardless of whether sound in a scene is generated by characters talking and moving, by recorded sound effects or by music, all sound is musical and, as such, is either loud or quiet, high-pitched or low, fast or slow, and rhythmic or arrhythmic. Musically speaking, it is the job of theater collaborators to orchestrate all this sound, which means, essentially, that they must tie the aural track to the plot, characters and action. Anecdotally, Tyrone Guthrie, the great English director, would occasionally sit in the back row during run-throughs, his back to the action, simply listening to the performance. His theory was that a performance must, on some level, tell the story of the play purely with sound and with no help from the pictures. With this aim in mind, this assignment encourages students to explore the full range of musicality.

Many students are interested in musical underscoring, no doubt because of the role it plays in film, a medium with which all students are more familiar than theater. And, indeed, underscoring can be effective. Play one nonverbal scene three times, each time with a different musical underscoring, and you will experience three distinct stories. Early in the exploration of musicality, I dissuade students from underscoring an entire scene (or play) with one continuous song, a technique well known to them because of its use in music videos. While such an approach might be effective for certain stories, it is also limiting. The problem with the technique is that it doesn't allow for any other form of sound, or, for that matter, silence; hence, the story is simply a picture in relation to one static musical element. I push students interested in underscoring to a more complex use of it, suggesting they use the underscoring selectively and in conjunction with other musical elements. For example, imagine a scene that begins nonverbally, which is underscored fully, followed by a scene with no underscoring but in which the dialogue is carefully orchestrated. The juxtaposition of these two musical approaches—these two movements, as it were—could be effective, the former serving as an introduction to the plot, the latter as the play's complication. Perhaps the underscoring returns at the end of the resolution, but it now has new meaning after the events of the complication. Though still a simple structure, this is far more complex than the original MTV approach.

Orchestrating dialogue also falls under the rubric of musicality. Take any short section of dialogue and ask two actors to read the text with no variation in pitch, rhythm or the tempo. The result will be language devoid of dramatic meaning. Now take that same section of text and give the actors specific musical instructions—"speak the first three lines quickly and loudly, pause after the third line, then resume quietly and much more slowly but building in tempo to an explosive final line"—and the text begins to take on meaning. Of course, the text will still seem lifeless if the musical directions are not linked to character and action, and many will choose to explore the action of the scene first; but eventually it is crucial that the musicality of the dialogue be carefully considered. I'm fairly certain that when Tyrone Guthrie was apocryphally turning his head and listening to a performance, it was primarily to focus on the musicality of the dialogue.

As was the case with space, there are no limits to the way musicality can be used in the theater, and I encourage the young storytellers to expand their idea of the musical possibilities open to them.

SPECTACLE

By the time the class gets to the final tool, *spectacle*, our young storytellers are armed with five powerful tools and are filling the space with personal stories that are well plotted and imaginatively staged. Adding spectacle is really quite easy at this point. As I define it, spectacle is comprised of all the technical elements that help one tell a story: scenery, lights, sound and music, costumes, makeup, props, etc. Some of these elements have already been implicated and discussed in either *space* (scenery, e.g.) or *musicality* (sound and music), and those that haven't already been discussed have, nevertheless, been used as over the weeks students increasingly take the initiative to use the light board, bring in costumes and props and, occasionally, use makeup as well. This assignment demands that each student create a piece that treats all spectacular elements fully, and that all those elements support the story. Aristotle was distrustful of spectacle, saying writers often used it to hide deficiencies in plot, character and action. For better or worse, little has changed in 2,500 years, and the same caveat must be used today when approaching spectacle. The most wonderfully horrific monster makeup is not going to make the audience appreciate a deeply felt story of a teenage werewolf; only solid plotting, clearly defined actions and engaging characters can do this. However, if all those other elements are clear, then the horrific makeup will be largely effective and, in fact, might very well be what the audience goes home talking about.

When spectacle is not tied to the story, it is gratuitous; when it is tied to the story, it is a powerful tool. The trick, as with the other tools, is to link a play's spectacle to its plot, character and action. Costumes should help us understand the character of each person in the play; light and sound cues can be effective not only in establishing time and place, but in highlighting important plot turns—dramatic light and sound effects, for example, are often linked to a play's climax. Plotting the journey of one's spectacle is as important for a storyteller as is plotting the journey (or arc) of each character. When theater critics speak glowingly of a design being a character in itself, it is usually because the design moves with the plot, visibly telling the play's story as effectively as the interactions of the characters. When spectacle is used this way, it is not just in support of performances but coequal to them.

CONCLUSION

First Year Directing at PHTS is not merely an introduction to the art of directing, but a detailed examination of all the components that make up a theatrical performance. Some of the topics covered are far removed from the usual course of study for an actor. The section on *plot*, for example, is probably more likely to be taught in a writing program or a film school than a drama school. And while the section on *action* clearly relates to the task of performing, how can studying *space* and *musicality* really be of use to the student who considers herself primarily a performer? The answer to this question comes in several parts. The most obvious answer is the one given in the introduction to this chapter, namely, that examining the whole helps train effective collaborators. Without a doubt, because of their interdisciplinary training in general, and Directing classes in particular, PHTS actors understand what goes into making an evening of theater and should, therefore, be adept at working with different kinds of directors on different kinds of plays. They should also be skilled at taking a director's conceptual ideas and turning them into character and action—an ability every director loves in an actor—and are thus well suited to work on new plays and conceptual restagings of classics, both of which benefit greatly from having "thinking" actors who can effectively collaborate with a director.

The fact that actors become good collaborators as a result of interdisciplinary training might in itself be enough to support the approach, but there are other benefits as well, especially in the way the class introduces ideas and concepts that will become important in their actor training. Most importantly, the holy trinity of story (plot, character, and action together) prepares actors for the detailed action and objective work that they will be wrestling with in their acting classes for years to come. Similarly, as mentioned in the conclusion to the Space section above, grappling with space as a visual component of theater helps actors appreciate and develop their ability to sculpt space as performers. Finally, one fact that becomes obvious to all students in First Year Directing is how useful it is to have actors with physical and vocal control, as they can really help tell a story clearly. This experience encourages the actor to develop the discipline necessary to master physical and vocal production. In essence, by putting themselves in the shoes of a director, the actors learn just how dependent the dramatic story is on their craft as performers.

Finally, an interdisciplinary approach aims to train storytelling artists, not just actors, directors and designers. This is an important distinction. In film, it is common for the writer to also be the director or for an actor to also direct or produce a film; accordingly, in film school training it is not considered odd for everyone to study writing, directing, editing and producing. In fact, it reflects the fluidity of the film profession. The theater, too, is beginning to blur the formerly distinct lines that separated the various collaborators, and—in the performances of John Leguizamo and John Cameron Mitchell, for example—the writer/director/actor is becoming more and more common in theater as well. At PHTS, it is not uncommon to see the same student direct a play one week, design sets for a classmate three weeks later, and play the leading role in yet another colleague's directing project three weeks after that—and excel in all three! If asked whether she considers herself an actor, a director or a designer, she would most likely consider the questioner with puzzlement. Such students don't delimit their talents along traditional lines, nor should they. In embracing theater in its entirety they are preparing for the day when they will change the way theater is made in America.

RECOMMENDED READING LIST

Aristotle's Poetics, S. H. Butcher, trans., New York: Hill and Wang, 1961.

Bartow, Arthur, *The Director's Voice: Twenty-One Interviews*, New York: Theatre Communications Group, 1988.
Interviews with twenty-one American directors. A great window into the process of making theater.

Bloom, Michael, *Thinking Like a Director*, New York: Faber and Faber, 2001.
Perhaps the best single textbook out there on directing.

Shahn, Ben, *The Shape of Content*, Cambridge, MA: Harvard University Press, 1957.
A beautiful and clear discussion of the relationship between form and content in all art. Written by a painter, but very applicable to the theater artist.

States, Bert, *The Pleasure of the Play*, Ithaca: Cornell University Press, 1994.
A very detailed and intelligent analysis of *Aristotle's Poetics*, applying its principles to modern and postmodern theater.

FRITZ ERTL is a theater director and educator. He has produced or directed world premieres of plays by, among others, Erik Ehn, Neena Beber and Paula Vogel, and has worked at theaters such as Berkshire Theatre Festival, BACA Downtown and HERE. At New York University, where he teaches, Fritz has directed many productions, including *Pentecost*, by David Edgar; *The Pains of Youth*, by Ferdinand Bruckner; and *Mad Forest*, by Caryl Churchill. Most recently he directed the world premiere of *Youth in Asia: A Techno Fantasia*, by Steven Drukman, a project he and the author co-evolved with dramaturg Una Chaudhuri. Fritz has been teaching at NYU since 1990, and in that period has taught a wide range of courses, including various dramatic literature classes, Dramatic Theory, Acting, Script Analysis, Director/Designer Collaboration and First Year Directing.

NEO-CLASSICAL TRAINING

Louis Scheeder

To really think onstage may very well be
the most important thing.

—LEE STRASBERG

THOUGHT IN ACTION

In Neo-Classical Training, we consider the text to be "thought in action." This concept supports the presentation of classical texts, principally those of Shakespeare, in an immediate, physical, emotionally charged present. We think as we speak, and the task is to train the actor to equate thought with speech—to prepare and train the actor to think while in a heightened emotional state, so that the language of Shakespeare is not merely articulated but possessed by the actor; so that it is lived—as opposed to learned—in the present theatrical moment. The challenge facing actors today is how to create a clear and simple present, one that is generative, in that it literally propels these classical texts to a viable, forceful, present tense. The actor as character creates thought through language by coining words, phrases and sentences—as opposed to reciting speeches. Language and thought are not separate; rather, the language of Shakespeare is the thought of the character—his creations quite literally speak their minds.

The basic tool of the actor is action, the internal process by which the actor *plays*—i.e., mentally and emotionally enacts a psychological drive rendered in verbal form to achieve what he or she wants, needs or desires at any given moment. When the actor plays a specific action, the unit of text comes alive. The action is the breath of life that provides the psychological oxygen that stimulates the brain. Emotional preparation buttresses and supports the devotion to action.

Shakespeare wrote *heightened* language that demands a heightened emotional state. In Neo-Classical Training, students first work to attain heightened emotional states by using nursery rhymes. The focus, at first, is on achieving a full emotional life without paying attention to meaning. Once the students attain competence at achieving a heightened emotional reality, they can explore how their emotions inform work that is centered on text rather than subtext. They quickly learn that emotion colors and informs the most rudimentary text, and they can then apply their heightened emotional accessibility to inform and enrich text. Students must imaginatively (and privately) explore their deepest fears and their greatest desires in this quest. With Shakespeare, passions are elevated: the plays demand both extreme love and deadly hate, as opposed to pedestrian likes and dislikes.

Actions stem from the actors' imaginations—from somewhere within them. Indeed, it is preferred that actors not hew to a preexisting *through-line* or conception of the part, scene or play. The through-line is a goal toward which the actor works during the rehearsal process, as opposed to a road map that is followed. The idea of a fixed, preexisting through-line is inherently dangerous, in that it derives from a heritage of scientific rationalism. When an actor establishes or fixates on a through-line too early in the process, she may begin consciously or unconsciously to censor actions—to think about what is appropriate—and may consequently fall into the trap of thinking, "If I really want X, I would never do Y." The wild beauty of late sixteenth- and early seventeenth-century plays lies in the inconsistencies, incongruities and contradictions of their characters. Indeed, actors must be free to grasp what may seem, initially, to be an *inappropriate* choice; such a choice often leads to an upsetting, fantastical, but important theatrical decision.

It is vital to remember that there is no *right* response. (We do, however, maintain a preference for one specific genre of action that I will address later.) Rather, there are a plethora of responses, none of which should be negated. The meld of the psychological drive in verb form with articulation of the text as uncensored thought—the playing of an action—can always and, indeed, should always change and develop as actors interact with each other and as their perception of the characters' needs, desires and wants expands and develops. Characters in Shakespeare—even in the smallest parts (see Francisco in *Hamlet*, for instance)—are rarely consistent. Given the antithetical nature of Shakespeare's writing, characters invariably contradict themselves at least once in any given scene. An extreme example of this is the famous Beatrice/Benedick encounter, after Hero has been spirited away, in which Beatrice contradicts herself as she vacillates between her love for Benedick and her disdain for men before realizing that Hero's plight is uppermost in her mind.

The convergence of seemingly random action with small units of text, while important for the work itself, is also vital in overcoming one of the great stumbling blocks in university-based training: the desire on the part of students to *get it right*. Within academia, in spite of the numerous courses espousing critical thinking and open-minded inquiry, there still exists a desire to succeed with the right answer. This tends to be tied up with questions of social construction—one of the great challenges is to break through socially imposed or constructed patterns of thought. Too often, students still respond with the "appropriate" response instead of the unpredictable, unscientific and inappropriate response. In short, an intense focus on action allows students to move away from received or preconceived *ideas* that are inculcated by cultural influences and enables them to realize the specific and individual emotional life of the characters being portrayed.

Ideally, art should be generative; it should produce something new. If acting is an art, it is therefore generative and must produce a new rendition of a scene or a production that has not previously existed. However, it is far easier to think about something that already exists in the mind or previously on a stage or in another's performance than it is to actually create something. The fascinating thing is that you can't know ahead of time what the thing you are creating is going to emerge as or become. Thus, every scene, every project becomes a blank sheet of paper. Neo-Classical Training strives to develop actors who will find the uncensored, unpredictable, generative response, as opposed to the socially conditioned or historical response, which is often imbricated with questions of character.

The notion of character, like through-line, is something at which one arrives through an internal rather than a mimetic process. A character is the sum of the actions that the actor plays; that is, after all, how we perceive people in real life—by what they do, by their actions. However, the characters in Shakespeare are so deeply embedded in our culture that even someone who has never read, heard or seen a play is likely to have a preconceived or received concept of the more famous among them. By focusing on the primacy of action, the personal internal response, students will draw away from fixed, external ideas and begin to find the truth of the character within themselves.

Action, however, must serve the text, for the goal is to generate the text. Setting aside concepts and interpretations, as well as fashionable schools of critical or political thought, at the end of the day one has a series of words that must be translated off the page and into the corporeal and spiritual realm of the actor. A focus on the text will ultimately lead to a sense of the internal working of the character, for, if the words are thoughts, they are not some external problem to be overcome; rather, they represent the innermost workings of the characters' minds. If one accepts that the words of the text are thought, there is no need for a subtextual current that flows silently under the river of words. What is needed is a firm commitment on the part of the actor to breathe life into words with action.

Words are the coin of our realm, and the challenge is to bear down, embrace the words, and wring from them what one can. Ultimately, they will, in their contradictory workings, reveal to us what we need to know. As John Barton has said, "The character is the text, the text is the character." And the text includes not only what your character says but also what is said about your character. The fine combing of the strands of text is the way to character.

While I have stressed the importance and value of the internal act—the generation of action—training students with these texts also calls for strict attention to what are sometimes considered to be the mere externals of training—stage combat, Alexander technique (to rid the body of external habits), movement work (to allow bodies to express internal complexities) and speech technique. We have adopted the speech and voice techniques developed over the past several decades by Robert Neff Williams, first at Columbia University and then at the Juilliard School.

ANTITHESIS AND IAMBIC PENTAMETER

The two facets of Shakespeare that are essential for work on Shakespeare's texts are an understanding and application of antithesis and a comprehension and appreciation of the complexities of iambic pentameter. Antithesis is the rhetorical contrast of ideas by means of parallel construction of words, clauses or sentences. It is the linguistic and thematic device Shakespeare used to construct his works. If there is a Hamlet, there is also a Laertes whose father has been murdered; parallel worlds of the court and the tavern coexist in *Henry IV*, Parts 1 and 2, while Hotspur stands in opposition to Hal; in *The Winter's Tale*, the scene shifts from the court of Sicilia to the sheep-shearing festivities of Bohemia; *Twelfth Night* and *The Comedy of Errors* abound in split selves—the examples are legion. The rhetorical device is interesting, however, not just for its literary merits but because it serves as a marker for actors to play contrasting, contradictory and antithetical actions, as well as to develop antithetical points of view about what they are saying—processes that are internal and help bring the text to its full contradictory life. Antithesis also serves as a reminder that, in the world of Shakespeare, we do not proceed gradually or realistically. *Transitions*, beloved of actors, are neither necessary nor desirable in Shakespeare. Rather, the actor must hurtle forward, skipping through time in a hyperreality of forward motion; the winter of discontent is made glorious summer, not spring, as nature and realism would have it. Antithesis also enriches the emotional life of the actors as they learn to work for contrasting extremes of emotion, rather than the single extreme emotion of which the young actor is so often enamored.

VERSE AND PROSE

Students often ask, "What, exactly, is verse, and how does it differ from prose?" A short answer is that prose follows the rules of grammar, while verse adheres not only to grammar but also to additional principles that serve to heighten the auditor's attention to the rhythm of the language. As Shane Ann Younts and I noted in our book, *All the Words on Stage*, verse can "assist the actor not only with meaning and syntax but with acting intentions and emotional clarity." The interplay of word and metrical stress is revealed when words are set in patterns against the rhythmic arrangement of five iambic feet. However, the homogeneity of iambic rhythm would turn into a thumping bore without deviation, and it is Shakespeare's exploitation of variation and difference that gives vitality and interest to the iambic line. Once the rhythm is established, author and actor work together to reveal the thought processes of the character to the audience.

For those who might wonder whether this attention to Shake-speare's use of poetic meter contradicts my earlier emphasis on internal processes, I would respond that rhythm itself is an innate and internal force, not an external representation; it is something that is felt and perceived rather than seen or viewed. Iambic pentameter is the heartbeat of Shakespeare's text, and rhythm is the invisible series of heartbeats that produces energy. In each play he wrote, Shake-speare seems to have confronted, investigated and mastered yet another variant to the standard iambic pentameter line, so that, by the end of his career, these variant rhythms—unstressed endings, soft endings, contractions, slurs, elongations, short lines, shared lines, caesuras, epic caesuras—can be felt, perceived or sensed internally by the audience, as opposed to merely heard or observed. These variants present the keys and clues to the working of the characters' thoughts. However, I would hasten to add that work on verse cannot proceed independently of work on actions and emotional honesty. Ideally, they are imbricated, as work on voice should be intertwined with work on speech and language.

In order that students may fully appreciate the complexity of Shakespeare's command of verse, I recommend that they listen to and explore the rhythms of jazz, which also gives form to the flux of life with its embrace of the 4/4 beat and repeated choruses—it mimics the arbitrary regularity of the iambic pentameter line. When there is agreement on structure, musicians and actors free themselves to move around within that structure and exert tensions against the beat at the same time as they observe it.

Training, if it is to advance, should ideally function as a laboratory in which hypotheses are posited, tested, refined and retested. How actors should handle Shakespeare's verse has been subject to such proofs. Experiments with verse speaking—or, in keeping with our general theory, verse thinking—have enhanced student training in recent years. I offer one example that has led to an upending of received ideas about approaches to the verse: For many years, it has been standard practice for those who advocate clarity in Shakespeare to urge young actors to play through to the end of the thought or sentence, rather than the end of the verse line, which provides a smooth, natural and reasoned presentation of the text. However, it also presents what is, in reality, a studied unnaturalness; for in real life we do not recite fully formed sentences; in the heat of argument, we often do not know where a sentence is going to end when we begin it. The technique of playing through to the end of the sentence fosters actors who speak magnificently phrased, well articulated lines that some-how seem memorized and learned rather than lived and created.

There are a multitude of reasons why characters might well adjust their thinking (I prefer not to employ the word *pause*, as it implies an interruption rather than a redirection in the flow of action) in the midst of an argument—for characters are always rhetorically in argument. The speaker might suddenly have a better idea, or momentarily search for the perfect expression, or fear that he or she is about to provoke the hearer to physical violence, or decide to change tactics, or feel the need to rearticulate or refine the thought in order to win the argument, or lose his or her place, or lose the thread, or become distracted, or seek for the perfect word or phrase or inten-tion—speakers are, after all, in action all the time. As Shakespeare developed his use of iambic pentameter and moved from the end-stopped line, in which the thought is completed at the end of the verse line, to the use of enjambment, in which the thought wraps around and ends in the middle of the next or succeeding line, he moved toward speech and language that was internally driven rather than externally imposed.

Recently, a group of high school teachers asked me what could be done to get their students to not stop at the end of the printed verse line. They were somewhat flabbergasted when I responded that their students' tendencies were instinctively correct because, in real life, people often don't know the end of the sentence when they begin it. In other words, we think as we speak. As acting training has become centered in the academy, one of the dangers of the academic mindset is the encouragement of students to "know what you're going to say"—as opposed to living in a spontaneous environment. However, all too often, for reasons of social construction, we tend to *perform*—to speak lines in keeping with the dictates of social construction with-in which we find ourselves. Shakespeare's characters (and those of every other dramatist) should be free of such modern encumbrances.

POSITIVE ACTION AND PERFORMATIVE SPEECH

Earlier, while discussing the idea of action, I alluded to a preference for a specific genre of action. While training is a practical area in which one imparts techniques of concrete skill, the theoretical should also be acknowledged. Two concepts are critical to the acting of Shakespeare in the present: positive action and performative speech.

These concepts have supported, refined, and energized the creation of Thought in Action.

Positive action means that the actor/character focuses on the success of the enterprise rather than allowing the fear of failure to enter the mind or consciousness—every character plays to win at every moment. If, as has been said, "In a good play, everyone is right," then argument and conflict will necessarily follow. Every scene contains a problem, and an argument will occur as to how to best resolve the problem. Students should always be engaged in rhetorical conflict, which is fully realized by a commitment to specific actions. The text states the problem; the job of the actor is to play for a solution to the conflict, not restage or reify the problem by lamenting that it exists. If the character is right, he or she will not sympathize with the other character's point of view or argument; rather, he or she will enter into passionate conflict in order to bring the other person around to his or her viewpoint, to win the argument. When characters play to win, they, by definition, avoid playing the problem. The inclination of creativity—both onstage and in life—is to celebrate and to praise life and existence.

Lady Percy's first line in her encounter with Hotspur in Act II, Scene 4 of *Henry IV*, Part 1, can set the tone for the scene: "O my good lord, why are you thus alone?" The natural tendency of many actors is to restate or lament the circumstances of the scene by ignoring scansion and stressing the *why*, instead of playing the line actively and positively: "O my good lord, why *are* you thus alone?" This sense challenges Hotspur and opens up the possibility of conflict; this attack stresses that the emphasis is on the other person in the scene, rather than the self, and allows the actress to begin to formulate the key questions: What do I want from him? What do I want him to do? How will I go about getting him to do what I want him to do? The actions taken to accomplish these goals will delineate the relationship between the two parties much sooner and more effectively than endless speculation about the state of the marriage and their past. When characters play to achieve what they would like the world to be, rather than what has been, when they think in terms of the present, rather than bemoan the past, the attention of the audience moves toward the future and they, in turn, anticipate and participate in a solution and resolution of the theatrical event.

I should hasten to add that *positive* action does not imply something Pollyannaish, nor does it advocate simpering. All characters—Iago, Iachimo and Richard, Duke of Gloucester, as well Viola, Rosalind and Beatrice, not to mention Othello, Hamlet and Lear—want something, and all must strive to attain it. With positive action, the characters hang on not only to the hope but also to the belief that they will get what they want. When they fail to achieve their goals, the effect will be psychologically and emotionally devastating; when they achieve their goals, the effect will be miraculous, exhilarating and transporting.

Positive action is also quite useful in helping the student understand why a character speaks in extensive monologue as opposed to dialogue. Though it could be argued that an exception to this exists in certain set speeches, characters typically do not know that they are going to continue at what might seem an inordinate length. Nonetheless, they want, need, desire—must have—something so intensely that they are able to marshal, nay, cannot resist marshalling a series of arguments that will enable them to read the slightest crack in the other character's armature. They intend to exploit it so that, in their heightened emotional state, they will triumph and seize their goal or prize.

A commitment to positive action functions as an antidote to the predilection of many young actors to dwell in the past rather than the present or the future. This tendency is understandable because so much of contemporary acting training pushes the student to look backwards instead of ahead. A fixation on past emotion or a character's history fosters students' obsessive concerns with character biographies, the given circumstances of a scene, and other irrelevant questions, such as, "How many children did the Scottish couple have?" While speculation about Hamlet's course of study at Wittenberg may be fascinating, it too often distracts from focusing on how his actions reveal or counter his espoused philosophy at a given moment in the play. The inordinate amount of time that is spent on the past stops the actor from focusing on the future. Emotional connectedness ideally should free the actor to move forward. However, it often mires actors in the past, forcing them to relive or reexperience things that have nothing to do with the text at hand or the action of the play. They often play the emotion rather than the scene.

Perhaps the car analogy is in order here. When students, being young, begin to work on emotional preparations for scenes, they will occasionally indulge themselves and wallow in the emotion, rather than preparing and then turning to the task at hand, which is the scene itself. Students need to consider their emotional preparation as the starting of the engine; they still need to drive the car—put it into gear, use the directional signals, steer with the wheel, etc. However, when the actor is grounded in the past, it's like driving using the rearview mirror exclusively, focusing on what has been done in the past rather than on the present moment or on what one wants in the future.

The theoretical work of philosopher J. L. Austin has proved quite useful in helping students to think about acting in the present. In *How to Do Things with Words*, he presented the concept of the performative utterance. Austin did, however, reject "stage speech" from his theoretical investigation. His declaration that "a performative utterance will, for example, be *in a peculiar way* hollow or void if said by an actor on the stage" is, unfortunately, all too often true. Austin seems to describe an actor out of touch with his text—an actor with a perceived absence of action or intention. While Austin considered stage speech "*parasitic* upon its normal use," his theories are nonetheless extremely useful to the ideal form of speech on the stage. Austin's description of performative speech describes language that is active and is involved in the performance of an action, as he referred to the "performative utterance as not, merely, saying something but doing something," and as not a true or false report of something. Austin's linkage of action—the doing of something—with language describes the solution to the perceived problem of language in Shakespeare's plays.

Austin provides a vocabulary that allows us to speak and live with language in the present. In his book, he isolates those "utterances" which are neither true nor false that do not "describe" or "report" anything. The utterance of such a sentence is the *doing of an action*. The active utterance is, then, not normally described as *just* saying something. To invoke Austin's terminology in such performative utterances as the marriage ceremony, betting, and the christening of a ship, the speaker indulges in the act as he utters a performative sentence—a "performative." Austin goes on to note that "perform" is the "usual verb with the noun 'action.'" Thus, the issuing of the utterance is the performing of an action. The goal is not to merely say something but to do something, as a performative act rather than a descriptive narrative.

The difference may be experienced in a piece of text such as, "This is I, Hamlet the Dane," which, when delivered as a referent to the speaker—that is, as utterance devoid of action—is comical and meaningless, but when directed as a performative at Laertes—that is, when coupled with action—can be menacing, revolutionary (he finally declares himself the rightful inheritor of his father), or any of a hundred different effects. Invoking Shakespeare's text as performative utterance allows actors to play stronger and more clearly defined actions. Another example is Queen Margaret's line:

> I here divorce myself
> Both from thy table, Henry, and thy bed,
> Until that act of Parliament be repealed
> Whereby my son is disinherited.
>
> —*HENRY VI*, PART 3 (ACT I, SCENE 1)

Her performative utterance *does* something. It allows the actress to play the text and create a divorce, regardless of whether she has the legal, religious or moral grounds to do so. The actress does not play, "I would like a divorce," or, "I wish I could divorce you"; rather, she performs an action and thereby drives the play forward. It is perhaps not a logical act on her part, but if the people in these plays were logical and performed with care and forethought, they wouldn't be in the situations they are in.

Shakespeare is at his richest when performed both positively and in the present tense. An example of this is the scene from *A Midsummer Night's Dream* in which Helena pursues Demetrius, a scene that can benefit enormously from an application of Austin's theory. Helena pledges her love to Demetrius with the text:

> And even for that do I love you the more.
> I am your spaniel; and, Demetrius,
> The more you beat me I will fawn on you.
> Use me but as your spaniel: spurn me, strike me,
> Neglect me, lose me; only give me leave,
> Unworthy as I am, to follow you.
>
> —*A MIDSUMMER NIGHT'S DREAM* (ACT II, SCENE 1)

There are several options open to the actress. In the first instance, she can *say* the line and assert her attentiveness and faithfulness; in the second, she can *act* as if she is his spaniel, i.e. she can metaphorically act as a dog, with the attendant mimetic representation of bodily movement that would stand for dog. In the final instance, however, she could embrace Austin's concept of the "performative utterance" and actually become a spaniel. Thus, a performative reading of the text suggests that she will neither say nor act "as if," but rather become a spaniel by the act of saying so. After all, stranger transformations occur in the play before its completion.

The careful reader will have noticed that the textual examples I have chosen are all in the present tense. This is the challenge Shakespeare presents to actors—how to create a clear and simple present, one that is generative and brings the text to a viable, emotionally rich, forceful present.

ENDNOTES/SOURCES

Epigraph:
(Page 269) Rice, Robert, "Actors Studio: Article V," *New York Post*, May 17, 1957.

RECOMMENDED READING LIST

Austin, J. L., *How to Do Things with Words*, Cambridge, MA: Harvard University Press, 1975.

Harbage, Alfred, ed., *The Complete Pelican Shakespeare*, New York: Penguin Classics, 1974.

Rice, Robert, "Actors Studio: Article V," *New York Post*, May 17, 1957.

Scheeder, Louis, and Shane Ann Younts, *All the Words on Stage: A Complete Pronunciation Dictionary for the Plays of William Shakespeare*, New York: Smith & Kraus, 2002.

Wright, George T., *Shakespeare's Metrical Art*, Berkeley, CA: University of California Press, 1988.
For those who wish to delve further into both the history of iambic pentameter and Shakespeare's magisterial development of language, I would direct the reader to George T. Wright's comprehensive work.

LOUIS SCHEEDER is an associate arts professor and the founder and director of the Classical Studio in the department of drama at New York University's Tisch School of the Arts. He has directed Off-, Off-Off- and on Broadway and at regional theaters in the U.S. and Canada. He served as Producer of the Folger Theatre Group, was assistant to artistic director Terry Hands at the Royal Shakespeare Company, and was associated for several years with the Manitoba Theatre Centre. He teaches acting privately in New York and has conducted workshops nationally and internationally, including South Africa and Cuba. He is coauthor, with Shane Ann Younts, of *All the Words on Stage: A Complete Pronunciation Dictionary for the Plays of William Shakespeare*. He received his BA from Georgetown University, and his MA and PhD in performance studies from New York University.

ARTHUR BARTOW joined the undergraduate drama department at New York University's Tisch School of the Arts as chair in 1990, and from 1995 to 2006 was the department's first artistic director. He is the author of *The Director's Voice*, now in its seventh edition from Theatre Communications Group.

Among his producing credits are the Off-Broadway production of *Modigliani* by Dennis McIntyre, for which he was co-producer, and the premiere of Elizabeth Swados's Helen Hayes Award–winning *The Beautiful Lady* at New Playwrights Theatre in Washington, D.C. As artistic director of the Theatre at Riverside Church in New York City, he presented the first production of the critically acclaimed play *Short Eyes* by Miguel Piñero (whom he discovered while Piñero was incarcerated at Sing Sing prison), as well as the New York premieres of *Are You Now or Have You Ever Been* by Eric Bentley and *Leaving Home* by David French.

During his years as associate director of TCG, he developed the TCG/NEA Fellowships in the Arts for directors and designers and created *ARTSEARCH*, the national print and online employment bulletin board for the performing arts. He has chaired theater panels for the New York State Council on the Arts and the National Foundation for Advancement in the Arts, and was executive vice-president of the Stage Directors and Choreographers Foundation.

He began his theater career as an actor, performing on and Off-Broadway and across the country in such roles as Neil in *Fiorello!* (national company), Friar Lawrence in Wally Harper's *Sensations* (Off-Broadway) and Cornelius in *Hello, Dolly!* with Betty Grable (national company). His credits also include roles in a wide range of regional productions, including Pemberton Maxwell in *Call Me Madam* with Ethel Merman and Warren in *On a Clear Day You Can See Forever* with Shirley Jones, Nancy Dussault, John Cullum and John Raitt.

He earned his BFA and MFA in drama at the University of Oklahoma, where he was also a pupil of British soprano Dame Eva Turner.